LADS BEFORE THE WIND

LADS BEFORE THE WIND

EXPANDED EDITION

KAREN PRYOR

To my father, Philip Wylie

Fourth edition
1st printing, October 2000

Cover design by Codesign
Book design by C. Linda Dingler
Unless otherwise credited, all photos by Sea Life Park.

Library of Congress Control Number: 00-135037
ISBN 1-890948-04-7

CONTENTS

Their appearance is generally hailed with delight by the mariner. Full of fine spirits, they invariably come from the breezy billows to windward. They are the lads that always live before the wind. They are accounted a lucky omen. If you yourself can withstand three cheers at beholding these vivacious fish, then heaven help ye; the spirit of godly gamesomeness is not in ye.

Herman Melville, *Moby Dick*

FOREWORD

by KONRAD LORENZ

Karen Pryor, nee Wylie, spent eight years as a professional trainer of porpoises at Sea Life Park, Makapuu Point, Oahu, Hawaii. She is, and was from her childhood on, one of those who derive an inexplicable primal joy from just watching animals, from which she has gained an intuitive knowledge of their behavior as a whole or as a system.

One can, indeed, gain insight into some parts of that system by laboratory experimentation. One can, for instance, investigate the learning faculties of an animal without studying all of its biology. The behaviorist school of psychology has thus studied a part or "subsystem" of organisms with notable success. On the other hand, one can approach animal behavior from the side of a wider frame of reference, the widest being the functional unit which consists of all the species of animals, plants, and bacteria living together in the same area. That kind of system is called an ecosystem; the science investigating it is called ecology.

Between the ecological and the behavioristic approach to animal behavior there are all kinds of intermediates. It is the free choice of any scientist, whether he wants to investigate the workings of a fly's nervous system or the ecology of a continent. In principle, the branches of research concerned with the smallest and those which deal with the largest of living systems are equally legitimate and can prove to be equally rewarding. There is no difference in value or in exactness between, say, biochemistry and ecology.

There is, however, the postulate that in studying a small subsystem pertaining to a living organism, the investigator should remain conscious of the wider frame of references given by the larger system. Some behavior students are open to the reproach that, in their extreme concentration on the process of learning by reinforcement, they neglect to consider the rest of the organism, which is equally worthy of investigation; the extremists among them even regard as "unscientific" any behavior study not concerned with the contingencies of reinforcement. This, of course, is a fallacy, as it excludes from scientific consideration everything that makes a pigeon a pigeon, a rat a rat, or a man a man.

Ethologists, on the other hand, try to understand the behavior of any animal species in the terms of a system of interactions and even in the wider frame of reference represented by the ecology of the species. Though it is the avowed program of ethology thus to study the behavior of a species as a whole or a system, and although learned behavior undeniably constitutes an intrinsic part of this system, ethologists tend to be interested more in the phylogenetically programmed behavior patterns of a species than in its learning processes. At least, I hardly know of an ethologist who has brought to bear, on the object of his ethological study, the whole arsenal of methods devised by the behaviorist school to study the processes of learning.

However, there is one ethologist who has indeed done so and with unique success—Karen Pryor. Being gifted with the unreflected joy in animals which, as I said, is the prerequisite of unbiased observation, she is a born ethologist. Being also endowed with a highly analytical mind—an inheritance from her father, Philip Wylie—she is capable of drawing exactly the right inferences from her observations. It was her fate—and a lucky one for science—to be confronted with the necessity to "train" porpoises. She used the wonderfully subtle methods of Skinnerian conditioning in order to control and shape the behavior of her porpoises so that they performed really spectacular acts for show. Kenneth S. Norris, the greatest living authority on whale and porpoise behavior, pays her the tribute of calling her a superb trainer.

The point of her tale, however, lies in the fact that she did not confine the use of her faculty of training her porpoises to make them perform incredible circus acts. What she did was to use the conventional training techniques to get into contact with her animals. She deliberately used Skinnerian techniques as a means of communication.

The fact emerges, amazing to some and a matter of course to others, that the animal *enjoys* learning and that the active role in operant conditioning is played by the subject of the experiment rather than by the experimenter. The story of how a porpoise can teach its teacher how to teach is not only highly amusing but supremely instructive to the student of social communication. Karen Pryor's tale of how she learned to train porpoises explains what the process of operant conditioning really is, and how a conditioned behavior pattern can be "shaped," or brought under stimulus control. In fact, the book can—and I hope it will—be used as a textbook on animal learning in general, and on Skinnerian conditioning in particular.

The essential value of the book, however, is contained in the fact that here is an ethologist who uses all the subtlety of conditioning not only as an end in itself, or only to study the contingencies of reinforcement, but as a tool to gain knowledge about the animal as a whole. Karen Pryor does not even try to keep up the current fiction of not believing that highly evolved animals like porpoises or dogs have subjective experience and an emotional life closely akin to our own. She declines to ignore or deny her conviction that indeed they have, and what she describes in this book is the interaction between two kinds of living creatures which, different though they are, share that faculty of experiencing pleasure and pain which is the essence of our mind and soul—whatever that may be. She does not, however, minimize the difference between man and porpoise. Her observations prove to the hilt that the stories about the almost superhuman mental faculties of porpoises, about their possessing something like syntactic speech, in short their being altogether cleverer than man, all are pure inventions or, at best, self-deceptions of uncritical observers. Yet, as so often is the case, the truth about an animal is far more exciting and altogether more beautiful than all the myths woven about it. There are parts in Karen Pryor's unadorned story which are truly moving. One incident nearly brought tears to my eyes. A female porpoise who (I intentionally say "who" and not "which") had struggled for some time with a learning problem had obviously begun to suffer from her inability to solve it. When, with the help of the trainer, she suddenly succeeded in getting the point, she did something which no porpoise had ever been observed to do—she swam up to the trainer and stroked her with her flipper, a gesture of endearing caress which is often observed among friendly porpoises but never had been recorded as being addressed to a human being.

The most impressive and, from the scientific viewpoint, indubitably the most important chapter is the one about the "creative porpoise." In two cases porpoises had been trained to expect reward whenever they succeeded in inventing an altogether new form of behavior. To grasp the fact that it is not any particular pattern of behavior which is going to be rewarded, but that the desired action should be some form, *any* form of movement which has *not* as yet been reinforced, requires a feat of abstraction quite unexpected in any animal.

It is clear that this book is of the highest scientific significance. If I have stressed this, before discussing its other merits, I have done so because some people adhere to the erroneous belief that anything of scientific value must necessarily be tedious. This book certainly is not. It is not only prvaded generally by a subtle sense of humor; it is exquisitely funny and even hilarious in parts. As I said, it is the story of the interaction between porpoises and people, and it is at the latter's expense that the reader has a really good laugh on frequent occasions. One of the funniest stories tells how the porpoises often succeeded in getting their trainers conditioned to reinforcing stimuli which they learn to send out in order to achieve their own ends, thus hoisting the humans by their own petard. Even more amusing, however, is the chapter about visiting scientists.

The book has still other merits which I should put last, but certainly not least—they are the sincere and warm love for all living creatures, the keen appreciation of their beauty, and, notwithstanding both, an unshaken and unsentimental adherence to scientific truth.

"I don't know what a porpoise trainer is supposed to look like, but I guess not like me." The author and Haole, a Hawaiian spinning porpoise, in Sea Life Park's Whaler's Cove.

1. BEGINNINGS

For eight years, from 1963 to 1971, I earned most of my living as a porpoise trainer.

I don't know what a porpoise trainer is supposed to look like, but I guess not like me. Most people (especially male porpoise trainers) think of it as a man's job. People next to me on airplanes tend to sit up a little straighter and say "You do *what*?" And it took the *What's My Line?* panel all ten questions and a big fat hint to guess my line.

I never intended to become a porpoise trainer. In 1960 I was married to a graduate student in marine biology, Tap Pryor. We were living in Hawaii, where the Marine Corps had sent us originally. We had three small children, and I was writing a book about breast feeding (*Nursing Your Baby*, Harper & Row, 1963). We were raising pheasants to help put Tap through graduate school at the University of Hawaii.

Tap was studying sharks. At no place in Hawaii was there a tank large enough to keep big sharks in. To do his research, Tap had to spend one whole summer in the South Pacific, on Eniwetok, where some tanks were. That was a drag. Lonely.

We had seen those huge commercial exhibits called oceanariums—the original one, Marine Studios, in Florida, and the second to be built, Marineland, in California. Maybe a biologist could do his work with large marine animals at one of these places? When Tap got his discharge from the Marine Corps, and we had a paid trip back East, home, we visited Marine Studios, Marineland, and the Seaquarium in Miami. It was discouraging. Public exhibits and private research didn't mix well. Experiments sometimes detracted from exhibits, and the scientists on the staffs of these oceanariums told horror stories of precious research animals being pressed into public shows just when the data collecting was getting good.

So Tap decided to build an oceanarium in Hawaii. Two oceanariums, back to back, one for the public—and Hawaii needed just such an attraction—and one for research.

We didn't have money; we were living on the G.I. Bill and that pheasant farm. We borrowed $500 from the Bank of Hawaii to build a scale model of Tap's idea. The morning newspaper kindly splashed the idea and a picture of the model all over the front page, and the project began.

Three years later, thousands of pheasants, hundreds of letters, and scores of Tap's trips to the mainland later, the idea was becoming a reality. On a barren piece of seacoast where once only thorny trees grew, Tap's dream was growing. A Hawaiian oceanarium, our oceanarium, designed by biologists, not businessmen, was under construction. An adjoining research oceanarium, sharing the public attraction's water supply, and inspiring the exhibit with creative, authentic, scientific ideas, was on the drawing boards. Tap had found investors for the public exhibit. He had also found scientists for the research institute.

Foremost among these was Dr. Kenneth S. Norris, a former curator of Marineland and a professor at the University of California. Ken knew all there was to know (then) about porpoises, and we needed that expertise, because you couldn't plan a public oceanarium without a porpoise show. Ken was also an expert on fish and reptiles, a biologist of national renown, and a very creative, imaginative man. He liked Tap's project, and helped plan it from the beginning.

The first actual building to go up, at Sea Life Park, was an innovation: a porpoise training facility, out of the public eye, designed just for the keeping and training of wild porpoises. Tap

Sea Life Park, surrounded by highway and looping entrance drive. Past the park, the training facility, offices, and the Oceanic Institute tanks and buildings. In the distance, the Makai Range pier, with the research vessel *Westward* alongside.

Park buildings, from foreground, going clockwise: the Ocean Science Theater, a temporary Man-in-the-Sea exhibit, the Hawaiian Reef, the entrance and gift shop, the restaurant, Leeward Isles pool, and Whaler's Cove. The Hawaiian village exhibit in the center. *Roger Coryell* hired Georges Gilbert, a French-Hawaiian fisherman and fine naturalist, to catch porpoises, as Georges had already done. There were eight animals of three species in residence.

Ken Norris provided a consultant on porpoise training, a psychologist named Ron Turner, who had worked with Ken on porpoise research projects and who knew all about the then little-known specialty of Skinnerian operant conditioning, a branch of learning theory that makes it easy to train animals.

Ron wrote a consultant's report on how to train porpoises. Presumably, any intelligent person could follow its guidance. Tap hired three intelligent people and set them to work in the training facility training the animals to perform for the public.

Three months before Sea Life Park was due to open, panic struck. Bulldozers were carving out huge pools. Buildings were rising. Advance tickets were being sold. And there was no porpoise show. The porpoises, in fact, had trained their trainers to give them fish for nothing.

Tap called California and spoke to Ken Norris. So much for science and theory and consultants; he needed a good porpoise trainer, and one who would come cheap. Where could we find one? "You're married to one," Ken said.

Me? I'd been an interested spectator throughout the growth of Tap's project. I'd typed letters, and cooked dinner for visiting investors, and watched with fascination when the first four porpoises, caught before the training facility was finished, were installed in a plastic swimming pool in my backyard. But what did I know about porpoises?

I did know a little bit about training animals. I had a marvelous dog, a Weimaraner, Gus, whom I'd taken to obedience school and to dog shows and won trophies with. Then Tap's father had sent the grandchildren a Welsh pony, and the pony had a baby, and the baby grew and had to be tamed and taught to work. I had ordered a set of harness by mail, tied the young stallion to a fence, looked up "harness" in the Encyclopaedia Britannica, and hung the harness on the colt until it fit the picture; and by and by I had the pony trained to pull a cart.

That was hardly preparation to train porpoises. But we always listened to Ken Norris; and he said I could do it if I studied Ron's report.

I sat down, after the phone call, with Ron Turner's training manual. It was written in thick prose and stiff scientific jargon. I could see why the people Tap had hired as trainers had been unwilling to digest it. It was exciting, though. Here were the rules, the scientific laws, underlying training. Suddenly I knew why I'd always had trouble with Gus on the "drop-on-recall" exercises. And why the pony, Echo, jibbed his head to the left on a right turn. I began to understand how training works. I could see that, given this handful of facts, this elegant system called "operant conditioning," one could train any animal to do anything it was physically capable of doing.

I sat up all night, for the first time in my life, and thought about what it would mean to be one's husband's employee. What it would do to my little children to have a working mother. What it would mean if Sea Life Park opened without a good porpoise show. And what tremendous fun it would be to try out Ron's manual and see how it worked.

I took the job. On the basis that I would work only a four-hour day (ha!) and that I would quit as soon as the shows were going well and other people could take over (ha! ha!). I had no idea I was about to get caught up in one of the major efforts of my life.

When Tap first started to plan Sea Life Park, a distinguished professor of marine biology at the University of Hawaii announced publicly that it was most unrealistic to plan an oceanarium with trained porpoises in Hawaii, because there were almost no porpoises to be found around our islands. As he put it, "Hawaiian waters have a very impoverished cetacean fauna." (The cetaceans are all the whale and porpoise tribe.)

It sometimes happens in biology that when an organism is declared not to occur in a certain region, it simply means that no one has looked for it there yet. There are thousands of porpoises in Hawaiian waters, of many different kinds, and quantities of whales, too. We eventually found at least thirteen species of cetaceans in Hawaii. We had nine of them in our tanks over the years. The very first animals I worked with were of three different species, and it was like working with three vastly different breeds of dogs.

There are in the world's rivers and oceans upwards of thirty different kinds of porpoises (or dolphins; Ken called them all porpoises, so we did too). The first four animals Georges caught, the ones which lived on my lawn in an Esther Williams swimming pool for a while, were "spinners." They belonged to the genus *Stenella,* and turned out to be true native Hawaiians, a local subspecies, *Stenella longirostrus Hawaiiensis.* Spinners are dainty little animals, half the size of TV's "Flipper," weighing about 100 pounds. They are graceful and attenuated, with long slender beaks, or rostrums, and big, soft, brown eyes. They are sleekly gray above and a charming pale pink below. They're called "spinners" because of a natural habit of throwing themselves into the air and spinning like tops before falling back with a splash. On the first day I reported for work, we had four spinners: Mele ("song"), Moki (a boy's name), Akamai ("smart"), and Haole (Hawaiian slang for "Caucasian"; Haole was unusual-

Michael, 6, Ted, 7, and Gale Pryor, 3, in the fall of 1963, befriending their mother's new pupil, Makua.

ly pale in color). No members of this species had ever been kept in captivity before.

Then Georges caught some bottlenose porpoises. The familiar porpoise used by all the mainland oceanariums is the Atlantic bottlenosed porpoise, *Tursiops truncatus.* Ours were Pacific bottlenosed porpoises, *Tursiops gilli,* bigger than the Atlantic version, much bigger than the little spinners, and rather stiff, clumsy animals compared to their Atlantic cousins. We called them bottlenoses, and sometimes bottlenecks and beetlebrains.

When I began training, we had two bottlenoses to work with, both males, Kane and Makua. They were large animals, 9 or 10 feet long, weighing at least 400 pounds apiece, gray all over, with short, thick rostrums, sharp little eyes, lots of stout conical teeth, and strong opinions.

The training facility consisted of a wooden building, a packed-gravel yard, and three tanks, joined together so animals could be moved from tank to tank through wooden gates. The spinners were in one tank, the bottlenoses in another. In the third tank, on my first day, were two more animals of the genus *Stenella.* These were patently not spinners. They were about 20 percent bigger than spinners, with hooked dorsal fins, and shorter, thicker rostrums. And they were covered with polka dots. On a basic ground plan of dark, slaty gray above and pale gray below, they were liberally splattered from nose to tail with light spots on the dark gray and dark spots on the light gray. The scientific name was *Stenella attenuata,* and they had no common name, so we followed Georges's lead and called them kikos, which is the Hawaiian word for "spots."

There were three trainers on the staff: Chris Varez, Gary Anderson, and Dottie Samson. Chris and Gary were husky blond giants in their early twenties, good friends, very excited about their work, and eager to make Sea Life Park a success. Dottie was a slender, sandy-haired schoolteacher, a few years older, sensible, cheerful, and devoted to the animals. The three of them not only trained the porpoises but scrubbed the tanks, broke the fish out of the freezer daily, doctored sick animals, took care of the training facility, and handled the streams of curious visitors that walked up to the tanks. Chris lived in the training building, which had a shower and a small kitchen, and he watched over the animals at night.

I don't know how they felt about having the boss's wife installed over their heads, but they were certainly very agreeable to me, and we had fun together from the beginning. It may have been a bit of a relief. They felt stymied by the animals, and perhaps were glad to have some direction; and if I turned out to be stymied, too, well, at least it would be my head on the chopping block now, not theirs.

Ron's manual had some ground rules which I put into practice immediately. Since the animals would be working for a food reward and might not work if they got too full, it was important to find out how much each animal liked to eat, every day, weigh his food carefully, and give him just that much. (That was my first budget fight: getting $40 for a scale out of the front office.) Record keeping was important, too, to keep track of health, food intake, and training progress. I forbade visitors or interruptions during training, and we built a little platform so visitors could overlook the work area without being close enough to disturb the trainers.

The manual described training in terms of one long daily training session, lasting perhaps several hours, for each animal, during which he would gradually get fuller and fuller of fish. That didn't make sense to me. I knew that my dog and pony learned more in several short sessions than in one long one, and short sessions were less fatiguing for the trainer, too. We decided to have three daily training sessions, spread as far apart as was practical.

It also seemed both impractical and unnecessary to train each animal separately. We decided to handle the spinners in a bunch, and the kikos as a pair, and train only the two bottlenoses individually. Dottie and Chris were to share the spinners, Chris and Gary would handle the two bottlenoses, and I would take on the kikos, which were nervous, recalcitrant, "untrainable" animals that hadn't made any progress at all so far.

The other animals had made some progress. The spinners had discovered that they got a fish every time they did their spin. At first they had been spinning spontaneously, just in play among themselves (and mostly at night), but they had learned to spin deliberately whenever a trainer came up to the tank with a bucket of fish. The bottlenoses would play with a ball, voluntarily, and would rise halfway out of the water to take a fish from your hand. One of them, Makua, was learning to ring a bell by pressing an underwater paddle with his nose.

Makua charmed visitors by rolling upside down and presenting his broad gray tummy to be tickled, and both bottlenoses seemed to enjoy it when we slipped into the water with them for a dip after work. They would swim alongside and allow us to put an arm around their substantial waists or to hold on to a dorsal fin and take a ride around the tank.

A porpoise's skin is firm and smooth, exactly like a wet inner tube. Makua and Kane felt like big animated beach toys, warm, buoyant, and resilient, throbbing with a great steady heartbeat and regarding us with a calm and merry eye.

Kane had an unfortunate infirmity which meant that he could never be a performer. Shortly after capture he had had the misfortune to jump or fall out of a full tank into an empty one, a very rare occurrence, as porpoises have quite a lot of sense about not jumping in the wrong place. Perhaps the fall onto a hard surface damaged his muscles on one side; in any case his tail section bent permanently to the left. It seemed to cause him no pain, but it was unsightly and made him clumsy. We could not return him to the ocean in that condition, so he was a pensioner, keeping Makua company for the present and destined to be a practice animal for new trainers.

Agreeable though the bottlenoses usually were, Chris and Gary warned me that they could be bullies. Angered by some training misunderstanding, Makua, particularly, was likely to strike the trainer's hand or arm with his heavy rostrum and to open his mouth, showing his four rows of quarter-inch-long, sharp teeth, while he swung his head about threateningly. Also once or twice he had deliberately knocked the fish bucket out of the trainer's hand and into the water.

The spinners, by contrast, never offered any threat or fight;

Chris, Gary, and Tap watching Dottie play with Makua and Kane. Porpoises feel smooth and resilient, exactly like a wet inner tube. Most porpoises enjoy being hugged and patted.

withdrawal was their response to anything they didn't care for. Dottie had done a wonderful job of gaining their confidence. She swam with them often, stroking and playing with them, and all but Moki were completely "hand-tame." They would come to be patted and even allow themselves to be caught and held and lifted from the water without fear.

The two kiko porpoises, Hoku ("star") and Kiko ("spots"),

were never to become tame. They eventually learned to tolerate being touched, but they never solicited patting and obviously preferred to be left alone.

Taming is one thing; training is another. We had to start applying this new conditioning system in Ron's manual as fast and as well as we could.

Classical or Pavlovian conditioning is an unconscious process. The animal reacts to a stimulus, perhaps without even knowing he is doing it, because of the consequences that always follow that stimulus: the dog salivates when the bell rings because the bell is followed by food. Operant conditioning is a different proposition. The animal learns that he can produce a desired stimulus —food, for example—by actions of his own. He is the initiator, the operator.

Animals seem to enjoy this. I think they like to be able to make things happen for themselves, in this way. Many of the behaviors which we used later in shows were spontaneous actions of the animals, which we rewarded, or "reinforced," with food until the animal began doing them on purpose to make us give him a fish, and at least some of these actions were, I think, deliberately offered in the hope of new reward.

The first crucial step in Ron's manual was to establish a signal that means "food is coming." It's important to be able to communicate to the animal exactly what it is that you like about what he is doing. If he jumps in the air and you then throw him a fish every time, he will soon learn to jump on purpose. The fish, however, inevitably reaches the porpoise's mouth after the jump is finished. The animal thus has no way of telling what you liked about that jump: was it the height, the splashing reentry, the part of the tank he was in, or what? He may think they all count, and get hung up in undesirable fixed patterns. He may never come up with exactly what you want. He may reach it very shakily, by trial and error.

Circus trainers can get around this by correcting the animal physically, with leash or bridle or whip, until they have exactly the action they want; but we could not do that.

Spinners vs. kikos: Our two species of *Stenella*, posing with Tap. The kiko, on the left, *S. attenuata*, has speckles all over, a blunt, white-tipped rostrum or beak, handsome black facial markings, and sickle-shaped fins. The spinners have gray backs and pale pink undersides, straighter fins, and much longer, thinner rostrums.

The manual said we must establish a signal, a signal that means "food is coming." Then we could signal to the animal and tell him *exactly when* he was doing the right thing. Ron suggested the sound of a police whistle. It is loud, clearly heard by a porpoise above or below water, not easily confused with anything else in the environment, and it's a response which a human being can emit rapidly. You can blow a whistle, for example, noticeably more promptly than you can press a buzzer with your finger.

Once the animal has learned the meaning of the whistle, you can use it to mark all kinds of actions at the very instant they occur. You can reward the jump exactly at its peak every time, reinforcing or strengthening the likelihood that the animal will jump for that peak, and thus go higher and higher. You can strengthen a very small response, blowing the whistle, for example, every time the animal turns to his left, until in a few minutes you have an animal pivoting in a tight circle leftward.

This is called "shaping." By strengthening some small response, you can, with careful planning, "shape" an elaborate behavior, something the animal might never have done spontaneously, such as tossing a ball directly into a basket or standing on its head and waving its tail in the air. With the animals' natural behaviors, and the things we could shape, there were certainly plenty of possible behaviors to work on.

The first step, for the trainers, was to make sure all the animals were correctly whistle-conditioned. Ron gave elaborate instructions for this. We were to feed the animals their rations for a day or two, without attempting to reward any action, pairing the blast of the whistle with the arrival of the fish, every time. Then, gradually, counting the seconds, we were to make the whistle precede the fish by a brief instant, and then by a larger instant, until the animal was conditioned to expect food when he heard the whistle, even if the food did not come right away.

I started with the kikos, Hoku and Kiko. Hoku, the male, had, in addition to his spots, two diagonal stripes of gray on his sides, a handsome and apparently natural marking.

Hoku and Kiko were more than just two animals of the same species that lived in the same tank. They were a pair, a couple, lovers literally until death. They swam together, ate together, worked together. When they swam, they almost always "held hands," each touching the tip of a chest or pectoral fin to the other's. The fins stayed overlapping and pressed together through every maneuver, rising to breathe, turning, swimming fast or slowly. Hoku was very chivalrous. He tended to keep himself between Kiko and any potential danger, and if a fish fell between them, he always let Kiko eat first.

We were using smelt, shipped in frozen from the West Coast. Unlike any fish caught in Hawaii, smelt were steadily available, cheap, nourishing, and small. A kiko could eat about ten pounds of smelt a day, which amounted to about a hundred fish, allowing the trainer plenty of individual reinforcements without having to resort to the messy business of cutting fish in pieces. We began at once dividing each animal's food into three daily amounts to get them used to eating in that pattern, and we started each training session by the clock, at a fixed time, to create an agreeable sensation of anticipation in the animals, a nice "must be about time to eat" feeling, which should facilitate training.

Even the simple task of whistle conditioning turned out to be very demanding of the trainer. You had to be sure that the whistle meant nothing except "food is coming." Therefore, as you stood by the tank blowing the whistle and throwing the fish, you had to think: Don't blow the whistle at regular intervals—as soon as they've finished the last fish, for instance. They will start to expect the whistle at regular intervals and will be disappointed if it doesn't come, or disregard it if it comes at the wrong time. Don't blow the whistle more often when they are swimming toward you or looking at you; keep it varied, so that sometimes they hear it from one end of the tank, sometimes from the other, sometimes when in motion, sometimes when still, so they will not start hanging around in front of you, or doing any other particular thing which you later might not want them to do. Don't let the fish follow the whistle at a regular interval, or arrive in a regular place in the tank, or right in front of the animal every time, lest he come to expect that, and stop "believing" the whistle if the fish doesn't show up exactly where and when he is used to it.

It is astonishing how easily we ourselves tend to develop habits. I found that keeping all these necessary variations straight in my own mind took a lot of concentration. Furthermore, since I was conditioning two animals, I had to throw at least two fish, each time, and I was awkward at first. On the second day, however, I was rewarded myself. The whistle was preceding the fish by anything from a split second to four or five seconds, and when Hoku and Kiko heard the whistle, they visibly startled and then began to search for food. That "startle" was my reward. "Aha! They hear the whistle—they know what it means now. I'm communicating." The first barrier was broken.

Meanwhile, Dottie, Chris, and Gary were going through the same procedure with the other animals. Of course, sometimes we were doing this simultaneously, and whistles were sounding all over three tanks. There seemed to be no practical way to avoid this, so we dismissed the problem. Let the animals discover for themselves that only the whistle sounding from the side of their own tank was meaningful for them. Indeed, the porpoises, with their wonderfully acute hearing, quickly caught on. Sometimes a trainer's whistle at one tank would cause a flurry of activity in the other tanks, but if no fish followed, the activity immediately died down.

When the whistle conditioning was accomplished, and we knew for sure that each animal understood what the whistle meant, it was time to lay out a training program: to finish up what had been started, and to decide on and build up a repertoire of behaviors that would add up to interesting shows. But what kind of shows? I needed to do some fast thinking.

Designing a porpoise show is one of those tasks for which naïveté is probably an advantage. If you don't really know what has been done before, you're not tempted to copy. If you don't know what *can* be done, you're not limited by ideas of what *can't* be done.

Ken Norris had often expressed his dissatisfaction with the standard porpoise shows that consisted of an accumulation of unrelated tricks like a circus act. We thought Sea Life Park shows should be built around a theme, or story line, with each trained behavior occurring for some sensible reason.

Tap had created two performance arenas in the park, Whaler's Cove and the Ocean Science Theater, each with a designed-in theme. Whaler's Cove was a large outdoor pool overlooking a magnificent view of the ocean and of two offshore islands. Here the show should be Hawaiian-flavored and historical, leaning on the oceanic background of the Island people and on the historical importance of the whaling industry in Hawaii. The Ocean Science Theater was a building, or at least a roof, suspended over a circular glass tank with seating three-quarters of the way around it: an underwater theater-in-the-round. Again, framed by the roof and by the cement back wall of the tank, was a magnificent blue backdrop of rough ocean water. Here the emphasis would be on porpoise biology and research. Would it be possible to create two wholly different shows with only seven usable animals?

One morning I hiked through the construction area and sat down on the slope overlooking Whaler's Cove, in the area where seating for about a thousand people would soon be built. In front of me was an irregular-walled cement pool, about 300 feet long and 100 feet across. At the left end was a small artificial island, and across the right end stretched the foundations marking the future location of a five-eighths-scale replica of a whaling ship. The ship, complete with masts and rigging, would provide the platform from which the porpoise trainers would operate. Visitors would also be allowed to go on board and view the animals through portholes from below deck.

It was easy to decide that the spinners should go in Whaler's Cove. They were bona fide, authentic Hawaiian porpoises, in the first place. Also the spectacular spin would look best out under the sky, rather than under the Ocean Science Theater's roof.

I sat in the midst of my future audience and looked at my future stage. It certainly was a big one. One could do something with the island, on the left, and with the ship, on the right, but the main activity would have to take place in the middle, an expanse of water nearly 100 feet across. I would need the kikos and at least one bottlenose up at the Ocean Science Theater. Could I fill up Whaler's Cove with four little spinners?

Color. Color would help. A pretty Hawaiian girl in a bright bikini, with flowers in her hair. The gentle spinners could certainly be persuaded to swim and play with a girl in the water; that was something people hadn't had a chance to see before. The girl could dive in from the railing of the ship, swim across the water, and land on the island, accompanied by the animals. That would utilize all of the stage. The porpoises could spin in unison to welcome her arrival. Several of them spinning at once would also fill up that big space. In fact, they could do a lot of things in unison, like a corps de ballet.

Thus two of what were to be the three principal elements of

the Whaler's Cove show presented themselves: the girl and the spinners working in unison. The third element, one or more trained small whales, would have to wait until Georges started collecting whales.

What we needed, then, were several behaviors which the animals could perform handsomely in unison, besides the spin. I thought of another jump spinners sometimes make, a head-over-tail flip, which we might be able to catch. Then there was tail walking, balancing half out of the water vertically. That might look like a hula. Maybe we could get the spinners to wear leis while they did it. Finally it occurred to me, looking at the empty pool and imagining it full of water and spinners, that when the animals dash about chasing each other in play they often are clear of the water in the leap so typical of the whole family that it is called "porpoising." A single animal porpoising, though pretty, is not spectacular, but five or more arcing in unison, side by side, might be something.

Stringing this stuff together onto some kind of story line would be a job for another day. At least I had an idea of what we could begin training the animals to do.

At the Ocean Science Theater the task seemed less amorphous. There were two holding tanks behind the cement back wall of the glass show tank, and we had two kinds of animals, kikos and a bottlenose. We would give a scientific demonstration, in two acts, on two general subjects, using as demonstration material whatever behaviors I could think of that would be effective in that tank.

"A porpoise," as Ken Norris once said, "is a creature of the interface." Breathing air, and being forced to surface often, he lives his life at the place where air and water join. Our spectacular glass-walled tank made the most of that fact. For the first time, people would be able to see above and below the water simultaneously, to watch not only a leap into the air but the underwater rush that led up to it and the curving finale of the trajectory, again underwater. The huge sheets of glass, costing thousands of dollars each, that made the tank walls were sup-

Whaler's Cove, with seating for 1,000 people. In the background, Rabbit Island and a promontory with a lighthouse, Makapuu Point. *David Cornwall*

ported by the thinnest of vertical members and had no top rim at all. Air, water, and glass met at the top of the tank in a visually very satisfying way. Given good water clarity, which we were almost sure to have, the tank would be like a big blue room.

The surface of the water was also visible from all but the two lowest rows of seats, thanks to a clever architect and good sight lines. Across the back of the tank and around the holding tanks in the rear was a solid cement platform, interrupted by the huge ring of pillars which held up the roof. That platform and the water surface constituted a stage of sorts, from which the trainers could work and where additional action could take place. Then there was that big roof overhead, shaped like a limpet shell or a tent, rising to a peak in the middle. Tap had planned a training platform, a narrow ramp sticking out over the water, which could be lowered to water surface or raised to the ceiling. Could we get a porpoise to jump all the way up to the rafters? We could try.

Powerful Makua, of course, was the animal for that high jump straight upward. He would be the Ocean Science Theater's first star.

Tap and Ken were anxious to have a sonar demonstration. Much of Ken's research had to do with porpoise sonar, or echo location, the sensory system which allows these animals to perceive objects in the water by sound rather than by sight. A calm, fearless bottlenose would be the animal of choice for that demonstration too. We would figure out some way to blindfold Makua, and then the audience could watch through the glass as he retrieved objects and perhaps located a bell to ring or some other target by sonar. That was certainly a training task of immediate priority.

Makua was already learning to ring a bell with his nose. That could be used as a sonar target, as a demonstration of training methods, or for the old circus "arithmetic" gag, in which the animal apparently adds and subtracts and counts out the correct answer by (in this case) ringing a bell. It might be nice to do the stunt and then repeat it and give away the secret by showing the audience how the trainer cues the animal to start and stop counting.

Makua sometimes made a clumsy, splashing leap which might be developed into something. We would watch him for other naturally occurring behaviors that could be used in the show.

Then there was talking. Have to have a talking porpoise, right? Porpoises normally make two kinds of sounds: the rat-ta-tat-tat of echo location and the peeping, birdlike whistles which are their form of social signaling, comparable to the clucking of hens or the barking, whining, and growling of dogs—a collection of little sounds which convey emotional states. These sounds, made in the water, are seldom audible in the air, at least not to the human ear.

You can, however, shape airborne noisemaking. If the porpoise is trained to stick its head in the air and make noise with the blowhole open, it is capable of a vast range of airborne barks, yells, and shrieks. Maybe we could shape Makua to stick his head into the air and say "Aloha."

Now, how to use Hoku and Kiko? They would be a graceful contrast to Makua and should perform by themselves, as a pair. Perhaps they could jump through a hoop held above the water. What could we do to show off their agility and speed underwater? I thought of patterns of hoops, hung vertically or horizontally in that transparent blue room, through which the animals could circle and slalom and loop the loop. I wondered if we could train them to swim at top speed around the tank. No matter what they did, it would be pretty and would lend itself to narration about the biology of the animal and what its life is like in the wild.

I looked at the interface line, where the surface of the water would meet the glass, and realized how lovely it would be to see a pair of animals in an arcing jump right against the glass. Suppose we extended jumps of some sort from the glass inward, all the way around the tank? Then Hoku and Kiko would arc into the air, across one bank of glass, under the water across the next section, into the air and under again, around and around the tank, lacing through the interface in a continuous, flowing line. It seemed to me that this would be very beautiful.

I climbed the ladder to the deck of the Ocean Science Theater, at the back of the tank, and counted. If we extended a bar 3 or 4 feet inward from each angle of the tank, which was in fact a hexagon, not a true circle, we could have six jumps at about 15-foot intervals. Just the ticket.

Finally, for a finale, a ball game. Makua and Hoku and Kiko could be taught to knock a ball around. Suppose we had a real water-polo game, *Tursiops* vs. *Stenella*, with goals on each side of the tank and a fish to the team that scored? It seemed to be a workable idea (there was a tremendous problem in it, however, which we were not to discover until training was almost complete: the animals were going to take the game seriously).

I could see at once that it would be important for the animals to come out of their holding tanks and go back in, obediently. Training the OST (Ocean Science Theater) animals to go through gates on command was going to be very important. We would have to add a session of gate training to the schedule, every day, until we were sure the behavior was reliable.

So a show plan took shape, and we could begin training in earnest. We had about three months until opening day. About nine-tenths of what I now know about training I would learn in those next three months.

2. SHAPING

Hoku and Kiko were whistle-conditioned. They knew a little bit more, too. They were willing to pass through the gate into the next tank, having experienced this on tank-cleaning days; and they liked to play with a ball, pushing it around with their noses. I used the whistle to shape the behavior of striking the ball strongly and striking it in my direction. The animals seemed to enjoy that, and it became a good way to end a training session on a note of success.

The first serious work on the agenda was the six-bar jump for the Ocean Science Theater. The first step for that, of course, was to get the animals jumping one bar. Hoku and Kiko were living in an oblong tank, in which they swam back and forth all day, so I began by putting a rope in the water, down one side of the tank, across the bottom, and up the other side, figuring that as the animals passed over it, I could reinforce them until they were passing over it on purpose, and then I could gradually raise the rope until they were making a jump over it.

However, when Hoku and Kiko saw this strange object in the middle of their tank, they declined to pass over it. Never mind if it was 8 feet below them and quite inert; it looked like a kiko trap to them. For the entire day they circled at one end of the tank, the end they happened to be in when the rope was first installed.

I tried everything that crossed my mind: reinforcing them for circling nearer the rope, baiting them over it with fish, ball-playing in such a way as to promote accidental crossing of the rope, throwing the fish reinforcement on the far side of the tank. Nothing. If a fish fell on the wrong side of the rope, they went without that fish. If the ball was knocked into the far side of the tank, that was the end of the ball game, unless I went and got the ball back myself.

It was infuriating. I was never going to get that jump developed unless they actually swam across the rope so I would have something to reinforce. I didn't have time to wait them out; they might avoid the rope for days. I wasn't inclined to let them get so hungry that their fear would be overridden by desperate need.

Finally, feeling a bit of desperate need myself, I grabbed up an aluminum beach chair that was sitting by the tank and threw it into the water next to the pair of porpoises. That harmless chair surely had to be a more fearsome object than the rope on the tank floor.

Indeed, Hoku and Kiko were appalled, and scuttled across the rope to the far end of the tank; as they did so, I blew the whistle, and threw them several fish, which they were not too frightened to eat.

Now, of course, there was a chair in the tank, scaring my porpoises. Eight feet down. I had to go indoors, change into a bathing suit, get into the tank, and dive down and get my chair back, while Hoku and Kiko circled nervously on the far side of the rope.

The second time, I had enough sense to tie a line on the chair so I could retrieve it without a swim. Again I dropped the chair in, by the porpoises, and Hoku and Kiko fled back to their original end of the tank, across the rope, getting reinforced for doing so.

The third time, Hoku and Kiko dashed across the rope as soon as they saw me lift the chair. Chairs might eat porpoises for breakfast, but that rope on the bottom of the tank had not leaped up and grabbed them. It was demonstrably harmless. They began using the full length of the tank again. After a few more reinforcements they were crossing the rope on purpose, taking their fish and then turning and dashing right back over the rope again and looking for more fish.

When they seemed relaxed, I "put them on a schedule." This is a crucial and often by-passed rule of training. The animals had learned something: crossing the rope is good for a fish. Now they had to learn that sometimes they would have to cross the rope two or three times for a fish. The first time they crossed it, and didn't hear a whistle, they seemed confused; did they hear wrong? Reluctantly, they tried again. Success! The whistle blew. Another try—no whistle. With more confidence, they quickly offered the response again. "It's okay, see, if you don't hear the whistle, just hurry across the rope again; you'll hear it this time, maybe."

Even with green, frightened animals you can in a single short training session get to the point where they will perform their new behavior with zest, two, three, or even more times, for a single reinforcement. Again, as with the whistle conditioning, I found it was quite a chess game for me. Ron's manual told me I had to keep the schedule randomized, sometimes reinforcing the first crossing, sometimes every other crossing, sometimes letting three crossings go unreinforced, sometimes reinforcing several in a row. I kept it up until the animals crossed the line eagerly and repeatedly, even if they sometimes had to perform three or four times before getting reinforced.

A random schedule of reinforcement, curiously enough, is more powerful than a fixed schedule. If Hoku and Kiko had spent an hour crossing the rope, getting a fish, crossing the rope, getting a fish, they might have got bored, or lazy. If, at any point, they had begun abruptly *not* getting fish—let us say, because I had decided they now had to cross the rope in unison—they might have quit working in disgust. The behavior would be "extinguished."

Ron Turner explained it to me once this way. If you have a car that always starts when you turn the key, and one morning you turn the key and it doesn't start, you will try a few more times and then give up, assuming something is wrong with the car. Your key-turning behavior extinguishes rapidly. If, on the other hand, you have an old clunker that almost never starts easily, and one morning it doesn't start, you may turn the key and pump the gas for twenty minutes before you finally quit. You are on a long, random schedule. That's the kind of persistence I wanted to build into Hoku and Kiko.

Once the random schedule was gently and gradually established, Hoku and Kiko dashed over the rope eagerly when I first showed up with my bucket, because they knew the first crossing might be reinforced. If it wasn't, they kept working, with speed and excitement, never knowing which crossing would be the lucky one. Furthermore, I could make it even more exciting by occasionally rewarding them with a double handful of fish instead of a single fish each: a jackpot. In fact, I developed a personal habit of always ending a training session with a jackpot, under the no doubt anthropocentric theory that it took some of the sting out of the session's having to end at all.

The power of random reinforcement is what makes slot machines fun, and roulette wheels. In animal training, getting that variable schedule established is absolutely crucial if you want to go on to higher things without losing momentum.

Once it was done, in this case, I raised the rope so that it hung halfway under the water instead of along the tank floor. Now Hoku and Kiko had a chance to make mistakes. Being timid, at first they sometimes swam halfway over the rope and turned and dashed back; and sometimes they swam under it. They got reinforced only for passing right across it. However, they had learned that if you don't succeed, you can try, try again. Therefore, without discouraging them, I could let them go unreinforced for wrong responses and select just the responses I liked.

In a few sessions, they were making no mistakes, I had the

rope at water level, and they were jumping over it very prettily. It was no trouble to slide a 4-foot-long aluminum bar under the rope, like the bars they would soon be jumping at Ocean Science Theater, and then remove the rope and have them jump the bar instead.

In this simple task there were lots of details to be tidied up. The animals had to jump *over* the bar, not off the end of it. I also wanted them jumping precisely side by side, not one ahead of the other, or too far apart. I wanted them jumping in one direction only, left to right. Each of these things had to be established and then put on a random schedule. Each had to be treated as a separate training task. If one held back a reinforcement because the animals were not exactly over the bar, and then held back the next reinforcement because the animals were not strictly in unison, though they *were* over the bar, confusion and disaster soon resulted. It was hard to remember to take one step at a time.

It could go very fast, though. One could clean up two or three loose ends in a single training session, but it was absolutely crucial to keep everything straight in one's own mind and not to be tempted to work on two or three demands during a single chance for reinforcement.

Raising the bar presented another fundamental problem every porpoise trainer runs into. Hoku and Kiko learned to make a big jump over the bar very nicely when it was just at the water surface. I raised it a measly two inches above the water—and they refused to jump at all. *Now* what?

It seemed to be a problem in perception. To a porpoise, an object in the water is visible to the eye and also perceptible by sonar. Once the object passes above the water surface, it no longer registers on sonar, as far as we know, and it looks very different to the eye, broken into fragments by the tossing, glittering underside of the air-water interface. One must go slowly at this point, having perhaps several training sessions in which the target is just at the surface, now visible as the porpoise's activities stir up the water into wavelets, now invisible as the wavelets fall away.

Hoku and Kiko, with the bar just above water level. Hoku is fairly confident. Kiko is jumping late, and eying the bar nervously. I am laughing at Kiko and am about to reward her with a whistle blast at the peak of her jump.

Meanwhile the porpoise shifts gears, learning to judge the position of the jump from memory, and the height of the jump by sticking his head out and taking a look in the air before he makes his approach. He probably learns, too, to see with skill up through the water surface, much as some human fishermen can learn to see fish very well looking down through the same surface. It's quite a lot to ask, really, and it's remarkable how good the animals get at it.

So I put Hoku and Kiko's bar just above the water's surface, and they could see it some of the time. They thought they might be able to handle that, I suppose; anyway, they tried a few sloppy jumps.

Now I had to drop every criterion previously established—jump neatly, side by side, in the right place—and just work on the new criterion: jump the bar even if it is in the air. Once the new aspect of the task was accepted, I went back to being strict about all the other stuff, and in much less time than it took to train originally I soon had a nice double jump again, but with the bar fully in the air.

I called this "going back to kindergarten," and it became an accepted practice in all our training. When a new and difficult criterion was introduced—working in a strange tank, for example —all the rules about perfection that had been established would have to be set aside temporarily (perhaps for a day or two, perhaps for no more than half a training session) while the animal learned to accommodate to the new circumstances.

The strict trainer who cannot tolerate "going back to kindergarten" simply wastes time and causes stress, trying to force perfection from the beginning in a new circumstance when it will come back anyway once the new circumstance has been accepted. I have seen this happen dozens of times in a human situation. Here's an example: singers and musicians who perform splendidly in a rehearsal room then get yelled at for making gross errors with the music in the first on-stage rehearsals; yet they may be, for the first time, scattered in new groupings, standing on ladders, wearing huge costumes, and staring into spotlights. People or porpoises, it's the same problem. It's the "new tank syndrome," and you can lick it by relaxing criteria temporarily, by "going back to kindergarten." In the long run it is not time wasted, but time saved.

Once Hoku and Kiko's bar was above the water surface, and they were jumping neatly, and jumping two or three times, if necessary, for each reinforcement (that all-important variable schedule), I introduced a new criterion: jump the bar any place in the tank, wherever I've set it up. And then another: jump the bar even if it is a foot above the water, or 2 or 3 feet.

The next step was to get them to jump several bars. Before I could do that, Ron's manual said, I would have to teach them to jump the single bar *only* on command. It was back to Ron's training manual for me, to find out how *that* was supposed to be done.

Gary and Chris, meanwhile, were working with the bottlenoses, for the other half of the Ocean Science Theater show. Both animals were learning to play ball and to rise up out of the water and take a fish from one's hand, though poor Kane, with his bent tail, could not rise very high. Makua was supposed to be learning to press a lever, a simple behavior which can be used for all sorts of things: banging a drum, turning on lights, and so on. We were going to have Makua ring a ship's bell, which was mounted at the upper end of the lever in a cobbled-up arrangement designed by me (and badly designed) that clamped onto the tank side.

The tanks were well planned for this kind of work. Rather than being at ground level, like a swimming pool, they were raised just high enough to put the tank rim at the trainer's waist level. Thus you could get your hands in the water without leaning down, a convenience I much appreciated after watching trainers at another oceanarium, with tanks at ground level, being forced to work by the hour on their knees.

Training a porpoise to press a lever seemed like a straightforward "shaping" problem. One would reinforce head movements in the direction of the target, selecting stronger movements over weaker ones, until the animal was pressing correctly. Gary, however, had been working for three weeks to teach Makua to ring the bell with his nose, without success. Makua had developed a maddening error. He would come closer and closer to the paddle he was supposed to press, until you could barely see any space between his nose and the paddle, and yet he would not touch it. Gary had succumbed to the natural temptation to take Makua's nose and shove it against the paddle. When he did that, Makua usually swung his head hopefully out toward the pushing hand. If Gary pushed Makua's whole body, Makua, being an animal much concerned with his own rights and dignity, pushed back. He was not only much stronger than a person, but seemed to be, as he hung in the water, as balanced and immovable as a rock.

One morning I watched Gary train, and I thought about it until the cause of the problem presented itself. Gary, in his zeal, had been blowing his whistle to encourage Makua when he *thought* Makua was going to press the paddle. Makua had thus been reinforced many times for a behavior which might be described as: "Make Gary *think* you are going to press the paddle." Between them they had got this down to a masterpiece of almostness.

It took about ten minutes to overcome this. Solid though Makua was, the water he was in did move in a constant current, and as he hovered one millimeter from the paddle, sometimes he drifted into actual contact. I told Gary to put his hand on top of the paddle, so that he could sense even the slightest touch. Then he reinforced only those touches. In no time Makua was pressing Gary's hand on purpose, a behavior which immediately carried over to pressing the paddle whether the hand was there or not.

Then Gary could start rewarding him for every other bump, then for every third bump, until he was pressing the paddle repeatedly for each reward. Because he was now on a variable schedule, and bumping the paddle often and vigorously, the trainer could then select only those bumps that were vigorous enough to activate the mechanism and cause the bell to ring. By lunch time the clang of Makua's bell was ringing out all over Sea Life Park.

One day Tap was out with Georges on the collecting boat, and he saw a wild kiko fling itself into the air in a series of soaring, tumbling leaps of breathtaking beauty. He at once envisioned a kiko performing those leaps in the big space of Whaler's Cove. Since Hoku and Kiko were destined for Ocean Science Theater, I agreed to the capture of another kiko or two for Whaler's Cove. They could be trained right along with the spinners, and perhaps they would spontaneously show us that leap Tap had seen.

The first one to come in was a half-grown female whom Georges had named Lei, the word for Hawaii's flowered garlands. Lei was a dear little kiko, still quite small but with a full set of teeth; past nursing age, but not much past it. She had almost no spots, except for a few around her neck, hence the name; she acquired a full set of spots as she matured.

Lei was a typical adolescent. A flibbertigibbet. The spinners befriended her at once, nuisance though she was. She would rush up to Haole, the boss of the school, and accidentally bump into him, like a clumsy child. She tagged after Mele incessantly, getting in the way of Mele's busy social life. She quickly grew marvelously tame, the only really pattable kiko we ever had, and she ate well and soon learned to work for her fish.

Dottie and Chris had charge of the spinners. Besides trying to bring the spin under some kind of control, teaching the animals to stand on their tails and hula, and working on the unison porpoising, they were trying to get the spinners to wear plastic leis. And getting nowhere.

This behavior could not be trained in a group. Individual animals had to be shaped, first to approach the lei, then to put the beak or rostrum into it, then to raise the rostrum so that the lei fell around the neck as the animal stood on its tail and "hula'd," then to back down and slip out of the lei so the trainer could retrieve it.

Spinners are shy of strange objects, just as kikos are, and the bright-colored, prickly plastic leis were anathema to them. Days and days of work brought no results; each spinner rebelled when the lei touched its skin. Lei, the new kiko youngster, however, enjoyed playing with the leis and learned to wear one before she had been in captivity a month. She looked quite charming in a lei, too; pink flowers were especially becoming.

The only training problem was that after she had taken her lei off, she liked to hang it on one flipper and swim around playing keep-away. Keep-away is a favorite *Stenella* game. With something nonfrightening, such as a bit of seaweed or a piece of string, they will play for an hour, carrying it on a fin, letting it slip off and catching it deftly on the tail as they swim, pushing it with their noses, and stealing it from each other in wild passes and chases.

None of the spinners would play this game with Lei when the

token was that prickly string of flowers, so she drove us crazy playing it with the trainers, swimming temptingly close, with the lei draped over her pectoral fin, and then eluding the grasping hand. We had to get it back, lest it break and get clogged in the drains, or, worse yet, in some animal's stomach. Even timid spinners might well mouth and accidentally swallow the individual plastic flowers.

We had to introduce our first punishment: what Ron Turner called a "time out." When Lei wouldn't bring the flowers back, the trainer snatched up the fish bucket and walked resolutely away from the tank for a three-minute period. This spoiled the game, of course. After a few time outs, we found that Lei could be trusted to return the flowers at once when the trainer asked for them by sticking a hand in the water. Giving up the flowers was better than having to give up the training session.

Lei quickly picked up what the rest of the spinners had learned so far, except the spin. She couldn't actually spin, so she did a sort of flip-flop in the air when the rest went up. She was remarkably silly. The start of a training session or the arrival of a reward just for her would send her into spasms of delight, rushing about leaping and splashing and disorganizing the others. We could only hope she would become more settled as she got older.

Dottie finally took on most of the spinner training. Chris did some work with them, but he found the work exhausting and somewhat infuriating. It was necessary not only to keep track of five animals, but to keep track of where each animal was in each stage of training for each behavior. "*Haole is spinning well, should be on a variable schedule now, being reinforced for every second or third spin: Moki hasn't spun since Wednesday, give him a fish for every spin. Mele's getting lazy, just reinforce the higher spins.*"

The fact that all the animals heard the whistle meant that we had to tell them who deserved it by throwing or withholding fish to individual animals. They moved around a lot and stole each other's fish, besides, and it was all very confusing for the trainer, and of course for the animals, though they were making progress.

It's possible—in fact, desirable—to work on several different behaviors in a single training session, if you can find some way of doing so. We had a kind of tower with a platform on top, about 10 feet above the water, built beside the biggest tank. It had been intended as a spot from which to teach porpoises to leap up for a fish, but it made a fine platform from which to train spinners. You could see them better from up there, and get the fish to the right animal more accurately. Dottie used it, too, to aid in introducing variation into training sessions. She might start out training spinning from the tower, then come down to tank side and work on the hula and lei wearing, then go back up to the tower and spend some time picking up new stuff. The animals accommodated themselves to this, and it paved the way for training them to do different things on different commands.

The head-over-heels flip was the first new thing Dottie tried to pick up. She began reinforcing it whenever it occurred. She might be talking on the phone or scrubbing the fish bins, but she kept one eye on the spinner tank, and if she saw an animal flip, she'd blast on the whistle, wherever she stood, grab a fish from the nearest bucket, and run out and get the fish (hopefully) to the right animal. We all helped when we could. It meant walking around all day with your whistle in your teeth and a fish in your pocket, and it also required being able to recognize the individual flipping animal in the air, and again in the water to get the fish to him; and we all got good at that.

Lobtailing, or slapping the water with the tail flukes, is another common behavior which Dottie watched for and reinforced. There are degrees of lobtailing; a light tap on the water signifies impatience or annoyance; it may be repeated several times. A hard smack, which makes a loud, carrying "Crack!" both in the air and under the water, is an alarm signal. If one animal, in captivity or at sea, smacks the water hard, the whole school dives out of sight at once.

Our spinners often lobtailed once or twice when they expected a fish and didn't get one. Dottie began to reinforce that, and soon she had the whole bunch of spinners lobtailing with great enthusiasm, whipping the water into a froth and making a great commotion. It was funny to see.

We conceived of trying to get them to lobtail while proceeding in a circle around the perimeter of the tank. We didn't know how we were going to move the behavior to Whaler's Cove, where there would be no circle of walls to keep the animals on course, but it took an astonishingly short amount of time to get the animals proceeding in a tidy nose-to-tail circle in the training tank. The animals spaced themselves out to form a perfect ring, and any latecomer who perhaps was still eating a fish when the lobtailing started looked around for an empty spot and rushed over to fill it, for all the world like human beings taking up position in a folk dance.

The group porpoise or simple arcing jump looked like another big success. Dottie began reinforcing Akamai for porpoising. The other animals, hearing the whistle and getting no fish, began

"The group porpoise or simple arcing jump looked like another big success. . . . Haole paced himself and sprang into the air next to Akamai . . . one by one the others caught on."

watching to see what Akamai was doing. It was not long before
Haole paced himself and sprang into the air next to Akamai,
copying his arcing leap with perfect precision. He was reinforced
for that; one by one the others caught on. (Lei of course was last
and persisted in jumping too early or too late or in the opposite
direction for the longest amount of time.) It took constant attention to keep the group jump simultaneous and in formation; you
had to watch like a hawk to be sure, as the animals came down
and scattered, that you did not pitch a fish to any animal that
had goofed.

About this time, Georges brought in one more kiko, a fine handsome male named Kahili; the word refers to a patterned standard
made of feathers, which in old Hawaii was held up on either side
of a chief's chair.

To get Kahili acclimated and feeding, we put him with his own
kind, Hoku and Kiko. He was in fine shape when he came in, and
soon settled down and was eating well.

Kahili looked very handsome swimming near Hoku and Kiko.
Since we already had one kiko in the Whaler's Cove bunch, to
give us a chance at that big kiko leap, why not keep Kahili for
the Ocean Science Theater? If it was pretty to see two porpoises
going over a bar in unison, it should be even prettier to see three.

We whistle-conditioned Kahili and began training him with
the other kikos, on ball playing, gate work, leaping on cue, and
going over bars. Since Hoku and Kiko were accepting the bars
and the ball, Kahili was not afraid of them. What he was afraid
of, however, was Hoku.

It had not occurred to me that Kahili would be regarded as an
interloper. Among our spinners, animals formed pairs and had
their favorite swimming companions, but they also frequently
formed trios. Haole was the boss and was particularly in charge
of the only female, Mele, but he did not lay sole claim to her.
Though we rarely saw actual mating, there was a great deal of
sexual play and attempted copulation among all animals, and
this could be between male and female or between male and
male. In fact they were downright indiscriminate in the matter.

I assumed that kikos were equally liberal, and that Kahili would fit in comfortably with Hoku and Kiko; but not so.

Although Kahili was bigger than Hoku, he was downtrodden from the start. He was not allowed to swim side by side with Hoku, and most certainly not with Kiko. He had to follow a few humble paces behind. It was difficult for him to offer a behavior and get rewarded; Hoku stole his fish. Kiko and Hoku both cuffed him contemptuously with flukes or dorsal fins if he got in their way while they were working; and the streams of bubbles emerging from Kiko's blowhole at such moments gave us a clue to the frequency of porpoise scoldings that Kahili was receiving.

Perhaps if Kahili knew his job a little better he could work more confidently? We put him in Makua and Kane's tank (they ignored him) and began training him individually. Chris taught him to swim over a rope, then to jump over it, and then to transfer the behavior to the adjustable bar. Kahili worked vigorously when he didn't have Hoku and Kiko pushing him around. In fact he was a wonderful worker and would soon jump a bar 6 feet above the water.

Since Kahili had become both willing and accomplished, I put him back with Hoku and Kiko a few days later and asked all three animals to go over a bar together. Yes, Kahili would jump; but what we got was Hoku and Kiko making a lovely jump side by side, and Kahili jumping at the same time, next to them but well separated and with a cringing, cowering twist in the air, as if apologizing for daring to use Hoku's bar when Hoku was using it. Then, when he heard the whistle blow, Kahili ducked into a corner and made himself humble while Hoku and Kiko ate all the fish.

It was impossible. Short of hitting Hoku and Kiko over the head for being such snobs, I could see no way of rectifying Kahili's lack of status. We decided to put Kahili with the spinners and let him go to Whaler's Cove.

Owing to the arrangement of the tanks, our practice on cleaning day was to put spinners and bottlenoses together, and then bottlenoses and kikos together, draining and cleaning the tanks one at a time. Thus it happened that Lei and the spinners had never met Kahili.

The simplest way to move Kahili seemed to be to crowd him to one end of the tank with a net, which Dottie and I pulled, and then to have Chris and Gary pick him up and carry him over to the spinner tank and chuck him in. Kahili made no attempt to resist this, and so it was done.

Shock! Spinners scattered in every direction. Who was this stranger? Who was, in fact, this irresistibly handsome stranger? As Kahili toured his new quarters, both Mele and Lei rushed over to him and literally prostrated themselves in front of him. They lay across his bows, on their sides, or even upside down, so that he had to push them gently aside to swim at all. Kahili politely stroked the females with his rostrum, and they righted themselves and crowded on both sides of him, stroking his flanks with their pectoral fins and rising and falling with him, breathing with him in unison (which is a true sign of porpoise togetherness) and trailed by a curious and respectful group of male spinners. Kahili, poor outcast Kahili, was king!

It must have been great for Kahili. He remained the dominant animal in the Whaler's Cove group for years. He could choose his swimming partner (Lei, of course, being of his own kind, became the favorite as she matured). He could steal fish from anyone. He could chase and scold without being chased in return. He always had the best training position, right in front of the fish bucket.

It was not so great for Haole. Instantly deposed without even a fight, he moped prodigiously for two days. He picked at his food; he didn't join the others; he just floated about with his rostrum sticking out of the water, looking and no doubt feeling like someone who has just lost a fortune in a stock-market crash: a victim of unjust fate.

He had not lost all his status. He was still an animal to be respected, and since he was often the quickest to pick up new work, he was watched and copied by the others during training

The beginnings of wearing a lei: Dottie shapes a spinner first to bump a ring with its nose, then to lift the ring, then to "hula" inside the ring.

sessions. He continued to be the friendliest of all the spinners to human beings. He just wasn't the headman anymore, and I suspect life was never quite the same.

Kahili learned all the spinners' work quickly, though like Lei he never achieved much of a spin. The rapidity with which he had learned the bar jump suggested that he would have made a fine subject for individual shaping, but in Whaler's Cove we needed him only as part of the group (he never did show us that spectacular kiko leap Tap had seen in the wild, nor did any other kiko we ever had). Kahili did what he had to, but he never worked very hard; if the trainer didn't give him a fish, he could always commandeer one from another animal.

One might suppose that the presence of a bully and thief in a group would be detrimental to training. On the contrary. It was certainly detrimental to Kahili's training, but not for his victims. Having their fish stolen—confiscated might be a better word, since Kahili did it not by stealth but by threat—seemed to make the others work harder than ever for the next reward.

Following the rules for shaping, you can get virtually any animal to do anything it is physically and mentally capable of doing. All you need to do is figure out how to break down the behavior you have in mind into small enough steps so that you can train one step at a time. That's how circus trainers get an elephant to stand on one leg, or a tiger to jump through a ring of fire. There's a fancy name for it: successive approximation.

Shaping is a mixture of art and science. The science is in the process: establishing variable schedules, raising criteria one at a time, reinforcing accurately. People who are in the business of shaping behavior sometimes arrive through trial and error at an excellent intuitive understanding of this process. I have seen some superb shaping being done by football coaches, horse trainers, and symphony conductors.

The art of shaping, the game of it, is in thinking up what to shape and figuring out how to get there. Envisioning something new is surprisingly difficult. That is why you so seldom see a truly novel behavior in a circus act. I myself found it was much easier to use a standard behavior, such as jumping over a line, in several different ways than it was to come up with a behavior new in itself.

Once a trainer has invented something new, almost any other trainer can figure out a way to copy it. It would never have occurred to me that you could water-ski on the back of two porpoises, with one foot on each, but when some smart trainer did it at Sea World in San Diego, we were able to develop the same stunt. Again, this tends to make animal acts pretty uniform. Since any good trainer can duplicate any cute idea he sees, circus people, especially, have to strive for uniqueness by developing behaviors so difficult for the animals—tightrope walking, for example—that other trainers might not want to bother to try duplicating the act.

The path to the desired end point can take any direction; there are probably as many ways to shape a given behavior as there are trainers to train it. One trainer's recipe for a behavior might be quite different from another's. Someone else might have gone at Hoku and Kiko's bar jump quite differently from the way I did it. They could have been taught to jump in a particular part of the tank first, and then had the bar insinuated under them. One could have got them across the rope by moving the rope rather than by flushing the animals.

Traditional animal trainers rarely are aware of this: they think of their own series of steps as the only possible ones—this is the way you train a horse to bow, this is the way you train a bear to ride a unicycle—and they often guard their shaping recipes jealously and hand them down as family secrets. There are, indeed, knacks and shortcuts in some shaping recipes. The standard way to get a dog to do a back somersault in the air is to teach it to jump straight up, and then swat it across the rump in midair so you turn it upside down before it lands on its feet again. With praise, and food reward, the surprise to the dog is mitigated, and shortly it learns to jump up and fling itself backward to avoid the swat (you need a small, lively dog for this, of course; a fox terrier, not a Labrador retriever).

A dog backflip is almost always shaped the same way. Watch a dog act with this trick in it, and you can often see the swatting gesture of the trainer's arm reduced to a cue for the dog's behavior. That's the traditional shaping recipe; yet a trainer who didn't have that recipe could probably train a dog to do a back somersault in a number of other ways.

The most interesting single shaping job I ever participated in occurred several years after Sea Life Park opened. By that time we had two magnificent adult female false killer whales, Makapuu (named for a point of land off which she was caught) and Olelo. These animals, pitch-black, streamlined, about 13 feet long, were superb acrobats and could leap and fling themselves about in the air with the agility of a porpoise. I conceived of the idea of having the two of them jump across a line in the air, simultaneously but in opposite directions, their huge bodies crossing by each other in midflight. It is not a new idea; I have seen it done with porpoises and also with riderless horses, but I thought that with these photogenic animals it would be especially spectacular.

I took on the training of Makapuu, who was already performing in Whaler's Cove. Another trainer, an English girl named Jennie Harries, worked with Olelo in the training facility. First we each put a rope across the bottom, training each animal to cross it on command, and then raising the rope until the crossing became a jump. We trained Makapuu to jump from right to left, Olelo from left to right. Then we moved Olelo to Whaler's Cove (she was furious, hated it there, and sulked for two days).

Jennie and I began having individual training sessions in Whaler's Cove with each of our animals, one whale staying quietly right beside her trainer ("stationing," we called it) while the other whale worked, until each animal would jump nicely, in the correct direction, on command, over a line stretched several feet above the water, behind the reconstructed whaling ship in a back corner of the pool.

Finally we decided that the whales were ready to try it together. We each called our own animals to the side of the ship. I gave Makapuu the hand signal she had learned to obey, and Jennie signaled Olelo. The two whales plunged away in opposite directions, turned, leaped, one from the left, one from the right, over the rope—and had a 3,000-pound, 20-mile-per-hour head-on collision in midair.

Of course they refused to jump again. "No, ma'am! Not me!" We had to revamp the shaping plan completely.

We began training them individually again. This time I shaped Makapuu to jump not only from left to right but also at the far end of the rope, 40 feet away from me. I tied a rag to the center of the rope so that I could judge the distance better and shape her progressively farther away. Jennie did the same thing with Olelo, shaping her to jump from right to left, but at the near end of the rope.

After a couple of weeks, when the animals had calmed down

The double lei jump: "two spectacular animals, crossing each other in glorious trajectories way above the water surface, and almost brushing as they passed."

and learned the new rules, we asked them to jump simultaneously again, with the rope stretched just a foot or so above the water so that it wasn't much of a task. They soon jumped willingly, at the same instant, but a good 40 feet apart.

It took time: we could train them only for a few minutes a day, since they were also performing in four or five shows daily, doing things they had already learned.

Then we gradually raised the rope until the animals were both making a handsome, 10-foot jump. *Then* we kept the ends of the rope 10 feet up, but we sagged it in the middle; the idea had been arrived at after considerable discussion over coffee cups, and we could only hope it would work.

Sure enough, natural laziness caused both animals to drift closer and closer in their jumps, toward the low point in the center of the sagging line. Gradually "cheating" toward the middle, they learned to gauge each other's approach and to keep to their own side of center. Finally they were passing each other in midair with only inches to spare. We slowly pulled the line taut again until the center, like the ends, was 10 feet above the water, and we had what we'd been aiming for: two spectacular animals, crossing each other in glorious trajectories way above the water surface, and almost brushing as they passed. It remains, I think, one of the most stunning show behaviors we ever developed.

Shaping is fun. It is, however, only half of the training procedure. The other half is the establishment of the cues or signals that let the animal know what you want and when you want it. Psychologists call this "bringing the behavior under stimulus control." It is a tricky and exciting business. When you have good stimulus control, you have, in effect, a sort of language between yourself and the animal, and not entirely a one-way language. Your actions and his reactions begin to add up to mutual communication.

3. SIGNALING

Whose idea it was originally, I don't know: Ron Turner's, or Tap Pryor's, or Ken Norris's; but it was a wonderful idea. We trainers had been provided with an underwater electronic system for cuing porpoise behaviors by sound.

Most porpoise shows, like other animal shows, are run on hand signals: the animals learn that when the trainer points his hand straight out, he wants a tail walk; when he waves his hand to the left, he wants a jump through the hoop, and so on.

There are several reasons why sound cues are often better. First, a porpoise is a hearing creature more than a seeing creature; he discriminates and responds to sounds more easily than to gestures. Second, he has to be looking at the trainer to see a hand signal, but a sound can reach him no matter what he is doing. Third, hand signals inevitably vary from trainer to trainer. The animals can become so well conditioned to the signals of their regular trainer that they will not respond as well to someone else's signal, and the shows fall apart if the principal trainer is sick or has a day off.

We thought that mechanically produced underwater sounds, in addition to the other advantages, would vary less and should allow us to rotate trainers from day to day without detriment to the public performances once animal behaviors had been learned.

The sound cuing system, invented at considerable expense by a local electronics firm, consisted of a central panel of switches and amplifiers, and three portable underwater speakers, each controlled by a pedal, which could be plugged in by the tanks. Each switch on the panel turned on an oscillator which made a sound: a buzz, a click, a steady tone, low or high, a pulsed tone, and so on. Any sound could be sent through any loudspeaker. You could also get some wild effects by throwing two or three switches at once.

The sounds the machine made were not porpoise sounds, or anything like them. For convenience, the tones were all in the human hearing range and were the sorts of sounds easily differentiated by people. The animals could hear much higher tones than we could, and make much finer discriminations, but we needed tones that we could hear and tell apart. There's nothing more maddening (as I found out later while training a research animal), than using a cue inaudible to people, struggling with the porpoise for half an hour because today he suddenly seems to have forgotten everything he learned, and then finding out that the cue sound isn't working because of some electronic disorder—such as the trainer forgetting to plug the machine in—and the animal can't hear it either. Conversely, it was very useful to be able to hear the tone, say to oneself, "Oh-oh, *that* isn't the spin cue," and run back and correct the switch that you threw wrongly.

All of the animals had behaviors that were ready to be put on cue. Makua needed to ring his bell when he was told to, and to continue ringing it until he was told to stop. He also had learned to jump into the air and come down sidewise with a big splash, a behavior whaling men call breaching. He needed to learn when to do that, and above all when *not* to, since it was inconvenient if he did it right next to you when you weren't expecting it, and soaked you from head to toe.

The spinners needed cues for spinning, flipping, porpoising in unison, lobtailing, and the hula. Hoku and Kiko needed a cue for jumping bars. We trainers got together, chose sounds from the switch panel for each behavior, and labeled the switches.

So, with Ron's book in one hand and a bucket of fish in the other, so to speak, we started training cues, beginning with teaching the spinners to spin on command. Or, as Ron put it, we started "to bring the behavior under stimulus control."

First, you get your fish, and you hang the speaker in the water, and place the pedal on the training platform, and go inside and turn on the equipment and throw the right switch, and then go back outside and put your ear in the water (since you can't hear the cue sound on the air), and press the foot switch briefly, to make sure the sound is working. Then, when you take position on the training platform, the animals, seeing that it's breakfast time and the trainer is here, begin to spin, one here, one there. Nice high brisk spins, because you have shaped them to be so, and several spins for one fish, if necessary, because you have put them on a variable schedule for that behavior.

So, you turn on the sound for thirty seconds, and you reward with both whistle and fish every spin of every animal that occurs during the time the sound is on. Then you turn it off for thirty seconds and ignore every spin, no matter how spectacular, that occurs when the sound is off.

Now what happens in the textbook is that the animals begin to spin more often when the cue is on, and less often when the cue is off, until off-cue spinning has become "extinguished," and all the animals spin vigorously when the cue goes on. From being a meaningless sound which they ignore, an "unconditioned stimulus," the cue sound has become the signal for spinning, a "conditioned stimulus."

What happened in fact, at least with our spinners, was that the animals spun less and less when the cue went on, and instead went over and inspected the loudspeaker. When the cue went off, they threw themselves into the air in spasms of hysterical spinning, faster and faster, higher and higher, and when they didn't get rewarded for that, they stopped spinning altogether. It seemed as if they recognized that the cue sound had something to do with their getting fish at some times, and not at others, but that they blamed this discouraging event on the cue sound.

We had to go back to reinforcing all spinning, until they were enthusiastic about spinning again, and then once more introduce the cue sound, this time with the cue-on periods *much* longer than the cue-off periods. Still we saw some animals spinning perfunctorily when the cue went on, and spectacularly when the cue went off. Eventually we came to consider a big show of off-cue behavior as a sign that an animal was at least beginning to notice the cue, and would soon "catch on."

It was evident when each animal did catch on. Haole was the first; after four or five cue-training sessions, he began to startle when the cue went on and then to spin promptly and with vigor. Other animals soon followed; perhaps some of them recognized the cue and some of them just went up whenever Haole did. Anyway, we began to get good on-cue spinning.

Then we had to extinguish off-cue spinning, deliberately and cleanly. A stopwatch was helpful here. If they didn't spin for ten seconds, you could turn the cue on, let them spin, and reward them. Then you started to wait ten seconds again. If someone spun, you started counting over again, until eventually a ten-second period would pass with no spinning in it, so you could put the cue on again. It was as if we were using the cue—the *chance* to spin and earn fish—as a reward for the behavior of "not doing anything for ten seconds."

Gradually one could shape that period of not spinning into a longer and longer time. We found that when the animals would go for periods of up to a minute without offering a hopeful off-cue spin or two that the behavior was for practical purposes "on cue." You could count on the animals to spin on cue and count on them not to spin—or at least not to spin and expect a fish for it—when they didn't hear the cue sound.

Training the animals to porpoise in unison on cue followed the same procedure. We rewarded porpoising, for a few minutes, until all the animals were porpoising. Then we introduced a cue sound, a sound quite different from the spin cue. What happened? All the animals spun. At this point any sound from the loudspeaker meant "spin" to them.

Since we were using a continuous cue, since our cue sounds meant "keep going until the cue falls silent," we now learned that we could use the cue to say "No!" It was easy to tell, from the platform, whether the porpoises were preparing to porpoise in unison, or to split up all over the tank and spin. The porpoising cue went on, the animals looked as if they were going to spin, and before they left the water, the trainer turned the cue off, leaving a lot of surprised animals milling around. The cue went on again, and if they made even a half-hearted attempt at porpoising, the cue stayed on, they heard the whistle, and as the cue went off they were happily eating their fish.

The animals had learned to spin on cue, and *not* to spin off cue. Now they had to learn to porpoise on cue and *not* to porpoise off cue, and also *not* to spin on the porpoising cue and *not* to porpoise on the spin cue. Training the *do nots* was fully as important as training the *do's.* I have seen many a dog and horse trainer overlook this fundamental fact. You do *not* have full control over the behavior just because you can order it up when you want it; you must also make sure it is no longer offered spontaneously when you did *not* ask for it. The army sergeant whose platoon will advance under fire when he tells them to is still in a bad way if they may sometimes advance when he didn't tell them to. In fact a primary function of drill teams and marching exercises and so on is not only to bring specific behavior under stimulus control, but also to establish a pattern, a habit, a skill, even, of responding on cue and not responding in the absence of the cue.

Porpoises can generalize (so can many, many animals). By the time our group had learned to spin reliably on the spin cue and to porpoise on the porpoising cue, they had also learned that "cues mean *do* something," "*no* cue means do *nothing*," and "different cues mean do different things."

It took days and days to teach the spinners the first cue, and many sessions to get the second cue down pat. The third cue, a sound for the lobtailing behavior, was pretty well established in a morning. The animals had become "sophisticated" about cues; from now on it became much easier to teach those individuals not only underwater sound cues but hand signals or any other kind of command.

Ron's manual showed us one more refinement: the limited hold. This was a method for producing instant rather than dilatory response. At first, when we turned on the spin cue, some animals didn't get around to spinning until the cue had been on for ten or fifteen seconds and the other animals had spun and were eating their fish already. So we started with the average time—about fifteen seconds—that it took for all the animals to spin on cue, and we turned the cue on for just that long. If Moki, say, was pokey, and didn't spin in fifteen seconds, the cue went off and he was out of luck.

A stopwatch helped the trainer stay honest; it was always tempting to leave the cue on just a little longer when you saw that your dilatory animal was just about to jump. If you succumbed to that temptation, however, you could end up with the animals training *you* to leave the cue on longer and longer.

Animals have a good sense of time. Soon every animal began to hustle a little. Some jumped as soon as the cue went on, and everyone jumped before the fifteen seconds were up. Then we shortened the cue-on time to twelve seconds. Again, the laggards were out of luck. Again, they had to learn to hustle. We found that we could tighten up this "limited hold" to the smallest length of time in which the animals could physically accomplish the behavior. When our shows opened, the spinning in Whaler's Cove was on a three-second limited hold. The trainer punched the button, and bingo! six animals dove out of sight and then flew into the air all over the place. It was dramatic. Since the audience could not hear the underwater sound cues, it was also mystifying. The trainer didn't seem to do anything, the narrator was just rambling along, and yet the animals exploded into action at exactly the right instant, over and over again.

We explained and demonstrated the use of underwater sound cues in the Ocean Science Theater, and yet I often heard people in the audience wondering how we got this magical control at Whaler's Cove. Once I heard a European psychologist firmly telling his companions that we had to be using electric shock to make all the animals leap so promptly.

We had a lot to learn about using the sound equipment. Eventually we had very sophisticated, sturdy, compact equipment which we treated with deftness and deference, but at first!—it was otherwise.

The equipment was bulky and full of gremlins, and we beat it about dreadfully. One of the first things we discovered was that if you stepped on the pedal while the underwater speaker was out of the water, you broke the speaker, and it would cost $40 and take two weeks to fix. Then we discovered that the cue machine didn't like fish scales. Smelt have tiny little scales that get all over everything, and our hands were always covered with them (except Dottie's; she was both ladylike and sensible, and wore rubber gloves). Every light switch and doorknob in the training facility was coated with a layer of dried fish scales, and soon the cue switches were ringed and rimmed with the little scales, which worked their way down into the innards of the switches so they didn't operate. Later, when we began using tape cartridges to make cue sounds, the problem was even worse.

Then we discovered that, sturdy though the pedals were, they could break; and they could also get full of salty dampness and start giving you shocks. We discovered that speakers deteriorated if they were left in the water overnight, but that the initial setup of bringing your speaker out in the morning, dangling it into the water by its own cable, and keeping it there by putting a brick on the cable where it crossed the tank rim, was a pretty dumb idea. The cable connections wore loose. Sometimes the brick fell off, and the speaker, quite a heavy item, suddenly descended to the bottom of the pool, jerking itself out of its socket at the other end. Also Makua and Kane liked to grab the speakers by the cable and swim away with them.

So a man had to come out from town and devise stout metal straps to which the speakers could be bolted and thus hung in the tanks, and we all got another lecture about respecting equipment and washing the smelt scales off our hands before touching anything. These things seem very obvious now, and if any of us had been craftsmen, or experienced with tools and with using delicate equipment, I suppose we'd have had fewer surprises; but we were novices. And each time we got a surprise, we lost a day of training time.

Nevertheless, the sound cuing equipment was worth all the headaches. Makua quickly learned to ring his bell on cue, and to breach on another cue. Hoku and Kiko learned to jump their bar on cue, and not off cue. When they had done that, I put a bar to the left of me and a bar to the right of me, turned the cue on as they approached the first bar, left it on, and they went right ahead and jumped the second one. From two bars they went to three, and I was feeling pretty smug about my cue control until I discovered one day that while the cue meant "continue jumping bars" to them, it did not really mean "start now": they were starting exactly at seventeen-and-a-half-second intervals, whether the cue went on or not.

This is called "superstitious behavior"; the animal has picked up and is responding to some stimulus in the environment that actually has nothing to do with the cue—in this case, a time interval. In fact, for the interval to become well established, I had probably unconsciously picked it up, too, and was putting the cue on every seventeen seconds or so, exhibiting some superstitious conditioning in myself.

Sometimes superstitious behavior is useful. The spinners tended to suppose that they were more likely to get rewarded in one part of the tank than in another. Thus when they had all performed helter-skelter in the air, they would split and zoom to their own "lucky corners" to look for fish. We really didn't care where they went, but it made it easier to reinforce accurately;

you could tell that Kahili would be at home plate, Mele at first base, Moki out in right field, Haole in the middle, Akamai on your left, and Lei was the one rushing around like a maniac from place to place. The animals' superstitious locating of themselves did provide an extra cue as to who was who, and so no doubt became a kind of two-way conditioning, with the trainer learning to expect to look for Moki out there and Kahili right here, an accident that was beneficial all around.

Everything was going well except for Makua's blindfold training. He would have to be blindfolded to exhibit his underwater sonar or echo-location ability. On Ken's recommendation we were using rubber suction cups that stuck over the animal's eyes. We went through a lot of design changes. We tried using purchased suction cups designed to hold ski or surfboard racks onto the roof of a car. We tried using those suction cups but modifying them by grinding them thinner so the suction wouldn't be so strong. We tried casting suction cups out of silicone rubber. We tried making a fiberglass blinker that would cover the animal's eye without touching it; the blinker was held in place with suction cups that went on the animal's head, not directly over his eye.

No matter: Makua was having none of it. As soon as he saw the suction cup in Chris's or Gary's hand, he got ugly and began threatening with his teeth and striking with his rostrum. He *was* menacing, and the trainers were justifiably unnerved.

As head trainer, I had to cope with whatever was stumping Chris and Gary. I gave them Hoku and Kiko, who were making good progress on several behaviors now, and went to work myself on the bottlenoses.

Over the years, interviewing and hiring training staff, I learned to ask each person if he had had any long exposure in his life to large animals. I was not looking for training experience, but for some previous personal experience of the sight of large teeth. There is something in all of us which flinches from the approach of a large animal's tooth-lined jaws, something which can be overcome only with daily exposure. It didn't matter what the potential trainer's experience was, whether playing with a German shepherd or bridling and riding a horse or working on a dairy farm. If he'd been around big animals, he could take the sight of a porpoise, snapping its jaws in threat, in his stride. A city child, however, whether high school dropout or graduate zoologist, was apt to flinch involuntarily from a large-toothed animal with its mouth open, and to flinch often enough and clearly enough to encourage bullying behavior from the animal.

I decided to practice blindfold training on Kane, separating him from Makua for the first sessions. First I tried shaping him to sit still right in front of me and allow me to cover his eyes with my hands, one eye and then the other and then both. No problem. In addition to a whistle and fish reward, I rewarded him with stroking, which he loved. I deliberately refused to stroke him in the normal course of events, but I patted him vigorously after every whistle and before tossing the fish.

Then I rewarded him for allowing me to touch his body with one of the rubber suction cups. I showed it to him, I touched it here and there on his body, I rewarded him from time to time as I did so, until he was completely used to it—horse-training methods. Psychologists call it "habituation."

Finally I stuck the suction cup on Kane's back. Catastrophe! Kane broke away and went crashing and leaping all over the tank, trying to dislodge this nasty thing clinging to him. In due course he did dislodge it, and I retrieved it with a net. Then he would not come near the suction cup again.

So I revamped the shaping recipe. Now I trained Kane to press his rostrum against my right hand for prolonged periods, no matter what I was doing with my left hand. I counted the seconds, shaping a ten-second press, a twenty-second press, while I touched, tugged, and poked him here and there with my free hand. When the pressing behavior was well established (we called it "stationing," and learned to use it for all kinds of things) I used my free hand to stick and instantly unstick the suction cup from his back. Since he had learned to "stand still

Blindfold training. I am touching Kane's forehead with the suction cup. Kane is suspicious. He's making me reach for him, and his nearest eye (under shadow of wrist) is squinted shut.

no matter what" he stood for it. From there we rapidly progressed to putting the suction cup anywhere on his body (not his head) and to Kane swimming away with it and bringing it back for me to take off. He had learned that the sticky little thing was harmless, and that I could be trusted to take it off for him.

It just took patience then to get him to tolerate its presence over an eye; and when we'd reached that stage, I switched to Makua.

As soon as Makua saw the suction cup in my hand, he put on his show, rapping my arms and swinging his jaws about. But I had learned something from Gus the dog and Echo the pony stallion, after all; they had both been bold, aggressive animals too. The first time Makua rapped my hand, I was frightened and angry, and I rapped him right back on the rostrum. I couldn't possibly hit him hard enough to hurt, but my intent was clear, and to make it clearer I yelled "No!" and slapped the water with both hands.

Makua sank down about 3 feet and emitted a huge bubble of air underwater. This, I think, is something a porpoise does when it is surprised, though not frightened, by some unexpected turn of events. I have often seen an animal do it when it first notices some change in a prop, or when it suddenly "catches on" to a training idea that has been puzzling it. I was once on a ship that nearly bumped a large whale. When the whale noticed the ship, suddenly so close, it emitted a huge bubble of air as it startled and dove. The behavior always reminds me of a cartoon character with a balloon over its head and a bunch of question marks and exclamation points in the balloon.

Makua gave up trying to strike me after I hit him back, but he still swung his head about with his jaws open; so the next time he did that I grabbed my fish bucket and walked away, giving him a time out for that performance. When I returned, Makua was lolling about with a "Gee, what did I do?" air. He soon gave up all his threatening behavior.

Makua's training then followed Kane's. Soon I could put the blindfolds over both eyes while he stationed in front of me; and I was looking forward to being able to ask him to do things with the blindfolds in place.

He still did not *enjoy* the necessity of having his eyes covered, whether by suction cups or by blinders. One morning when Makua was being particularly sulky and recalcitrant, he suddenly let out his breath and sank to the bottom of the tank, where he lay motionless. A half-minute passed, and then a minute. I became most alarmed. Had he died? It certainly looked like it. I rushed off to find Chris to help me get Makua up again. When Chris looked in the tank, he laughed. "Makua's just sulking. Look at him—he's watching us." Sure enough, through the water surface I could make out Makua's little eye, regarding us wickedly.

Playing possum, Chris told me, was something he had seen several times when a bottlenose was displeased. The first time he saw it he too thought the animal was dying. He jumped in and pulled it up, only to have it take a breath and sink right to the bottom again, more displeased than ever at being hauled about so. He pulled it to the top five times before it became clear to him that the animal was sinking on purpose.

I can't imagine what earthly value this behavior pattern is to a Pacific bottlenose porpoise which spends most of its life in water about 3 miles deep and could hardly sink immobile to lie on the bottom every time it felt miffed. But they sure did it in our tanks.

Once Makua was down there, there was not much I could do. Time outs had no effect; indeed, by sinking, he was giving *me* a time out. There was no way to punish him. Oh, I could have got a long stick, perhaps, and poked him until he came up, but the trouble with that approach is that it makes the subject mad, he gets more resistant, you have to increase the vigor of your punishment to get a reaction, and pretty soon you are resorting to cruel and unusual means, or to violence. That is the nasty trap built into negative reinforcement which we can see operating around us all the time, from treatment of criminals to escalation of bombings. I wasn't about to get involved in that chain of events.

So I dipped into Ron Turner's manual and read and reread the sections on extinction. How do you get rid of a behavior you don't want?

You can punish the undesired behavior; that was out.

You can let it die away by itself for lack of reinforcement; but that wouldn't work this time. As long as Makua persisted in this behavior when I brought out the blindfolds, he *was* getting reinforced. He was postponing blindfold training, which was what he wanted. Besides, he could and did stay down for five minutes at a time, and one could lose an awful lot of valuable training time waiting for him to come up.

You can interpose some incompatible behavior, training the animal to do something else that can't be done while lying on the bottom; but that is what I was trying to do anyway.

The word "extinction" cropped up quite a lot in the business of bringing behavior under stimulus control; when the behavior is occurring on cue, it is extinguishing off cue. There was the answer! I would train Makua to lie on the bottom on purpose, in response to a sound cue. Then I would extinguish the behavior off cue. Then when I *didn't* want him to play possum, I wouldn't give him the cue.

The next time Makua sank himself, I blew the whistle and threw him a handful of fish. He emitted his large, astonished bubble, and surfaced and ate the fish. We went back to blindfold work. By and by he got mad and sank himself again. I reinforced it again. By the next day he was sinking over and over, and I began requiring a certain length of sinking time and giving him a time out if he came up too soon. Soon I had the sinking behavior stretched to a reliable thirty seconds, and I introduced a sound cue. Makua rapidly learned this, having already assimilated two other sound cues, one for ringing the bell and one for breaching.

At last spontaneous sinking disappeared. Makua sank on command a few times at the end of each session, and he buckled down and wore his blindfolds like a gentleman when asked.

The submerging turned out to be an amusing performance behavior. It was corny, but it was funny. In our glass tank the audience could see Makua above and below water. As he stuck his head out at the training platform, the narrator might explain that the trainer had asked Makua to do something, but forgot to say "please"; and then the cue would go on, quietly, and down Makua would go to the bottom, sinking tail first and lying there, the picture of hurt pride, until the trainer "repaired the error," turned the cue off. Makua bounced happily to the surface, and the trainer surreptitiously rewarded him with a fish.

Porpoise sonar was first postulated in 1945 by a collector at Marine Studios in Florida who noticed that Atlantic bottlenose porpoises could invariably locate and pass through the holes in his nets, even in the muddiest inshore waters. To follow up on this observation, William Schevill and Barbara Lawrence, researchers at Woods Hole, installed a porpoise in a muddy salt-water pond for a summer, and began to investigate whether or not the porpoise could indeed "see" without using its eyes. Visibility in the pond was nearly zero; a white disk disappeared from sight when it was 2 feet under the water. Yet the porpoise not only navigated with ease but located targets and even selected a larger piece of fish over a smaller one, or a favored variety of fish over one less favored, from a considerable distance.

During this procedure an underwater microphone picked up sounds coming from the animal, percussive sounds which grew closer together as the animal approached the target, ending in a creaking noise like a squeaky door. Further investigations by Dr. Winthrop N. Kellogg, Ken Norris, U.S. Navy scientists, and others have since demonstrated that what the porpoise does is to send out from its forehead a beam of sound, which bounces off any solid object in front of the animal, making echoes. The animal picks up the echoes, apparently not with his ears but with sound-carrying channels in his lower jaws. He can then translate the echoes into a sort of mental picture of the object. He can tell how far away it is, how big it is, and quite a lot about its shape and consistency. His sonar gives him a sort of TV picture of what is in front of him.

A porpoise can be trained to locate by sonar an object as small as a beebee on the floor of the tank. He can make size discriminations so fine that we would have difficulty making them visually. He can judge materials to the point of being able to tell an aluminum square from a copper square of the same size and thickness. He can most especially well "see" air bubbles; when a porpoise "looks" at a human swimmer, he may be far less conscious of the body outline than he is of the air spaces in the swimmer's lungs and sinuses.

We thought that public demonstration of this interesting capability could be easily made by covering the animal's eyes, so that he plainly couldn't be using them, and then requiring him to find fish, locate targets, and evade obstacles while blindfolded. One would be able to see the animal making scanning motions with his head, sweeping the water with a beam of sound like a person moving a flashlight beam around a dark room. With the aid of a good hydrophone (underwater microphone) the audience would hear that part of the sonar sound which is audible to human beings and could notice the sound becoming louder and sharper as the animal closed in on its target. This was what we were aiming at for the Ocean Science Theater.

Makua was no genius about using his sonar. Perhaps using sonar in the confines of a cement tank is quite different from using it in the open ocean. He took his time about learning to find and ring his bell while blindfolded, but he finally did learn to do so, and also to pick up small objects and return them to the trainer.

Eventually we trained animals of several species to wear blindfolds, and then to echo-locate for our audiences. A small false killer whale named Ola was probably our star sonar animal. By the time Ola came to Sea Life Park, several years after we opened, we had good hydrophones plugged into the P.A. system at Ocean Science Theater. Ola was pretty noisy, anyway. The audience could hear every pop and click and squeak as Ola, blindfolded, zoomed around the tank picking up on his nose a bunch of rings that were slowly sinking and "scanning" the tank floor, very evidently, if any rings went to the bottom before he got to them.

I always liked to hear an audience fall silent as one of our echo-locating animals "looked" for a lost ring that had settled to the bottom. When the animal "saw" the ring and homed in on it, the clicks over the hydrophone got louder and louder and then stopped abruptly as the animal deftly nosed the ring off the floor. The audience invariably gasped in unison and then applauded. That gasp always gave me a thrill; they saw and heard what had happened, and they understood.

Sea Life Park grew and grew. The Reef Tank was almost finished, so Georges went fish collecting.

When the Reef Tank was filled with water, there was a prob-

The Hawaiian Reef exhibit. Visitors descend a spiraling glass-walled corridor to view a living coral reef, with all its inhabitants.

lem; several windows leaked ferociously. They didn't just dribble water, they sprayed streams of water clear across what was to be the public viewing corridor. The tank had to be emptied and the windows resealed.

Meanwhile Georges arrived with a load of colorful reef fish that had to be put somewhere; they would not live forever in the *Imua*'s bait wells. As many as possible were installed in aquariums, bathtubs, fiberglass bins, whatever was available, up at the Reef Tank. Could the rest of them be put in the training tanks with the porpoises?

Why not? Porpoises, after all, have seen fish before. They should not find the sight disturbing; and it seemed unlikely to me that our animals would eat the reef fish, many of which were nasty, prickly things with spiny fins, and most of which were considerably larger than the smelt and little mackerel our animals seemed to prefer.

Half the reef fish went into Makua and Kane's tank, the other half into Hoku and Kiko's tank. The fish headed right for the central drains which afforded a bit of shelter.

Makua and Kane said "yum yum yum" and ate up all the reef fish in their tank in the twinkling of an eye. Hoku and Kiko refused to swim over the populated drain in their tank for two days.

I still had in my mind's eye a vision of Hoku and Kiko passing intricately through underwater hoops. A vertical arrangement was difficult to manage in our shallow training tanks, so I decided upon a sort of slalom, a chain of hoops through which the animals would pass, left to right, right to left, like children playing "Go in and out the windows." This would show off the suppleness and grace so characteristic of kikos, and would also fill up the Ocean Science Theater tank visually in a satisfying way.

The stiff yet bendable plastic pipe used in landscape irrigation systems could be bent into splendid 5-foot-diameter hoops, lightweight, sturdy, and waterproof. We "liberated" some of this pipe

No matter what I did, Hoku and Kikŏ avoided passing through the second hoop.

from the Sea Life Park construction site and made up a bunch of hoops.

When I had the animals going through one hoop well, I added a second one, at an angle, and tried to get them to go through that one after the first. No luck. They carefully avoided the second hoop. I tried hanging it so close to the first hoop that they practically *had* to go through it, and yet they would weasel out of the gap, unless there was no gap at all, in which case both hoops looked like one, anyway.

If I gave them no fish unless they went through both hoops, they stopped swimming through hoops altogether, and the behavior extinguished. What was wrong? Surely they weren't afraid of the second hoop? Why couldn't they figure it out—why did they work so hard to *avoid* the second hoop?

I plunged back into the manual and finally even called Ron Turner long distance. It seemed that what we had was not a single behavior but a "behavior chain." A behavior chain is a series of behaviors, each one of which is rewarded by the opportunity to do the following one, until the end is reached. And a behavior chain, curiously, has to be trained backwards.

To train a slalom through several hoops, I had to train, first, the behavior of passing through a single hoop in a single direction, from left to right, and then *put that behavior on cue*. That hoop now became the last hoop in the chain: with my six-hoop plan, it would be hoop 6.

Now I put another hoop in the water, hoop 5, coaxed the animals through it, and rewarded them for swimming back and forth through it, until they were comfortable. Then, when they swam through hoop 5 from right to left, instead of giving them a fish, I turned on the "hoop" cue. They knew what that meant; swim through hoop 6 from left to right, and you'll get a fish. Thus the cue for hoop 6, left to right, was the reward for hoop 5, right to left.

When they would go through both hoops easily, I started turning the cue on as they approached hoop 5, and leaving it on as they went through. If my timing was right, they went through hoop 5 and then turned and went through hoop 6. If my timing was wrong, they ducked around hoop 5 and went only through hoop 6, but when they did that I could correct them by turning the cue off before they finished the behavior. Soon I could hang both hoops in the tank side by side, put the cue on no matter where the animals were, and they would position themselves and take hoop 5 right to left and hoop 6 left to right, every time.

Now I could introduce hoop 4 in front of hoop 5, use the cue as a reward for passing through that new hoop, left to right, and so on, until we had a handsome slalom of six hoops, having backed all the way up the behavior chain to hoop 1.

The six-bar jump, which has already been accomplished, was of course also a behavior chain, one I had trained successfully through dumb luck. Just by accident, before I tried to get the animals to jump two bars in succession, I had already taught them to jump one bar on cue, and one bar in any part of the tank. It was not difficult for them, then, if they jumped a bar, and the cue was still on, and there was another bar in front of them, to go ahead and jump that one, too. The hoop chain, with its necessity of reversing direction each time, was not so obvious, and skipping the business of putting the behavior on cue first was fatal. Ron pointed out to me that if you start the chain from the front end, and then add the new thing, you are asking for an animal to do something he knows, go unreinforced, and then try to get reinforced by doing something he doesn't know. You have to *end up* with the guaranteed sure thing.

The best behavior chain I ever saw was accomplished by a white rat that had to go up a little ladder, cross a platform, climb a rope, cross a bridge, get into a little box on a pulley, release the pulley, lower himself and his little elevator box paw-over-paw to the floor, and finally press a button and get his food pellet. The only practical use I've found for the knowledge of behavior chains is that it seems easier and faster to memorize poems and musical pieces if you start with the last sections and work forward from the end.

A curious thing happened to the chain of hoops behavior when we eventually got it into the shows. In the training tanks, which were shallow, there was not much water above or below the hoop chain. At Ocean Science Theater, which was 14 feet deep, we hung the chain through the middle of the water, with 5 or 6 feet of water under and over it. Hoku took to going down the chain underneath Kiko, instead of beside her. He paced her exactly, turn for turn, tail beat for tail beat, but under the hoops, not in them. One day, narrating a show, the solution to this problem suddenly occurred to me: I signaled the trainer and the assistant and said to the audience, "We'll lower the hoops to touch the bottom. Then Hoku can't possibly go under them." The assistant slacked the rope, the hoops sank 6 feet, the trainer turned on the cue, and as Kiko went through the hoops, Hoku neatly positioned himself and paced her down the chain, turn for turn, tail beat for tail beat—*over* the hoops. It was hilarious, and we kept it in the show, letting Hoku run under the hoops, lowering the hoops to the bottom and letting him run over them, in every show.

Opening day, planned for January 1, 1964, eventually took place February 11, owing to construction strikes and bad weather. Our budget was predicated on money flowing in as well as out from New Year's Day on. Even if the turnstiles weren't turning, porpoises had to be fed, people had to have paychecks, and bills had to be paid. With each delay we got broker. One of our suppliers had a credit manager named Wolff, and we used to joke, when he came out to the Park site, that the wolf was at the door; but it wasn't so funny for the people in the front office.

We trainers, however, were blessed by delays. Every day that the opening was postponed gave us one more day of training. The spinners were in good shape. They moved up to Whaler's Cove about a week before Christmas: Haole, Moki, Mele, and Akamai, the spinners, and Lei and Kahili, the two kikos. Dottie soon had most of the behaviors we had trained going well in the new location: the spin, the hula with Lei wearing a lei, the porpoising in formation.

It was intriguing to discover that the behavior, developed in the training tank, of six animals slapping their tails on the water while circling the tank edge could be transferred perfectly to the open water of Whaler's Cove. Without any tank walls to guide them, the porpoises nevertheless formed a perfect circle and motorboated around it, nose to tail, as long as the cue was on.

Our five-eighths-scale model of a whaling ship, christened the *Essex*, had been installed on its concrete base in one end of Whaler's Cove. It was from the *Essex* deck that Dottie trained, with her fish bucket on the railing and the cue machine beside her. The ship was stunning, a detailed smaller copy of a real whaling ship that had sailed out of Honolulu in the early 1800s and been sunk by an angry whale.

Herman Melville heard the story from an *Essex* survivor in a bar and based *Moby Dick* on this true incident. We chose to name our ship after the original *Essex* because we were on the side of the whales.

The ship itself was a labor of love, designed by marine architect Ernie Simmerer and built by craftsmen at the Pearl Harbor shipyard who had a wonderful time laying aside the welding and drilling of modern shipbuilding to use old-time skills to construct the upper two-thirds of an old wooden ship down to the last yardarm and belaying pin. The rigging was correct, and the ship flew a replica of the original captain's flag of the old *Essex* and the thirty-star American flag of the period. (When the Park opened we got at least one complaint a week at the ticket house that the flag had the wrong number of stars on it.)

We wanted someone to swim with the porpoises in the show, and someone showed up. Sculptor Al LeBuse was working on the site, making a charming gold-leaf porpoise for the finial of the flagpole at the Park's entrance (I wonder how many people ever notice it, 100 feet in the air? It's still there now) and making carvings for the gift shop we planned to open. His lovely Hawaiian wife, Lani, hung about the training facility helping out and patting the porpoises. Lani proved willing to be hired as the swimmer. I worked out a show script in which Lani would dive off the ship, swim to the island in Whaler's Cove, escorted by the porpoises, and sit on the island while the animals went through their behaviors. Then she would slip into the water and play with the porpoises as the low-key but charming high point of the show.

The island gave us another idea: why not have a porpoise race? The animals could start from the ship and race across the pool, around the island, and back. If we could develop speed, it should be quite dramatic.

To train this, Dottie began with a homemade sound cue: a long, warbling blast on the whistle, quite different from the short, sharp chirp we used as the conditioned reinforcer. (The day she started to train it, the cue machine was broken, hence the substitute sound.) Any animal that by chance swam toward the island after Dottie's warbling blast was heard got a chirp-whistle and a fish, the fish thrown well ahead of it to encourage hunting in the direction of the island. Dottie (like all of us who trained spinners) shortly developed a fantastic throwing arm and could pitch a fish 100 feet or more with considerable accuracy. In a few days all the animals rushed toward the island when they heard the warbling blast which was the "race" cue.

Then we put Lani on the island with a bucket of fish, and she rewarded the animals by throwing fish in back of the island. Soon they were going all the way around the island and coming back to the ship for the reward.

There was no need to establish a strict limited hold; the animals hurried off and hurried around the island in order to get back for the fish. Habitually they made the run at speeds of about 15 knots, roughly 18 miles an hour—a scientist later clocked them with a camera. This is fast enough to look downright startling, and the race became a dramatic feature of the show.

Moki, who always marched to a different drummer, soon discovered that he could rush off purposefully with the others, then double back just as he reached the island and be the first one at the ship to steal other porpoises' fish. We gave the animals a time out if anybody else tried it, but Moki did it with such crafty style, making a perfect imitation of the revved-up start and the brakes-on finish, that it was funny to see and we left it in the show.

Up at the Ocean Science Theater, construction was far from complete, and we just had to pray that the animals would have at least a few days to become accustomed to new surroundings before they had to perform before audiences.

I had planned a show in which Makua and the kikos would work together at first, ending up with a joint water-polo game, followed by Makua doing a solo sonar demonstration and his various other behaviors. Then the kikos would do their fancy six-bar jump and chain-of-hoops swim. We had also trained the kikos to jump high in the air together whenever they heard the sound of applause; we all stood around the training facility clapping vigorously and recording it on tape, to make the cue. Our idea was that the audience itself would be the cue for a finale behavior of high repeated jumps.

When the animals had learned to bat a ball toward a goal,

Dottie training Hoku and Kiko to play water polo.

Makua's goal being at the left end of the tank, and Hoku and Kiko's goal at the right end, we put them together in a training tank to try to train a real game of water polo. Would they understand that competition was involved? Could we actually reward them for making goals, rather than for just hitting the ball right? Would it be a *real* game?

We began to "play," the ball in the middle and one trainer for each team, with whistle and fish bucket at opposite ends of the tank.

It took the animals about three training sessions to figure out what was happening. Aha! The idea was not just to make goals, but to keep the ball away from the other team.

The trouble was, nobody told them about any rules against foul play. The game instantly turned into an all-out melee over possession of the ball, with Makua crashing into Hoku and stealing the ball, and Hoku and Kiko ganging up on Makua, ramming and swatting him and doing their porpoise best to drive him off the playing field.

There went our water-polo game! Porpoise warfare was *not* something we wanted to demonstrate to an audience. I revamped the show plan, designing it so each species would work separately, and we were careful to keep genuine competition out of training situations as much as possible henceforth. Makua, Hoku, and Kiko were good buddies, in normal circumstances; but when forced to compete for rewards, they turned into no-holds-barred entrepreneurs, and we couldn't encourage that!

Letter from Tap Pryor to stockholders:

January 6, 1964

Dear . . .

Forgive the form letter . . . we're pressing hard toward opening Sea Life Park. . . . the first preview is scheduled for January 24th, when Assistant Secretary of the Navy, Jim Wakelin, Admiral Hayward, and the Interagency Committee on Oceanography have scheduled a special visit . . . barring bad weather, it appears that we will open within our budget and with a slim but adequate fund reserved for working capital. Fortunately, new exhibits differ from other businesses in that a particularly high volume can be predicted in the early weeks. . . .

Tap was already much involved in planning and developing the proposed research institute which was the real raison d'être of Sea Life Park. Porpoise research was projected, and ambitious offshore projects based on Cousteau's undersea pioneering. We hoped for a laboratory on the sea floor, for a small submersible to study fish behavior, and for special salt-water facilities, such as oceanarium-sized tanks, that are not available at ordinary marine laboratories. Tap and Ken Norris thus had been cultivating potential users and sponsors of such facilities, of which the U.S. Navy certainly was one. The proposed link with the exciting field of ocean research and development was also one of the factors that made Sea Life Park intriguing to potential investors in the early 1960s.

Many, many times in the future we were to put on special demonstrations for high-powered groups of scientists, businessmen, and government people, pushing our product, which was innovative ocean research, and our facility, which was a unique and fertile blending of commercial and pure science organizations.

The demonstration on the 24th of January, before opening day, was the first of these adventures.

Admiral John Hayward, then stationed in Hawaii and a great friend to Tap's projects, had set it up; Secretary Wakelin (he and his wife Peggy were to become dear friends of mine) had agreed to bring his group, which was visiting Hawaii for some other reason, out to Sea Life Park for an hour.

As I stood on the deck of the Ocean Science Theater, with a microphone in my hand and my knees buckling with terror, here they came, hordes of VIPs in business suits and white uniforms glittering with gold, down from the Hawaiian Reef tank, where they had not seen much, since the exhibit was far from ready, along the path to the Ocean Science Theater. And what did I have to show them? Maybe nothing.

The Ocean Science Theater had been filled with water three days earlier, and we had moved Makua, Hoku, and Kiko down immediately to get them ready for this demonstration. There was an air leak in the plumbing system somewhere which we had not had time to fix, and that meant that the water was full of tiny bubbles. One couldn't see across the tank, much less get that crystal-clear impression of a "blue room" that I had imagined. We had managed to cobble up six bars extending from the glass walls of the tank for the six-bar jump; but the chain of hoops wasn't ready.

Tap wanted me to use Hoku and Kiko and not Makua. The members of the Federal Interagency Committee on Oceanography had certainly seen solitary porpoises ringing bells and playing ball before, and Makua's sonar work was definitely not ready yet. Hoku and Kiko, on the other hand, with their elegant appearance and fancy behavior chains, would be something new. So Hoku and Kiko it was.

And by now, dear reader, you know Hoku and Kiko. Here they were in a new tank, with never-before-seen glass walls, with a new holding tank and a new kind of gate, with the trainer standing in a new place on a wooden gangplank that hung threateningly out over the water. Let the cues sound different, too, because of the new echoes; what were the chances of Hoku and Kiko relaxing enough, in three days, to do *anything* right, much less a whole performance? Pretty slim.

I invented a little spiel about the nature of porpoises and the possibilities of porpoise research, and I prepared to give it as I watched Tap and Admiral Hayward seating their group in the stands. I don't think I had ever spoken over a microphone before, nor had I ever spoken to a large group, except as an actress in college plays, where I had a script, the protection of others, and terrible stage fright nonetheless. *This* time the stage fright was truly appalling, and Hoku and Kiko, though Chris on the training platform did his very best, made their contribution by swimming around staring out through the glass at the audience, and doing absolutely nothing they were asked to do.

In due course I would learn how to cover up for this event, but on that awful day I knew of nothing to say but: "Well, I guess they aren't going to do that either, heh, heh." *Finally* Hoku and Kiko stopped staring suspiciously through the glass long enough to go over the six bars, gracefully arcing in and out of the water against the glass, making the beautiful picture they were supposed to. I waved frantically at Chris to stop right there, to quit while we were ahead. I thanked the politely clapping audience and suggested they come back in a month to see what Hoku and Kiko could really do (I didn't have the courage to order them to *keep* clapping, and louder, please, so that Hoku and Kiko would do the applause jump). Then I yanked out the mike plug, raced down the ladder into the trainers' little sitting room underneath the stage, and took up smoking again.

Actual opening day was not nearly so bad. By that time we had the animals working pretty well. We held two previews, one for the press, their families, and representatives of the travel industry upon which our survival would depend, and one for our construction workers, their families, and the people of the nearby town of Waimanalo. Tap himself did the narrating at the Ocean Science Theater for these previews. With his by now extensive experience speaking to investors and other groups he could extemporize comfortably when the porpoises dawdled.

During the previews at Whaler's Cove we just ran through the behaviors the animals had learned. By opening day, I'd worked out a written script; Ocean Science Theater could be ad-libbed, but Whaler's Cove needed more structure. We tried the script a few times, and it seemed okay. The night before opening, Dottie and Chris decided that what Whaler's Cove needed was music. There was background music on a public address system all over the park, which we could plug into, but they thought Whaler's Cove should have its own music. When I came in the morning of opening day, they had picked out an excellent musical accompaniment to my script from Chris's collection of Hawaiian records. We took his little portable phonograph down to the *Essex* and plugged it in, setting it on top of the cue box while we took up position near it for the show.

We did that first show for our first real audience with Dottie training, Chris frantically changing records, and me narrating the script over the mike for a sentence or two, then holding the mike up to the phonograph for a little musical effect, then talking into it again, getting constantly mixed up, and once in my confusion holding the mike up to Dottie and treating the audience to a painfully amplified whistle blast.

Never mind; it was a great success. The music rose. Lani dived gracefully from the ship's railing into the gin-clear waters of Whaler's Cove. The porpoises swirled around her. When she landed on the island, they flipped into the air, in unison, and I paraphrased some of Herman Melville's charming lines about porpoises: "These are the lads before the wind; they swim in hilarious shoals, tossing themselves to heaven like caps in a fourth of July crowd. . . ."

The porpoises did the hula and perfectly performed their circling, tail-slapping maneuver, which we called a Samoan slap-dance; they raced around the island and climaxed the show by spinning, and then Lani slipped into the water with them, and they swam into her arms and towed her about as she held one or two of them by the dorsal fin. They surface-dived with her, in water-ballet unison, and again swirled close around her as she came up. I pointed out on the microphone that none of this part of the show had to be trained, that the animals did it out of love and for pleasure. I quoted Plutarch's opinion that the porpoise is the only creature that seeks friendship at no advantage to himself. The music rose and fell, the porpoises were beautiful and so was Lani, and people cried, including all of us on the deck of the *Essex*. Opening day was a success.

4. COLLECTING

Georges Gilbert, our first collector and our best, was a husky, handsome, gentle, humorous man in his forties, half French and half Hawaiian. He was a knowledgeable fisherman who could locate and collect unharmed virtually any fish in Hawaiian waters, from a three-inch butterfly fish to a school of lightning-fast tuna. Georges learned his porpoise and whale collecting techniques from Frank Brocato, collector for Marineland of the Pacific in California, who had invented a practical way to catch cetaceans in waters too deep and open for the use of surround nets.

Georges hunted from a leaky old fishing sampan, the *Imua* ("Imua" means, roughly, "forward!"), remodeled following Frank's system. A pulpit was extended forward from the *Imua's* bows, so that Georges could stand out over the bow wave with his catching rig and snare a porpoise playing in front of the traveling ship. A tall A-frame was erected on the aft deck so large animals could be winched aboard. The catching device consisted of a steel pole with a noose at the end of it, held open by a metal frame and stitched to a shallow net. When Georges dropped this arrangement in front of a traveling animal at just the right instant, the animal shot forward in fear, hitting the netting, breaking net and noose free of the rig, and drawing the noose tight around its own middle. The noose ran to a coiled line on deck which paid out as the animal fled, until Georges could work his way back from the pulpit, grab the line, and bring the animal in hand over hand to the side of the ship.

Some animals gave up quickly and let themselves be brought in almost without a fight. Others put up a ferocious battle. A little spinner, if determined, could pull the drifting *Imua* all over the face of the ocean. One courageous pilot whale fought so hard and so long, three hours in rough seas, that the rope noose began to cut into its skin, and Georges, with admiration and regret, cut it loose for the sake of its own well-being.

Georges, on the pulpit of the *Imua,* hunting a school of false killer whales.

Getting a line on a porpoise was not easy. Georges was remarkably skilled. Not until I saw other collectors try for two or three weeks to catch a spinner, finding the animals and getting in among them day after day, and yet every day failing to noose one, did I appreciate what a master Georges was. In 1962, before the training tanks were finished, Tap felt that for fund-raising purposes he needed to be able to say he actually possessed some porpoises. It was then that he had an Esther Williams plastic swimming pool erected on our back lawn, with a little pump pulling salt water from our beach. He gave Georges the order to start hunting. Four days later there were four healthy spinners in that plastic swimming pool. Four animals in four days is still Sea Life Park's all-time record for collecting.

Getting the noose on the animal was only the first job. Then the animal had to be safely delivered to our tanks. Being air-breathing, a porpoise can stay out of the water for hours or even days, provided it is supported properly so that its own weight does not cut off circulation in its flippers or internal organs, and provided its skin is kept constantly wet. A porpoise's skin and eyes are not designed to dry out. Any carelessness in this matter will result in cracked, peeling skin or temporarily clouded eyes. More important, a porpoise's cooling system is designed to work in water, not air. Insulated all over with a layer of blubber, the porpoise rapidly overheats once it is out of the water. The fins and tail flukes, where the heat loss is greatest, can get hot to the touch, so hot that water dries on them right before your eyes, like water on a hot stove.

Georges's system was to lower a canvas stretcher in the water, work the animal into position over it (his assistant, Leo Kama, usually jumped overboard to do this), and then hoist the stretcher aboard, hang it in a supporting rack, rig some shade over the animal if necessary, and detail Leo or another crew member to sponge or spray the animal with water continuously while the *Imua* headed for the nearest dock. Meanwhile Georges radioed ahead for a truck to meet the vessel and transport the new captive the rest of the way to Sea Life Park. If he was collecting in his favorite waters, off the Kona Coast of the island of Hawaii, he also called up a plane to fly the new captive from Kona to Honolulu.

Cetaceans almost always lie still and cease to struggle once they have been lifted from the water. As I wrote in a scientific article:

All of the delphinids . . . are apt to be docile upon capture. This often causes amazement; we are so accustomed to a captured animal struggling with all its might that the cetacean docility seems to imply wisdom or insight on the part of the animal. However, the porpoise's defenses, primarily flight and ramming, are impossible once the animal is out of the water. Exhaustion and the impact of two totally new experiences, being held out of the water and being separated from others of its kind, probably contribute to the newly captured animal's tendency to lie motionless. Though nearly immobile, a new captured porpoise or small whale is certainly frightened, and death from shock is not uncommon.[*]

Spinners and kikos are particularly high-strung and apt to go into shock; some oceanariums will not even attempt to capture animals of this genus because they are frightened so easily. Georges, however, as far as I know, lost only one animal from shock in all his years of collecting, and that one, inexplicably, a bottlenose. Georges always insisted on quiet movements and soft voices when a new animal was aboard the *Imua*, and sometimes he assigned Leo to sing and play the ukulele to the animal all the way home.

When a porpoise or whale arrived at the Park, there was quite a rigmarole to go through before it could be put into the water. First we had to measure it all over and record the measurements on one of Ken Norris's International Cetacean Congress forms. This elaborate data—distance from eye to blowhole, distance from tip of jaw to axilla (the porpoise's equivalent of an armpit, or finpit)—and much more helped to accumulate information about the range and characteristics of all the species we dealt

[*] Karen Pryor, "Learning and Behavior in Whales and Porpoises," *Die Naturwissenschaften,* 60 (1973), 412–420.

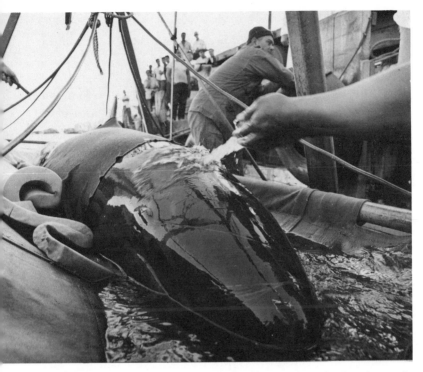

At dockside, Georges prepares to hoist the captured whale aboard a truck, while Leo keeps the whale cool and wet and a curious crowd watches.

with. The measurements had to be taken upon capture, not two or three weeks later when the animal might have lost or gained weight; but sympathetic bystanders and trainers often begrudged the extra time it took before the poor animal could be back in the water.

While one person took the measurements and another recorded them, two more would be doctoring the animal. A porpoise's surface skin is very delicate; you can draw blood with a fingernail. Wherever the animal had touched a hard object—the frame of the stretcher, the tailgate of the truck—it would be scraped and bleeding. Medication was applied to any such cuts or scrapes; someone drew a blood sample from the veins in the animal's tail, and the animal was given a massive injection of vitamins and long-acting antibiotics to help it overcome its stress and to protect against illness.

Porpoises are very susceptible to illness in captivity—particularly, oddly enough, to pneumonia. Out in the great wide ocean they hardly come near a germ, so their bodily defenses have dwindled. Our lungs are lined with cilia, little hairs which beat upward all the time to carry away dust and contaminants. The porpoise tribe have lost the cilia in their lungs. Our bodies are equipped with a rapidly mobilized white-cell production system to fight any infectious organism that gets into the bloodstream. Not so the porpoises'; their white-cell production is sluggish. We were to learn that a sick porpoise's white count might not start going up until the animal was actually on the mend.

A new animal coming into captivity, with no immunity and an inadequate defense system, was instantly exposed to all the pathogens human beings carry in their bodies: staph, strep, and all the rest. Even organisms harmless to us could cause trouble for a cetacean. *Escherichia coli* is a common human intestinal organism. It normally gives us no trouble, but I had two valuable whales die of *E. coli* pneumonia. We learned to expect new animals to get sick automatically, and to prevent it before it happened with protective antibiotics.

Once doctored, tested, and measured, the new animal was lowered gently into the waiting tank, usually with a trainer in the water and another alongside the tank to help. The porpoise might be stiff from hours of lying on the stretcher, in which case it would have to be supported for a few minutes before it could swim. Often new animals were confused and disoriented, and had to be prevented from blundering into the walls and hurting themselves. Being completely surrounded by cement is a baffling experience for a creature that has known only the boundless waters of the open sea. The sonar echoes alone, bouncing off tank walls from all sides, must make a newly caught porpoise feel as confused as you or I would feel if we were suddenly set down in a small place entirely surrounded by blazing searchlights.

We always tried to have another tamer porpoise or two in the tank when the newcomer was introduced. Porpoises are supposed to be marvelously altruistic and to help each other in time of trouble, but we found this to be pretty iffy. The tame animals might ignore the newcomer. They might avoid him. They might treat him as a plaything, to be bumped, teased, harassed, and if possible, raped. Bottlenoses were particularly disagreeable in this respect, and we learned not to use them as companions for any wild porpoise but another bottlenose.

Occasionally an animal would help a newcomer. For a while we had one small male kiko who was such a gem of a nursemaid that we kept him in the training facility on purpose to help newly caught animals. He would bolster the newcomer if it floundered, get between the new animal and the tank walls to keep it from bumping itself, and would even pass it fish and try to get it to feed. That was a unique animal, however. In general the advantage of tame companions was only that the new animal could see the other porpoises were not frightened, could see them feeding, and would learn by observation.

Eating dead fish instead of chasing down live ones is a tremendous change for a porpoise; dead fish are by no means recognizable as food at first. We would wriggle the fish in our hands, toss them as alluringly as possible right in front of the newcomer, even annoy it with them. Many an animal first discovered dead fish were edible when it snapped in irritation and accidentally closed its jaws on a fish.

The effort to induce a newcomer to eat would continue every few hours for days, if necessary. Some trainers were especially skillful in this matter, noting the slightest indications of feeding behavior—a turn of the head, a momentary relaxing of the jaws, a slight change of direction to pass closer to a floating fish, even a glance toward the fish. Each sign of hope indicated renewed effort until at last the animal might nose a fish, then mouth one, then perhaps carry one about for a moment, then finally swallow one. Once the first fish went down, more followed; and we would count the fish, one by one, that the animal actually ate; ten little smelt, twenty-five, up to the eighty or a hundred that made up a good day's ration.

Increased appetite after a day or two of not eating sometimes provoked feeding, but there was increased danger, too, with every day's delay. It may be that a porpoise gets most of its fresh water from food, even though it may also drink sea water. In any case, a porpoise that goes without food rapidly begins to dehydrate, and in a few days can die, not of starvation but of thirst.

As a porpoise gets dehydrated, its sides cave in a little, it begins floating higher and higher, and it also begins to lose interest in life and becomes less and less inclined to take a fish.

The size of the animal dictated how much time we had before the animal was in danger; a little spinner could not go safely for more than two days without food, whereas a pilot whale or bottlenose porpoise could manage pretty well for five days or a week.

When an animal had gone too long and not eaten yet, we had to force-feed it. Listless and inappetent, the animal could usually be caught just by grabbing it as it drifted by. Then one trainer held the porpoise still while another pried its jaws open and slipped a smelt head-first down the throat. Again, skill was essential; a clever nursemaid could reward the first voluntary swallowing with stroking and soft words and then gradually induce the animal to open its mouth for itself, to work the fish back with its tongue voluntarily, finally to move its head and take the fish itself, and at last to pursue the fish a few inches; when it would do that, it could pick up tossed fish and was on its way to good health. It was sometimes a painful business, especially with kikos and spinners. A spinner's hundred or more needle-sharp teeth nicked and scratched one's hands all over even if one wore gloves. It was a relief when the animal finally caught on.

Force-feeding an unwilling large animal such as a pilot whale was another matter. The water had to be lowered, and two strong men detailed to hold the animal. We put a stick in the animal's jaws to force them open, and then fed it liquidized food through a stomach tube. The animal learned nothing useful from this (although one or two reached the point where they would voluntarily swallow the stomach tube). Our only aim was to keep the

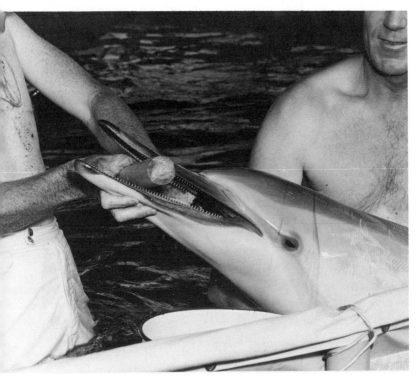

A dowel rod keeps the animal's jaws open as the men force-feed a newly caught spinner that won't eat. It's always an awkward business. There is no way to slip fish past those needle-sharp teeth without nicking your hands.

whale alive until it learned to feed more normally. Force-feeding a big animal was hard, disagreeable, occasionally dangerous work, and the preparation of the necessary 40 or 50 pounds of ground and blended fish daily was a messy chore too.

The presence of other animals often helped a newcomer catch on. Sometimes it was helpful to feed the other animals by tossing fish only in front of the new porpoise. Having fish stolen right across its bows over and over again could be sufficiently insulting to arouse ire, so that eventually the new animal would grab the fish just to keep these impolite strangers from getting it.

One of the fastest feeders I ever saw was Makua. Tap and I were there when he was introduced. When Makua was released into the training tank, he swam comfortably and negotiated the walls well. Kane, who had been caught some time before, was loafing in the middle of the tank, and Tap, who was in his bathing trunks, slipped into the water, put an arm around Kane, and began feeding him fish with his free hand. Makua regarded this situation—another big male bottlenose much like himself getting a free meal—and without a sign of fear insinuated himself under Tap's other arm and allowed himself to be hand-fed 15 pounds of fish as fast as Tap could get it to him.

Even with medication, a new animal had to be watched carefully, as indeed did every other animal, for the first faint signs of illness: a cough, a bad smell on the breath, a reduced intake of fish, or any tendency to play with the fish rather than gulp it down hungrily. The signs were small, and easily missed. Each of us had to become sensitive to the slightest change in our animals. Kent Burgess, head trainer at Sea World, once told me that every time he hired a new apprentice trainer he told him: "Sooner or later you're going to kill a porpoise." Harsh words, but true. Kane, poor crippled Kane, died of pneumonia because his new trainer thought the animal was refusing fish out of spite and failed to report it. The best medicine is the trainer's long experience. Many times we began treatment and saved a porpoise's life when the only thing that told us the animal was getting sick was the look in its eye.

Most new captives were in good shape and beginning to acclimatize within a week or ten days. A few, and pilot whales were a particular headache in this respect, just seemed to give up. Many of our pilot whales started out as "floaters." Instead of swimming, they hung motionless at the water surface, as if they could not go under. Gradually their backs got dried out and sunburned, blistering and peeling horribly. The trainers rigged shades and sprinkling systems and spread the whales' backs with white zinc oxide ointment to keep the sun off. In spite of force-feeding, the animals lost weight. As they weakened, they would list to one side or the other, until they had to struggle to get upright and get the blowhole out of water for each breath. We strung up all sorts of slings and braces to keep them upright, so they wouldn't ship water in the blowhole and drown. Chris and Gary spent many a night up to their waists in water helping one or another whale stay afloat.

There seldom seemed to be any primary injury which could account for this peculiar behavior of floating, which we sometimes saw in spinners and kikos too. It seemed as if the animal just wouldn't try; the look in the eye said "Let me die." We tried pep pills and stimulants. Once I even fed one pilot whale a quart of gin, with no observable effect.

Other oceanariums had not reported such problems, and pilot whales were a feature at more than one exhibit. They had problems, though, reported or not. It is a bit of a joke among oceanarium trainers that one famous pilot whale on the mainland actually consisted of a series of thirteen animals bearing the same name.

We had, inexperienced as we were at first, a pretty good record in keeping animals alive in captivity. Most of our captives pulled through. Almost always, when an acclimated animal got sick, we were able to cure it. In fact, over the first three years, we had a lower death rate among the porpoises than I later had with the Welsh ponies I was raising; and vets know a *lot* more about equine medicine than about porpoise medicine.

Many of the animals presently at Sea Life Park have been there for years. Our original vet, Al Takayama, was justifiably proud of the almost negligible death rate during his tenure.

Still, one cannot help but ask oneself if it is justified, this taking of animals from their home in the wild sea and subjecting them to the risks of captivity for the sake of scientific curiosity and public amusement.

I think it is, or I would not have been involved. So terribly little is known about cetaceans. They are among the last numerous large animals on the planet, and among the least understood.

The great whales are being hunted, perhaps to extinction, for the profits they bring when converted to margarine and cat food and fertilizer. They may be gone before we learn what there is to know from them. They may be gone before we recognize what we are doing to the sea itself by eliminating these huge grazers on the ocean's plankton pastures.

In many parts of the world porpoises are hunted for food or caught in fishermen's nets as an unavoidable part of the modern system of fishing for tuna, a system which kills (are you ready?) well over 100,000 porpoises a year off the coasts of Central and South America. Again, though porpoises, like whales, represent an important resource, it is one about which we know very little: one which many people are consequently all too ready to squander.

The struggle to understand how to keep porpoises alive has resulted in the development of good techniques. The U.S. Navy now routinely collects, keeps, and transports porpoises and small whales, and they do it without wasting animals. We are learning more about cetaceans all the time, and learning from them, too. Study of the porpoise's peculiar physiology has led to medical advances, particularly in the understanding of kidney function. Study of the porpoise's super sonar has led to sonar advances.

Perhaps as important, though, the keeping and display of porpoises in oceanariums has helped to awaken the public to the value of these animals. Conservation begins with understanding, and understanding can begin with personal contact: a child in the audience catching a ball that a porpoise threw, a governor or senator stroking Makua's ample belly. I feel sure that no "sportsman" who saw one of our shows ever went out again and put a rifle bullet through a porpoise at sea just for fun. National conservation efforts by an informed public have recently brought all cetaceans in U.S. waters under federal protection, so that today you need a permit and a good reason to go out and catch a porpoise. U.S. whaling has stopped, and the importation of whale products is now illegal, a first step to halting the slaughter on a worldwide basis.

We never grew used to seeing an animal die. The weakest new captive got as much loving care, as many tears blinked back if it wasn't doing well, as did a cherished star performer. We never stopped arguing and struggling to work out better systems of doctoring and diagnosing. We learned a lot about porpoises—perhaps enough to have helped hurry the day when they are no longer regarded, along with so much of the rest of the planet's wildlife, as just another consumer item.

Surely the most magnificent animals Georges ever collected for us were the false killer whales. We first heard of them from commercial fishermen in Kona, the fishing port on the "Big Island," Hawaii. "Hey, Georges!" came over the ship-to-shore radio: "Some lolo bunch of pilot whales is stealing all the fish off my long lines. Got two big aku yesterday, and wen' stole six mahi mahi today, cut 'em right in half. Why don' you come down here and catch dem guys? Give us plen'y trouble!"

Pilot whales? It certainly didn't sound like pilot whale behavior. Long-line fishermen set out a line holding a series of baited hooks to catch tuna (aku), mahi mahi (dolphin-fish, or dorados, a fish, not a mammal), and other species for the fish market. The fish they catch may weigh 50 or 100 pounds, no diet for pilot whales, which have small mouths and blunt teeth and feed largely on little squid. Georges went down to Kona to see.

What he saw were false killer whales (*Pseudorca crassidens*): black all over, like a pilot whale, about the same size (12 to 18 feet long), and traveling in schools. Otherwise, they were completely different. The false killer is a tropical cousin of the great true killer whale, that handsome subarctic animal which has become a popular oceanarium star.

The true killer is so called because he kills other mammals for prey: porpoises, seals, even other whales. The false killer is a ferocious predator, too, but he eats big oceangoing fish, not mammals. Georges on his first sighting of these gorgeous beasts saw one leap clear of the water with a 50-pound mahi mahi glittering crosswise in its jaws, which the whale then shook to bits and shared with other animals around it. No wonder the false killers were driving the fishermen crazy. A long line, with a bunch of big fish hooked on it, must have looked like a banquet table to them.

The first false killer whale Georges caught, Kaena (named for the point of land off which it was taken), never did very well, though it lived many months and performed, rather sluggishly, in Whaler's Cove. Kaena died of what an autopsy proved to be a longstanding kidney ailment which it perhaps had contracted even before capture.

The next one, Makapuu, was an adult female, named for the point of land off which she was caught, which is the same point of land on which Sea Life Park is situated. Georges himself, a truly gifted animal handler, taught her to eat, standing in waist-deep water and wriggling a mackerel at her so invitingly that she finally—after two days—swam into his arms and took the fish.

False killer whales are swift, elongated, streamlined animals, elegant acrobats, capable of flipping their 1,300 pounds in mid-air like a spinner and reentering the water without a splash. Makapuu learned to jump 24 feet straight up in the air for a fish. We had to hang the trainer from a bosun's chair in the *Essex* rigging to get the target high enough. I had joked about getting an animal to jump to the ship's yardarm, three stories high over the water. Makapuu did it.

False killer whales are volatile, passionate animals, performers supreme, complete with prima donna temperaments. They were the most beautiful but perhaps not yet the very best of all the strange species we found. The best was an obscure and homely species, *Steno bredanensis*.

One spring we had the ragged old *Imua* repainted. An elderly sign painter came down to the boatyard to put her name and Coast Guard numbers back on. Out of a feeling of esprit he also painted a life ring on the side of the cabin, with a porpoise jumping through it. Such a porpoise! It had a conical, pointed head like a lizard, bulgy eyes, big flappy flippers, and a humpy back, and it was splotchy brown instead of steely gray. As the *Imua* left the harbor on a whale-hunting expedition, Tap laughed and pointed at the painting and said to Georges, "Don't catch us one of those!"

Twenty-four hours later Georges was back at the dock with a porpoise that looked exactly like the painting.

It was *Steno bredanensis,* the "rough-toothed porpoise," Ken Norris told us when we called him long distance in California. There were specimens (skeletons only) in a few museums, and the animal had been known to science as it appeared in life only because, a few years before, several specimens had been stranded on a beach on the coast of Africa.

That first *Steno* was in a terrible state of shock. We could not get it to eat to swim or to pay attention to other porpoises. It was terrified. It was dying of fright. We thought that perhaps the only thing that would help would be another *Steno* for company.

Though the weather was bad and getting worse, Georges went back out to the piece of ocean in which he had caught the first *Steno.* He had not noticed the school until he was right on top of them; unlike other porpoises, *Steno*s swim under the surface, often rather slowly, coming up only to breathe. This makes them exceedingly difficult to spot.

To help out, we sent up a spotter plane. The plane located a school of *Steno*s, and Georges began maneuvering the boat among them.

Georges had been hunting whales when he came across the *Steno*s, and now he was fishing from the extra-long whale pulpit. In rough seas the whale pulpit was a hazardous place to be. As the boat rose, the pulpit would swing 20 feet into the air, and then as the boat fell, the pulpit would bury itself in an oncoming wave. Georges directed Leo, at the wheel, by a series of body and hand motions. Both of them had to gauge constantly the position of the animals, the travel of the boat, and the height of oncoming waves. A miscalculation could plunge Georges underwater. The pulpit, necessarily lightweight and rather fragile, could easily snap off and be carried under the boat, Georges and all, into the *Imua*'s propellers. Georges's life truly depended on the accuracy of the body-English communication between him and Leo.

The *Steno*s were not afraid of the boat, and indeed were riding on its bows. They were, however, avoiding the swinging pulpit, and with the base of the long whale pulpit in the way, Georges could not get at the animals that were right at the bows.

Over the radio came intermittent reports from Sea Life Park of the rapidly worsening condition of our captive *Steno*. Darkness was falling.

Suddenly, the spotter plane radioed that the *Imua* was drifting, and that there was lumber and wreckage floating all over the ocean around her. While the *Steno*s loafed around in curiosity, Georges and Leo had idled the *Imua*'s motors and set out to remove the whale pulpit. Plank by plank, they utterly demolished it, casting its pieces into the ocean.

When the pulpit was gone, and the motors had started up again, the school of *Steno*s obligingly began playing under the bows. In no time Georges had latched on to a fine adult male which he named Kai, or "sea," for the rough water in which he was caught; the naming of animals was always Georges's privilege.

Kai reached Sea Life Park long after dark and was put in with the failing female. She died a couple of days later of pneumonia, but perhaps her presence helped Kai to adjust; in any case, he never presented a problem, but swam and ate, and raised cain when he chose, from the very beginning.

A few days later, on May 16, Georges brought in another *Steno*, named Pono, which means "good," or "justice." It's funny how one animal will weasel its way into your heart, and another, similar in every way, will not. Kai was a fine animal, and we worked with him extensively, but no one ever got especially fond of him, whereas Pono, though she was a prickly soul and sometimes aggressive, was an enchantress.

Pono was as full of confidence in captivity as Makua had been. On the first morning after capture, when food was offered, she ate vigorously. Since there was therefore no need to devote all the day's fish to coaxing the new animal to eat, Kai, who was of course in the same tank, was put to work. His morning training session consisted of being shaped to ring a bell by pressing a lever with his nose. Two or three times he did this, and then Pono dashed up, shouldered Kai away from the bell, slammed the bell so hard she nearly knocked it loose, and stuck her head up expectantly for a fish.

No need for all the laborious days of whistle conditioning and shaping for this animal. We soon were joking that with *Stenos* all you had to do was write the training plan on waterproof paper and hang it in the tank. Not that *Stenos* were necessarily easy to handle. They bit people without compunction (especially the veterinarian). Wild, fresh-caught *Stenos*, on tank-cleaning day, would pick up the nets with their teeth and duck under them, or wedge themselves through closing gates without regard for their own skins, and all of this not because they were afraid to move to a strange tank but seemingly because they considered they had a right to select the tank they preferred.

One day, remembering Hoku and Kiko, I experimentally threw a beach chair into Kai and Pono's tank. They grabbed it, dragged it, swam under it, hit each other with it, wedged their heads under the arms. In ten minutes they could have written a book called *1,001 Things to Do with a Beach Chair.*

Stenos not only look quite unlike all other porpoises; they behave very differently, too. They have a tremendously long attention span and love a puzzle. They will sometimes go on working when they are too full to swallow another fish, just because the task is interesting. They are full of curiosity and utterly careless about hurting themselves if the injury occurs in pursuit of some *Steno* goal. Our *Stenos* were always covered with fresh cuts and scrapes from sticking their heads in the drains or up the water pipes or some place they shouldn't. They come into captivity covered with nicks and scars. As one reporter put it, "A *Steno* looks as if it had spent its finest hours fighting with a switchblade."

Some *Stenos* have a curious habit, when first captured, of cleaning their fish: gutting and deheading them before eating them. They would hold the fish in their teeth and bang them around until the heads came off and the insides fell away. When a *Steno* felt it thus had to clean every one of the hundred or more little smelt making up its daily ration, feeding it took forever, and the process made a mess of the water and the tank all around, besides. Luckily they gave up the habit, in due course, and swallowed their fish whole, like normal porpoises.

The rarest animal Georges ever caught came in before my tenure as head trainer, but I was there to see it.

From my journal, July 7, 1963
Georges radioed from Kona yesterday to say he saw a school of really weird porpoises of some kind yesterday and today, but they were very fast and he couldn't catch them. Little, like a spinner, but with blunt heads, and no rostrum, sort of like a pilot whale. Black all over except for white lips; he called them "clown" porpoises.

July 16, 1963
Georges caught one of the "clown" porpoises and it came in today. What a strange animal. We called Ken Norris, and he was very excited and is flying out from the Coast as soon as he can to see it.

Georges recorded sighting the school again.

At 8:05 A.M. on 16 July, 1963, the school was sighted again about ½ mile off Milolii, 36 miles S of the original sighting. The sea was calm and the skies clear. Water depth was about 600 fathoms. As in previous sightings, the school was swimming in an area of strong currents, indicated by foam streaks and roily water. . . . At 11:15 A.M. an adult was netted. After an initial dash and shallow dive, the line slackened and the animal briefly took up station below the vessel and on the same course.

Georges went on to report that the odd beast struggled very minimally when brought alongside to be maneuvered into a stretcher and hoisted on board. But then it had a surprise for the crew:

Its demeanor at this time clearly suggested caution. It periodically opened its mouth and snapped its jaws closed. This behavior was intensified when the animal was touched. After it was safely on deck it continued to snap from time to time during the short trip to Kailua-Kona. It also emitted a repeated "blatting or growling" noise by forcing air through the blowhole. . . . During the trip to the oceanarium its handler reported that it snapped at him every time the truck hit a bump.*

Both jaws of the animal were lined with strong, sharp conical teeth. The "demeanor" of the animal, immobilized as it was, yet "growling" and watching for every chance to bite, was formidable indeed.

Quite a few of us knew a bizarre animal was coming in and went to see it. At Ken's request, I made some behavioral notes for him, which were later published.

As the animal was being escorted along the edge of the pool it suddenly struggled free. In the next few seconds the animal dashed forward halfway around the tank, dived to the bottom, and leaped two-thirds free of the water at the point of introduction. [I was standing there, I remember. It bounded into the air and took a good look into the back of the truck in which it had just been carried.] Without slackening speed the animal swam in a tight figure eight at the water inlet [I swear it was looking to see if it could escape up the current flowing from the pipe] and then shot partly out of the water and snapped twice at one of us. [Me. Hanging in fascination over the edge of the tank, I was its nearest target, and it leaped for my face, teeth clashing, like a seagoing wolf.] There was only time to yell a warning when the animal leaped again and snapped at another person, 10 feet away. As the personnel backed nervously away from the tank edge, the animal took up station in mid-tank, apparently watching its captors.

The following day, the animal had calmed down and it cruised quietly about the tank. It showed no fear of humans and came to the side of the tank and allowed itself to be touched; however it would often snap its jaws and "growl" when we touched it or gestured at it. . . .

* Taylor A. Pryor, Karen Pryor, and Kenneth S. Norris, "Observations on *Feresa attenuata*," *Journal of Mammalogy*, 6 (1964), 37.

Unlike most newly captured cetaceans, this animal made almost no attempt to avoid an observer, but instead acted as if it expected the observer to move. If it were pushed as it floated by, it usually gave a short sidewise thrash of its flukes and then sometimes swam in a tight circle towards the offending party. . . .

When a whole mackerel was slipped into its mouth, it was eaten. After this the animal fed voluntarily upon fish thrown to it. It also accepted squid. . . . When given access to an adjoining pool, it passed without hesitation back and forth through the gate, again quite unlike other cetaceans, which usually exhibit fear of gates and must be trained or forced to go through them. *

On the day following capture, our chief maintenance man, Ernie Boerrigter, one of the most benevolent humans alive, put an arm into the tank to check an intake pipe, and the little "sea wolf" made a swift, jaws-open pass at his arm, from which he recoiled just in time. This was its last aggressive move toward people, though it often "growled" and had a curiously frightening habit of loafing in the center of the tank, watching us with one eye and patting the water surface with its pectoral fin in a sinister way, like an irritable man drumming his fingers on a tabletop.

But what *was* it? Ken Norris, one of the world's experts on cetacean classification, finally came up with the answer. It was a pigmy killer whale, *Feresa attenuata,* and was known to science from two skulls in the British Museum, collected in 1827 and 1871, and from a single skeleton collected at a whaling station in Japan in 1954. A rare animal indeed!

The *Feresa,* a male, became quite tame in a few days. (One tells a male from a female cetacean by the genital slits: two in the male, one in the female, usually.) Though the *Feresa* never solicited attention, he tolerated it. Chris grew brave enough to swim with him, and consequently so did I. I put a face plate on, slipped into the water behind the animal, and had a look at him underwater. Surprise! He was looking at me, even though I was directly in back of him.

* *Ibid.*

Porpoises, like horses, have their eyes on the sides of their heads. The field of vision does overlap looking downwards, which makes sense; it's the overlap that gives depth perception, and porpoises need that, looking down. It's amusing to swim under a school of porpoises and look up and see all those pairs of bright little eyes regarding you with interest. The *Feresa*, however, had eyes so situated that he had binocular vision not only downwards but backwards. When I stuck my head under water, I found him looking backwards into my eyes with both of his own, the only animal I ever met that really did have eyes in the back of his head.

The *Feresa* seemed mopey. We decided he needed company and put him in a neighboring tank with two pilot whales. He swam with the smaller of the two, but we noticed that sometimes he charged toward it at right angles. When he did that, the pilot whale avoided actual contact with a little burst of speed.

One morning, the little pilot whale was found dead. It had died from a single sharp blow at the base of the cranium, a blow our vet was at a loss to explain.

The true killer whale, of which *Feresa* was a distant relative, sometimes kills its larger prey in just this manner, by ramming it at the base of the skull. Could it be that our little sea wolf was as efficient a murderer as its big cousins? We were fearful, and isolated him again.

Still, he seemed so bored and lonely that we tried giving him company once more, this time a little spinner.

At first, the whale ignored the spinner, and the spinner was calm. Then the pigmy killer whale took up a cat-and-mouse game which was frightening to see. He stationed himself in the middle of the tank and made little rushes at the spinner. The spinner began circling the tank. The whale feinted, threatening to rush again. The spinner circled faster, until it was swimming at top speed, whistling in terror, while the *Feresa* pivoted in the center of the tank, watching the spinner (and no doubt laughing sadistically).

Spinners in the next tank were having hysterics too, frightened by the distress calls of their species mate. This clearly was not going to work. We returned the spinner to its own group.

So the *Feresa* lived alone. He died about a month later of an attack of pneumonia. Had his spirits been higher, perhaps he would have lived, but Georges was not able to catch him a species mate, we could give him no company save ourselves, and we were not enough. Ken Norris flew over from California to photograph and study the beast while it lived. During my years at Sea Life Park we deliberately never collected another.

There are more rare cetaceans in the waters around Hawaii which no doubt someone will come to know someday. We had a stranded infant pigmy sperm whale in our tanks for a couple of days, an odd little beast that looked just like a giant sperm whale. Our infant was only about 3 feet long. The adult, sighted occasionally, is a solitary animal, about the size of a pilot whale, but shaped like the giant sperm whale and closely related to it.

Another rare infant washed up on a beach turned out to be a little whale named *Peponocephala electra*. Ken Norris found a *Grampus* skull on one of our beaches, and more than once, at sea, collectors glimpsed but could never get a line on specimens of *Ziphius*, the beaked whale, a rare animal that looks faintly like a giant bottlenose twenty-five feet long.

Porpoises will occasionally reproduce in captivity; some oceanariums have had fair success raising their own replacement animals. It does seem that porpoises in captivity are more likely to have young if they are not working. Show animals, working at demanding tasks, may mate frequently, but rarely conceive. This may be analogous to the observation of many horse owners that mares which are being shown or raced often fail to come into heat. To breed them, you may have to turn them out to pasture for a month or more of rest. Marineland of the Pacific achieved a number of successful births by setting up a breeding colony of idle animals which were never asked to perform.

The Atlantic bottlenose porpoise, the only species for which we have extensive data, is sexually mature at around seven years (their estimated life span is between twenty and thirty years). Gestation is eleven months, and the single baby is born tail first, then boosted quickly to the surface for its first breath, either by the mother or by an attendant "auntie" porpoise. Like a colt or a calf, the baby porpoise is quite large in relation to its mother, and fully active from birth. It swims, clumsily but briskly, at her flank, partially towed along in her slipstream. It nurses like a colt, many, many times a day, but briefly. The mammary glands are in two slits on either side of the genital slit; while the baby is nursing the nipple protrudes, and the infant porpoise suckles just like any other mammal. There is a myth that the porpoise mother squirts her milk into her baby's mouth, but this is not so; the system called the letdown reflex makes the milk available, just as in any other mammal.

A baby porpoise nurses for nearly two years and does not begin to grow teeth and nibble fish until it is many months old. Ordinarily an adult female will have one baby every two years.

We had a number of births at Sea Life Park from animals of various species that were captured while pregnant and either

Mahina, the *Steno,* nursing her newborn hybrid baby, Mamo, fathered by a *Tursiops. Bob Hooper*

miscarried or delivered later. None of these infants survived. The first infant that lived and thrived was conceived and born in captivity. It was also the rarest of all the porpoises we ever had, a hybrid.

Mahina ("moonlight"), a *Steno*, came into captivity while pregnant, and shortly aborted. She was put into research tanks that had by then been built at the Institute, where she lived some of the time with a hot-tempered Atlantic bottlenose named Amiko, one of Ken Norris's research animals.

Kai was long gone, and at no time during Mahina's life did we have another male *Steno* on the premises. Imagine our surprise, then, when the trainers looked in Mahina's tank one morning and found a little tiny porpoise swimming by her side. She had had a baby.

It was a hybrid, half *Tursiops truncatus* and half *Steno bredanensis,* about as likely a combination, according to the taxonomic charts of porpoise relationships, as a cross between a sheep and a camel. Yet here it was, with a forehead like its father's but with its mother's nose, with something of Amiko's smooth grayness, but a hint of Mahina's blotchy brownness. A female, named Mamo ("favored one"), it thrived and grew, and in two years was much bigger than both its parents. At the time of writing, Mamo has just gone into training; it remains to be seen whether she will have all the temperamental virtues of both her parents, or all their faults. She is, indisputably, however, the rarest of porpoises: almost certainly the world's only "*Steniops.*"

5. TRAINING TRAINERS

As soon as the park opened it was apparent that the training department couldn't go on the way we were for more than a few days. We were running five shows a day at Ocean Science Theater, and five shows a day at Whaler's Cove, and constantly had new animals to care for too. It took three people to put on the Ocean Science show: a trainer, a narrator, and a backup man to open gates and handle props. It took four to handle Whaler's Cove; trainer, narrator, backup who changed the music, among other tasks, and the swimmer. Gary, Chris, Dottie, Lani, and I were running back and forth doing ten shows a day over the first weekend. Obviously we were going to have to hire some more people; and now, with the turnstiles clicking, we could do so.

Part-timers, full-timers, inexperienced youngsters for the most part, people applied in droves, and we winnowed them out as well as we could. We got a high school boy to help in the fish room and back up the shows, and a pretty hula dancer to fill in for Lani on her day off and to start to learn the Whaler's Cove narration. But what we needed were good people who could rapidly become either trainers or the kind of nimble, extempore narrators wanted for Ocean Science Theater. And at our rates of pay, that wasn't going to be easy.

My journal, February 17, 1964

I was running from Whaler's Cove to Ocean Science Theater this morning when I was overtaken by a job applicant, David Alices. He's been a seeing-eye dog trainer—I'm always scared of professional trainers, I don't want a slick, circus-type show and they sure aren't going to listen to me gabbing about behavior chains and conditioned stimuli. I asked him what else he'd done (besides training dogs and driving a truck for Coca-Cola) and he said on weekends he taught blind kids to ride horseback. Good! What really clinched it was that he said last month at home just for fun he had trained a guppy to jump over a matchstick.

A versatile trainer is rare. An innovative trainer, in the tradition-oriented world of animal training, is almost unheard of. David's blind equestrians and jumping guppy spoke to me of talent, and spoke truly.

David was older than the rest of us, thirty-four, a husky, very swarthy man of Puerto Rican extraction, though born in Hawaii. He had a deep voice with a chuckle in it, and blazing black eyes like a gypsy, and he took no nonsense from man, woman, or beast.

David rapidly learned to train both shows, which meant that Dottie and Chris could take a day off, now and then, which they'd been doing without, and that I could get home to my children on the weekends.

In due course, when I got the fancy title of Curator (Curator of Mammals, really—I was never responsible for the fish in the Reef Tank), David became my first head trainer. His dominating ways caused trouble with other departments, Maintenance and Sales, for instance, and he sometimes frightened those pretty young swimmers who cried if they were yelled at; but David was good for the porpoises, and a godsend to me; it was my battles he was fighting.

A few weeks after we opened, Lani had to quit. She was not physically robust enough to endure getting wet five times a day. Even in Hawaii, winter days can be chilly, rainy, and uncom-

Alongside the *Essex* a swimmer smiles at the audience from her canoe while the spinners leap behind her in unison.

fortable. Trainers and swimmers both needed strong constitutions to avoid catching cold after cold.

To mitigate the swimmers' problems, we decided to have at least two girls on the job, both of whom could narrate the Whaler's Cove show and swim with the animals. That way they could alternate, and neither one would have to swim five shows a day. We also built a small outrigger canoe, changed the script around to accommodate it, and had the girl make her entrance in the canoe from behind the *Essex,* instead of diving in from the railing. That cut her swimming time in half, and if the day was cold and blowy she could do the whole show from the canoe, feeding and patting the animals without getting in the water herself.

We got swimmer applicants by word of mouth or by newspaper advertisement. What a headache! The newspapers could not run an ad that specified race or sex. Yet for the tourists' cameras and the sense of the show, the swimmer really had to be female, pretty, and more or less Hawaiian in appearance. From our first ads, a lot of males and a lot of pretty blond girls made the trip out to Sea Life Park for nothing. Finally I found a phrase the newspapers would accept that got the point across: "Wanted: Polynesian mermaid."

Many swimmers came and went, and some came back again. Puanani Marciel, one of the first swimmers after Lani, stays in my mind because the animals loved her so. When she swam, they sometimes nearly hid her from sight, crowding around to be near. She was a proficient swimmer who loved to play in the water, diving and surfacing and swimming down to the bottom, and wherever she went the animals paced her and matched her movements exactly, in a kind of interspecies water ballet. She was gentle, and knew the spinners individually perhaps better than any of us. For years after she no longer worked for us she came back now and then to swim with the spinners, and they always seemed overjoyed to see her.

Puanani is also remembered with affection by some of our stockholders for having startled a board meeting one day by bursting in one door, twirling around the room, and leaving by the other door, dressed in nothing but a red bikini and singing, "I've got a date with Mel Tormé, I've got a date with Mel Tormé!"

Putting the canoe into the show led to a theatrical effect I was rather proud of. For dramatic reasons the girl could not get into her canoe until the show had started and the audience had been seated. It took some time for her to get organized, out of sight behind the *Essex*, and to get her canoe straightened out so she could paddle into sight. To cover the lapse, I wrote a piece of description into the script: "In the beginning, there were no people on these islands: only the plants, the birds, the wind, and the empty sea. From across the horizon the first Hawaiians came, in long double canoes, looking for new land. They brought food with them, water in bamboo bottles, pigs, chickens, dogs, and enough plants and seeds to start life again in some new land. Look out across the bows of our ship, the *Essex*. The lighthouse that you see marks Makapuu Point, a landmark today and a landmark to the ancient Hawaiians. Perhaps it was on a day like this [and then the narrator described the weather, whatever it happened to be] that those first Hawaiians came, past Makapuu Point, inside Rabbit Island, to land on these very shores."

Of course, historically, Makapuu was probably not the first landfall, but it might have been. The audience obediently noticed the lighthouse, and then found themselves looking out to sea. If the narrator handled it right, a vast, speculative silence fell over the crowd. For a moment, the ocean they were looking at was peopled by a vision of the travelers of ancient Polynesia. As they had this thought in their minds, the real girl in her little fishing canoe paddled into sight.

I used to drop by the show sometimes just at the start to enjoy that moment of hush before the canoe's entrance. It tickled me that a dramatic high point of the show consisted of ninety seconds in which, actually, nothing was happening at all.

Meanwhile Gary Anderson was doing less and less for us, because he was going back to school part-time. Sea Life Park was dedicated to education, and it seemed almost a duty to encourage Gary to finish getting a college degree. It was awkward, though, for the rest of us, having Gary come and go on an irregular schedule, and having him absent in the mornings when there was so much work to do getting the fish out of the freezer. Eventually Gary and I came to a disagreement about it, and I realized with a shock that since I was the boss I was going to have to relinquish my authority or relinquish Gary.

Horrors! That meant firing him. I'd never done such a thing to anyone, and hadn't a clue as to how to go about it, and slept very badly the night before, feeling like a heel. But I did it. It was painful. Gary admired Tap, was dedicated to Sea Life Park, and truly loved the porpoises, but he finally agreed he couldn't handle school and this job both.

Gary did go on with his schooling, and I got braver—or meaner—about firing. Usually it turned out that if we were not happy with an employee, he or she was much more unhappy with us, and upon being fired immediately fell into some much more suitable job, while, on our side, some much more suitable person walked in the door.

On February 20, a week and a half after opening day, Danny Kaleikini walked in and asked for a job.

By that time, the front office had scraped up the money for a tape deck for the Whaler's Cove music; Chris's phonograph had been retired from its exposure to salt air and fish scales, and that show was going pretty well. Danny, a handsome, articulate young Hawaiian man, built like a dancer, told me he was a nightclub performer; he had some ideas for our Whaler's Cove show and would like to be the narrator. I regarded this enterprising approach with considerable suspicion, since I was satisfied with the show, but I sat down with Danny for a quick lunch in the Park's restaurant, the Galley.

All the girls at the Galley food service counter were Hawaiians, mostly from nearby Waimanalo, and as Danny carried our tray to the table they beckoned me excitedly. "That's Danny Kaleikini!"

"Yes, the name is something like that."

"What's he doing here?"

"Well," I told them, "he is applying for a job at Whaler's Cove."

"Oh, you some *lucky*. Hire him, hire him!"

I didn't understand what all the excitement was about, since I hadn't seen a nightclub show in years, but I took the point. If Lei, Ilona, and the rest of the girls in the Galley knew and admired Danny, then he had to be good for Sea Life Park.

At that time Danny was headlining in the Tapa Room, one of the biggest supper clubs in Waikiki, with a show he'd designed himself, an authentic Hawaiian show, with no Tin Pan Alley music or out-of-place comedians, just Danny singing real Hawaiian songs, chatting about his grandfather, and even playing the prehistoric Hawaiian nose flute. He was backed up by good musicians and good and authentic hula dancers. It was then the only Hawaiian show in town that Hawaiians themselves cared for. I still don't know why Danny, who was working every night until past midnight, and had his own show people to cosset and worry over, was willing to work for us for pennies doing five Whaler's Cove shows every day; but he was.

Sea Life Park was an organization that believed in authentic rather than ersatz Hawaiiana, and Danny was a strong supporter of this cause. Perhaps too he approved of the idealistic aims of the organization, of our youth and dreams. (The average age of the whole staff, on opening day, was twenty-seven.) In any case, he gave up a lot of time. The first Whaler's Cove show wasn't until 11:15, which gave a nightclub performer time to sleep in the morning, but then the last show was at 5:15, which barely gave him time to wash off the salt spray, eat, and get into costume for his own first show. Danny kept it up for months. He contributed a lot of amusing and lively ideas to Whaler's Cove, and he set a pattern for the script which, if it was not my rather literary-poetic pattern, was one which could much more easily be followed by young Hawaiians on the staff. Soon Danny had trained two or three girls and boys to handle the narration as he did, word for word and pause for pause, rattling off streams of Hawaiian and Tahitian phrases and setting up the audience for each porpoise leap or spin with perfect theatrical timing.

Danny did more than tighten up shows for Sea Life Park. He brought out VIPs from the travel industry, on his own time, and took them around the exhibit. He boosted the Park on his own show. He worked with Tom Morrish, marketing director, making sales suggestions and opening doors for Tom in Waikiki. When even Danny's formidable energies could no longer encompass two full-time jobs as a performer, he resigned from the shows but stayed on as consultant, and eventually he became a stockholder and member of Sea Life Park's board of directors.

In the first frantic months of operations, show business sent us another gift, a girl named Randy Lewis. Randy's father was Hawaii's most famous disc jockey and newscaster, a radio personality named Hal Lewis, who called himself J. Akuhead Pupule. Randy, at nineteen, was a tall, pretty blonde with a good education and her old man's gift of gab. She wanted to be a porpoise trainer, and I thought she might also be a wonderful narrator.

Dottie and I by that time were splitting the Ocean Science Theater narration. We began the show with Makua and a rather thoughtful discussion of what a porpoise is. We had him show his teeth and his tail and come to be patted, to demonstrate his docility. We pointed out the blowhole and convinced the audience that Makua was a mammal, not a fish. We let him play ball with the audience, whacking the ball out over the glass so someone could throw it back. We discussed intelligence and training methods. We had Makua breach three mighty, splashing breaches, which often soaked the people in the front rows. Far from annoying them, this seemed to make people feel they had come into personal contact with the animal, and repeat visitors often sat in those front rows on purpose. We used the talking and the sinking-to-the-bottom behavior, and we had Makua "count" by ringing his bell, and then we blindfolded him and demonstrated his sonar.

None of these behaviors was particularly glamorous in itself. What made the show interesting was the information we crammed in and around Makua's activities. Everything he did taught the audience something about him, and about porpoises, and maybe about biology in general. What was usually on display was our own enthusiasm, curiosity, interest, and fund of information.

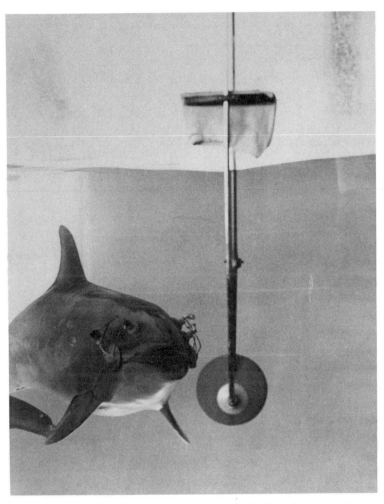

Makua, wearing blindfolds, locates and rings his bell at the Ocean Science Theater.

Furthermore, we were not ashamed to train right in front of the audience. The talking, "Say Aloha, Makua," was trained entirely during performances. So was the high jump, or "high rise" to the rafters. (Makua didn't make it to the rafters, but he could go 18 feet straight up.) Since Dottie and I knew both the animal and the training situation well, we could explain where we'd stopped last time in a particular shaping session, what we were hoping for this time, what the problems might be, and what the animal was doing and perhaps thinking. It put the audience on the edge of their seats, all right, and when an untrained behavior was first done right, to the obvious exhilaration of both trainer and animal, it made a thrilling show.

With Hoku and Kiko, we talked about the research potential of the animals, their great speed which seemed hydrodynamically impossible, and about porpoise behavior and communication.

As a finale we had taught Hoku to jump over a high bar, extended 8 feet over the water from the raised training platform. Kiko was not trained to make the jump. When Hoku was rewarded with several fish for this strenuous jump, he politely shared the fish with Kiko, and she grew to expect it. If he touched the bar as he went over, he was not rewarded, and when that happened, Kiko was apt to be most annoyed, and to chase him, chattering and streaming bubbles from her blowhole, all over the tank. It was the kind of thing that an audience could really enjoy, if you could make it clear ahead of time what to look for. This was porpoise communication in real life, not science fiction.

It took a lot of moxie on the microphone, though, to make all this clear to an audience. Dottie and I soon got over our stage fright. There wasn't time for it, with five shows a day, five days a week, audience after audience, some consisting of six hundred tourists who had to be encouraged to laugh and respond, some of six hundred schoolchildren who had to be intrigued into silence, and with weekend audiences of families and local folks who wanted to hear how all this related to them and to Hawaii. An

Makua's high rise was trained, like many show behaviors, entirely in the shows, with the narrator explaining the training process as it occurred.

Ocean Science Theater narrator either gave up or got good in a hurry.

Randy Lewis listened to our shows and read all she could find about porpoises. She soon was handling part of the show, and then all of it. She had great good taste; although wisecracks came naturally to her, she never made either the animals or the trainers the butt of her jokes. She had a marvelous facility for filling in the low spots in a show with lively talk, keeping the audience amused even though they had to sit idle for five minutes while Makua decided whether he was going to go through the gate or not, or while Hoku and Kiko dawdled because of some small change in the routine which had upset them. One could be standing clear across Sea Life Park and hear a roar of laughter rise from the Ocean Science Theater and know that Randy Lewis had just said the perfect thing again.

We all grew clever at coping with disaster: when the winch broke and the training platform fell in the water, or the cues suddenly didn't go on and we had to run the show with only the behaviors that didn't require sound cues, until the repair man arrived. Randy was the best of all of us at this, and I'm glad she was on the mike the day spring came to Ocean Science Theater.

Hoku and Kiko often dallied amorously during shows, but they could usually be called back to work by turning the cue volume up, or by slapping a fish on the water, or something. One day nothing worked, and the porpoises began to copulate, swimming belly to belly around and around the tank. Porpoises manage this business very neatly, but still, their occupation was obvious; and Randy had a wall-to-wall audience of high school girls and nuns. She said every interesting thing she could think of about porpoises, but finally even Randy ran out of information. "Well," she finished, "you came here to learn about biology, didn't you?" and hung up her mike and closed the show to tumultuous applause.

By our second winter of operation, Dottie had left to take a research job on the mainland, and Chris had moved to California. Chris's place on the training staff was filled by a husky, grinning,

Mormon missionary named Pat Quealy, a fine, bright young man full of Irish charm and good humor, who, in addition to missionizing in Tasmania, had been a cowboy and a roughneck in an oilfield. Pat Quealy and Randy Lewis ran Ocean Science Theater together, and he quickly learned to handle the narration as well as the training.

Dottie's place was filled by Ingrid Kang, a handsome Swedish girl married to a Korean history professor at the University of Hawaii. Ingrid had a degree in animal behavior from the University of Stockholm and came looking for a research job at the Oceanic Institute. They didn't have work for her, but I did, and Ingrid was wise enough not to turn up her nose at porpoise shows because they weren't "research." I think she knew from the beginning that the opportunity to learn about the animals was just as great, perhaps greater, in the thick of daily work with them as it would be in a "pure research" situation. Indeed, Ingrid now has her name as author or coauthor on more scientific papers than any of the trainers who were later hired to do "scientific" training alone.

Ingrid pitched in as third in command, under David Alices, and when he departed, after three years, she became head trainer. When I departed, Ingrid became curator in my place. Slow-spoken and thoughtful, self-conscious about her Swedish accent, Ingrid categorically refused to do any narrating, but she assimilated Ron's training manual without difficulty and quickly became a marvelous trainer and a gifted caretaker for sick or newly captured animals. Among our volatile crew of bright youngsters, Ingrid's maturity, confidence, and calm were extremely valuable.

She was a good teacher, too, and this was important. With our low salary scale, we could hire only young and inexperienced people, and this meant a lot of turnover. Some didn't work out, some found the long outdoor days too strenuous, some left to make better money driving trucks or dancing hulas. Boys got drafted and girls got pregnant and/or married. There were always newcomers who had to be taught the ropes, and Ingrid was a whiz at that, far more patient and persistent than I.

I kept my eye out for talent wherever I saw it. I picked up Kerry Jenkins at a lunch counter. She was in the next booth, describing, with vivacity and presence, the trouble she was having finding a job. She sounded like a narrator prospect to me, and she was a good one, and is still handling narrations ten years later.

Marlee Breese was an ex-babysitter of mine who turned into another super narrator. Diane Pugh I spotted at the stables where my ponies lived. She was out in the ring on a half-broken quarter-horse filly doing a very clever bit of training. She was a girl of unusual beauty, tall, dark, half English and half Cherokee Indian.

When she came out of the ring, I asked her if she could explain what she'd been doing with the filly. Most amateur horse trainers go along by guess and by gosh and achieve at least half of their results by luck. Diane knew exactly what she'd been up to. Although she wouldn't have called it "bringing behavior under stimulus control," she understood it. I thought she'd make a good porpoise trainer—and she has been one of the Park's senior trainers for six years now.

Jennie Harries was another horse trainer that I picked up at a stable, an English girl, visiting Hawaii for a lark, and an Olympic-level horse trainer and rider. When the Institute acquired tanks and animals of its own, Jennie was put in charge of them. We worked together over the years on a number of fringy, amorphous problems that were too speculative to bother the show trainers with, such as trying to get an animal to mimic sounds and trying to use horse-training methods to harness-break a porpoise. Like many talented animal trainers Jennie had a prickly disposition with people. She expected of others the same rigid standards of performance she set for herself, and she expressed herself with a forthrightness that seemed to the more easygoing to be arrogance. It made her more useful to me as a solitary worker than as a member of a show team, though she did help out with shows when needed, and it was Jennie and I together who trained the spine-tingling double whale jump.

My journal, Thurs., Oct. 27, 1966

Gregory said of Jennie today, all it takes [to be a good trainer] is guts, perseverance, and discipline. She has the whale jumping a bar out of the water—Olelo in the training facility, something 6 trainers in 6 months have not done with either whale. I explained how to do it, and it took her only two days. Thing is, she *knew* how fast to take the bar up. My heart turned over with pride when I saw her push the whale on up a foot in her first training session. She adores her; Olelo is a wonderful animal. "Thinking all the time," I remarked, and Jennie said, "Yes, she's really ticking over, you can see it," as Olelo cocked a canny eye at us and jumped again. There's the art of it. Skinner is all very well, but if you can't tell when your animal is thinking hard, you'll never make it.

Dec. 21, 1966

Jennie wrote an article which has been published in a French horsemen's magazine, on dressage training compared to whale training. It was an excellent piece, and the Gallic captions to the pictures were most amusing. Jennie hand-feeding Olelo: "Et la dresseur, n'est elle pas charmante?" also, over a shot of Olelo's bucket-sized mouth, "La premier différence de cheval et baleine est que la bouche de cheval est moins grand," and as the whale jumped a line, "Sauter: dressage ou ballistiques?"

There were many, many other good trainers over the years— Lyn Cowan, Carol Sorrell, Bob Ballard, Danny Kali. Some stayed with Sea Life Park, some went on to other oceanariums, and a couple became psychologists and switched from porpoises to people.

Most of the time, my training staff was composed almost entirely of women. There were a couple of practical reasons for this. First, our salaries were low, and it was easier to get girls at those prices than boys. Even very young men often had girlfriends or wives or children to support. They could not afford to

work for us long and could easily find higher-paying work else-
where. Second, in the late 1960s, the U.S. Navy opened a porpoise
research and training facility in Hawaii. In keeping with the
policy of most oceanariums, they hired only male trainers. David,
Ingrid, and I were busy turning everyone on our staff into skilled
trainers, and it began to seem as if every time some young man
started getting pretty knowledgeable, either the Navy or some
other oceanarium would come poaching and hire him away at
double the salary we could pay. I thought they were dopes for
not stealing Ingrid or Diane or Marlee or some of the other girls,
but they didn't. Not until 1972 were our trainers paid salaries
competitive enough to keep men on the job routinely.

I, on the whole, preferred women as trainers. Men, in general,
seemed to have a drawback: their egos. A man tended to feel that
when the animal didn't respond correctly it was defying him.
Then the man got mad. Not every man, but more than a few.
I have seen more than one male trainer throw a bucket of fish to
the deck or drive his fist against the nearest wall and then stamp
off furious, from a self-created ego battle with an animal.

The male trainers were also much harder for me to handle as
employees. Some of them resented being bossed by a woman.
Many of them took questions of status much more seriously than
the girls did, and would sulk or brag about any little thing that
meant a change of status to them, from a five-dollar-a-month
raise to being shifted from one show area to another. Once a
man began to think of himself as a "trainer," it became difficult
to get him to do necessary but menial work, such as scrubbing
the fish scales off the *Essex* deck. The girls usually did not have
that kind of pride.

If women, in general, had a drawback as trainers, it was their
kind hearts. The girls were willing, sometimes too willing, to let
an animal get away with sloppy work, to let it slide rather than
making it toe the line. It was to girl trainers, over and over, that
I had to say: "Don't sympathize with the animal, don't try to
imagine what it is thinking—you cannot possibly *know* what it

is thinking, so you can't use that as a basis for decision. Stop feeling sorry for the porpoise. Stick to the training rules."

I could teach the trainers what I knew. Who would teach me, though, when I ran up against something I didn't understand? I carried my puzzles around in the back of my head and picked the brains of every trainer or psychologist who came through the Park. When Ron Turner, for example, visited Hawaii briefly to help Ken Norris with an experiment, I dragged him out to the show tanks and exhibited two problems I'd been unable to solve.

At the Ocean Science Theater we had given Makua a partner, a beautiful lady bottlenose named Wela ("calm"). Our object was matrimony, but as far as I know Makua and Wela were never anything more than platonic friends. Wela was a fine performer, but she was often naughty. She took to refusing to go back in the holding tank. She would hover outside, but when you opened the gate she would whisk in and then turn around and whisk right out again before you could get the gate closed. Sometimes, with a wicked flash of the whites of her eyes, she would knock the gate from the trainer's hands, shoving her way through.

Ron watched with a jaundiced eye as I opened the gate, Wela went in, I blew the whistle and tossed a fish, and Wela on this instant whirled around and went back out again. "What are you actually reinforcing?" Ron said. "You're reinforcing turning around and going back out." So I was. A split-second error in timing was strengthening the undesirable behavior. Even if Wela didn't bother to eat her fish, she had been reinforced by the whistle, followed by the tangible reward not of fish but of freedom.

Once an animal has learned something, it will never entirely unlearn it, Ron pointed out. You can overlay the learning with new information, you can extinguish the behavior almost entirely, but you can never completely erase what has been written. Wela's trickiness at the gate was never entirely eradicated, but we reduced it considerably by reinforcing her not for going in the holding tank, but for going in and staying while the gate was closed. If she did duck out, Ron pointed out, we had to swing the gate open and let her go. Beating the gate was fun in itself; to encourage the behavior to extinguish, we had to have something nice happen if Wela did right, and nothing at all happen if she did wrong.

In Whaler's Cove I had another problem. The spinners were supposed to do the "hula," balancing on their tails half out of water, all together. They had taken, instead, to coming up and going down at different times. Whenever you blew the whistle you were likely to be reinforcing at least one of the animals just when it was going down, or after it had popped up and down several times instead of coming up and staying up. Ron again

With Ron Turner's advice, we finally managed to train a perfect hula. Lei, in the center, wears her flower lei.

applied the Occam's razor of operant conditioning: "What are you actually reinforcing?"

"Well, let's see. A long hula? A consistent hula? The start? The end? Mostly I just want them all to be up at the same time."

"Then don't reinforce them unless they are."

Presto! I started withholding reinforcement until that instant, however brief, when all six noses were in the air, ignoring everything else such as who was highest and whether they stayed up a long time or not. Sure enough, in a few days all the animals came up together and stayed up together. Except Kahili. As befitted the privilege of his authority, he always showed up at the last moment and then collected his fish first.

That simple rule of Ron's, to look, when things went wrong, at what you were actually reinforcing, bailed me out of a lot of problems from then on.

Visiting scientists were often very pleasant about taking time to teach me what they knew. Two professors from Reed College, Dr. William Weist and Dr. Leslie Squier, worked at the Institute during the summers, using elaborate electronic equipment to program the behavior of little fishes. Both of them called my attention to occasional research papers in the vast forest of psychological literature which might be of special interest to me—papers which I most certainly otherwise would not have seen.

Bill Weist put in hours and hours one summer teaching me how to set up training problems on his roomful of programing equipment. I learned about norgates and flip-flops and other obscurities—not enough to be an expert, but enough to know how the equipment worked and what it could and could not be used for, should I ever have a budget big enough to acquire some.

One night at a dinner party I was complaining to University of Hawaii professor Dr. Ernst Reese about the apparently insuperable problems of trying to record the events in a given training session, other than in narrative form. Ernie told me about a device called the event recorder, and then most kindly lent me one from his own laboratory. This interesting machine ran a roll of paper at a steady rate under twenty little pens, each of which made twenty little lines. Along with it came a panel of twenty little buttons. Every time you pressed a button, the pen it was hooked up to made a little blip in the line. Paul Bacchus, an Institute trainer, and I set out to use this device to record a single training session with a porpoise. We labeled one row of buttons for things the trainer could do—turn cues on, turn cues off, blow the whistle, give a fish, leave the tank side, and so on. We labeled the other rows for things the porpoise could do: the various behaviors it was learning, plus auxiliary things like eating the fish, splashing, changing direction, and so on.

We held a couple of training sessions. Paul quickly learned to punch the buttons with accuracy. We found, looking at the roll of paper after a training session, that from those little blips you could discover all sorts of things that were not apparent in the heat of the moment: for example, that the animal always slowed down when asked to turn right, or that the whistle was coming a little late. Here would be the blip on the line where the desired behavior had taken place, and here would be the whistle blip, not directly under the behavior blip, but a little farther on. The paper had had time to roll by, a half-inch or so, and the animal was actually getting reinforced after the fact. You could also see patterns, repeated clusters of blips, that could tell you that, unknown to you, the animal had slipped into a chain of offering three responses in sequence, no matter what commands or other responses fell in between. Fascinating!

At that time my original Welsh pony mother and foal had grown into a herd of a dozen or more, owned in conjunction with my father-in-law and pastured on the neighboring island of Maui. Each year we shipped the two-year-olds to Honolulu to be broken and sold (my idea of recreation, in these busy years, was to leave the porpoise training for an hour or two, round up a bunch of children, and go play at training the ponies. I don't know where I found the strength).

I decided it would be fascinating to try the event recorder on a horse-training session. Paul and I went to a nearby stable where

I was keeping a young Welsh pony filly, just arrived from Maui, gentle and tame but utterly ignorant. She wore a halter but knew practically nothing about being led around by it; main force was the only way to move her.

With a pocketful of grain I began the business of teaching the filly to move forward when I tugged on the halter and said "Walk"; to halt when I pulled on the halter and said "Whoa"; to back up; to turn left and right; and to trot when I urged her to hurry. Paul labeled his buttons and poked away on the keyboard, recording my voice cues and my reinforcements ("Good *girl*," and then a handful of grain). The session proceeded according to all my previous experiences: lots of tugging and hauling, and a certain amount of progress.

Afterward, we sat down in my office at the Park and studied the paper track from the event recorder. Eureka! It was instantly obvious that my voice reinforcements were almost always late, sometimes by nearly a second; I often spoke to the pony *after* she had taken a step or two, when she was again standing still. Also, many times the pony had made the correct response, but so briefly that I hadn't recognized it, and sometimes I confused the pony by giving her two tasks at once, such as going forward *and* turning.

We went back out the next day, and I made a firm effort to correct my timing errors, to work on one behavior at a time instead of jumbling them, and to pay sharper attention to the pony's hesitant and brief responses. In *fifteen minutes* I had a pony which would move briskly beside me on a slack line, no tugging or pulling needed, and which would walk, trot, halt, and back up on voice commands. Horses don't do much guessing; they won't jump the time gap for themselves, as a porpoise can, if the reinforcement is late even by half a second; but they are fabulous learning machines.

A professional horse trainer was leaning on the fence watching this session and snickering a little because I was committing the cardinal sin of the amateur by using food. When I was through, he asked how long I'd been working with the filly. "Two days,"

I said. "About fifteen minutes yesterday and fifteen minutes today." He spat on the ground and walked away, disgusted. He *knew* I had to be lying.

Our borrowed event recorder soon had to go back to the university, and I was never able to squeeze one of these $1,000 items into my budget, but I think now that the ideal situation for any trainer would be to work always with an event recorder and someone to run it. It seems to me to be not only a great time saver, but potentially a splendid source of new information.

Another horse trainer, a dear old friend named Al Reynells, taught me something that was to prove extremely useful with porpoises. One day he told me about "quick breaking," the gypsy or Indian way of turning a wild horse into a tame one in a few minutes. I flatly refused to believe it until I had a couple of demonstrations, one from Al and one from a Hawaiian horse trainer, Tommy Campos.

The system is this: the trainer puts the wild horse in a very small corral, perhaps 20 by 20 feet, just big enough so the trainer can stay out of kicking range. Then he stands in the center and threatens the horse from behind, either by cracking a whip or by flipping a rope at the horse's tail end. The frightened horse begins to run around and around the pen, but he cannot escape. The trainer, in the center, continues to threaten him from behind, urging him on.

Sooner or later, in panic, the horse will reverse direction. If he turns inward, he must momentarily come toward the trainer. At that instant the trainer drops his arms and steps backward, reducing the threat. In ten or fifteen minutes the horse "discovers" that the only safe place, the only place where he is not pursued, is next to the man. By the end of the session the horse may be leaning his head on the trainer and following him about like a dog. He feels safe only when he is literally in the trainer's hands.

This is no job for an amateur: you have to be able to read the horse pretty well, and to move fast yourself. It is also scary to see, because the horse is so terribly frightened at first. However, if one must take on a grown horse that was not gentled as a colt, and if one does not have time for the weeks, even months, it might take to gentle the horse by accustoming him to one little thing at a time, it is a very effective and useful measure.

I decided to have a go at "quick-breaking" a porpoise. We had a new bottlenose in the training tanks who had not shown any signs of getting tame. He avoided all contact with people, and his fearfulness was a nuisance if we had to doctor him or to move him to another tank.

One morning I put him in the smallest round tank and dropped the water down to about 3 feet, a depth in which both the porpoise and I could move around easily. Then I picked up a towel and climbed into the middle of the tank. The porpoise, alarmed, began to swim around the perimeter of the tank. As he swam, I pursued him by slapping the towel on the water behind him. Panicky, he dashed around and around, and then began turning and cutting back and forth. Each time his turns brought him toward me, I instantly pulled in the towel and stepped back from him. Then, as he passed and was going away, I stepped forward and started flipping the towel at him again.

At first it seemed as if nothing was happening. I saw none of the signs of slowing down that the horses I had watched began to give. But suddenly the animal swerved toward me. I laid the towel down and stepped back—and he rolled on his side and swam gently into my arms.

From then on he was tame. You could catch him, pet him, swim with him, hug him. As with the horses, the pursuit was not something he associated with the person; the feeling of safety was. The animal wasn't even afraid—and this surprised me—of towels. Without any sacrifice of his natural ebullience and spirit, he was permanently "broken." It was a most valuable technique, and in fact easier, because less dangerous to the trainer, with a porpoise than with a horse.

In 1965, to sharpen up everyone's training skills, David and I developed a weekly class in training for any staff members who

A ring full of Welsh ponies and children. I borrowed horse-training methods for the porpoises and applied porpoise-training methods to the ponies. Coca-Cola, ordinarily forbidden, was a good reinforcement for children and ponies both.

wanted to attend. I would talk about some aspect of operant conditioning, such as the reason that a variable schedule of reinforcement is more powerful than a fixed schedule, and David would talk about some aspect of the art of training, such as how to choose the likeliest prospect from a group of animals. The most valuable classroom technique we had, however, was "The Training Game," a device passed on to me by some visiting psychologist.

One person was sent out of the room. We selected an official trainer from among the rest of us, and we chose some simple behavior, such as "Write your name on the blackboard," or "Stand on one foot on a chair" or "Dance up and down and sing."

Then the "animal" came back in the room, and the "trainer," using a whistle, tried to shape the desired behavior. No talking was allowed. The subject was instructed to move around the room freely and to return to his starting place whenever he had been rewarded with the whistle. At first we gave the subject an M&M

or a Lifesaver every time the whistle blew, but we soon found that group approval and the sound of the whistle were reward enough.

Putting a novice behind the whistle was a quick and cheap way of drumming training laws into the novice's head without making some poor porpoise put up with an inconsistent trainer. It was a fast lesson in disciplined thinking. When the subject was a human being, there was no way for the trainer to say to himself: "The animal *can't* do this," or "The animal is mad at me," or "The animal is deliberately defying me," or "The animal is stupid." If that new trainer couldn't shape that human being to flap his arms like a bird, the fault could lie only in his training technique.

The groans of the other trainers when a beginner missed an obvious opportunity for reinforcement were informative. So were the murmurs and pleased laughs when the beginner made a smart move. If the trainer got up on his intellectual hind legs and claimed this task couldn't be done because of so and so and so, we gave someone else a chance at it. If it really seemed necessary to make the point even at the expense of the novice trainer's pride, David or Ingrid or I would take the whistle and shape the behavior in a dozen well-timed reinforcements.

When a new trainer achieved a nice piece of shaping, the cheers and applause as the subject finally accomplished the desired behavior were highly reinforcing for subject and trainer alike. The thrill of a quick accomplishment in training class also helped to sustain a trainer's morale in the slower business of shaping animals.

We could use the Training Game to demonstrate any aspect of operant conditioning, such as developing superstitious behavior at will, putting behavior on long schedules of reinforcement (there was the time we got a subject to turn the light on and off twenty times for each whistle), or bringing behavior under stimulus control.

Being the subject was an interesting experience; it brought home rather dramatically how baffled the porpoises must often feel. We learned that it was possible for an animal, even a human,

to show a response correctly without having any understanding
of what it was supposed to be doing. You could, for example,
condition someone to walk around with his fists clenched behind
his back, and he would accomplish it several times, correctly,
and then be surprised that the session was over, since he had
as yet no conscious knowledge of what he was being reinforced
for.

Once, working on stimulus control, we got a subject to clap
his hands every time one of the girls in the back of the room
blew on a kazoo. We all agreed, finally, that the behavior was
established on cue, and extinguished off cue, for periods up to
thirty seconds (and that's a long time, when you're standing in
front of a room full of people and doing nothing). Yet when we
stopped the session, we found that our subject did not have the
faintest idea that he had been responding to a cue, or what the
cue had been. As far as he was concerned, he had never "noticed"
the toot of the kazoo. Imagine!

The choice of behaviors to shape was a nice problem in itself.
Things that are socially "okay" to do were easy to shape. One
could always get a subject to write on the blackboard, first by
reinforcing movements toward that part of the room, then perhaps by reinforcing hand movements in the direction of the
chalk, and so on. Things that are not normally "okay," like standing on the table, took more time. David was exceedingly in-
genious about overcoming a subject's inhibitions. It was a lesson
to all of us in the art as opposed to the science of training to
watch David change his track in the middle of a shaping
sequence. For example, faced with the table-standing behavior
as a goal, and a subject that leaned against the table but could
not bring himself to move farther, David once solved the problem
by getting the subject walking around again, getting him walking backwards, and then deliberately backing him over a waste-
basket so that he tripped and accidentally sat on the table, thus
breaking through the taboo about being *on* a table.

It was interesting, too, to see who made a good subject and
who did not. Brains, at least introspective, intellectualizing brains,

were not of much use to the person playing the animal. The thinking person tended to stand and *think*, trying to guess what behavior the trainer had in mind, which was a big waste of time, since it gave the trainer no movements or behavior to reinforce. Egotistical people sometimes got mad, especially if they thought they had figured out what to do, and then the next time got no whistle for that action. (Porpoises get mad in the same situation. A human subject just looks sour and grumbles; a porpoise makes a big breach and splashes the trainer from head to foot.)

Easygoing, extroverted people who didn't mind looking a little silly made good subjects. On a TV panel show I once spotted the moderator as a potentially good subject, and demonstrated porpoise training by writing out what I was going to do and showing it to the audience, then getting the emcee moving around until I could shape him, with the whistle, to take the earrings off a lady on the panel and put them on himself. He was lively and unselfconscious, and it took about two minutes.

David, like all natural trainers, was excited when he saw a good prospect. One day in the training game I assigned a new swimmer, a lovely Hawaiian girl named Lehua Kelekolio, to be the subject. She was very quiet and reserved, and I thought the experience might be relaxing and helpful to her. One of the junior trainers had the whistle. Lehua got through the door, and was moving around and had earned one or two whistles, when David shouted, "Hey, that's one *good* working animal, lemme have the whistle!" and finished the training himself for the pleasure of shaping a sharp worker.

It was in the Training Game that I first became fully conscious of the differences between what the skilled operant conditioner knows and what the practical animal trainer knows: between the science of training and the art of training. We called it "Karentraining" and "David-training," and sometimes, for exercise, made lists on the blackboard. Things like whistle conditioning, time outs, and limited holds went under "Karen-training." Things like knowing when to quit and thinking up shaping recipes and choosing a good subject went under "David-training."

I became conscious of the existence of two vast camps of trainers: the psychologists, with their elegant, almost mathematical rules for training, but no rules for the "David-training" aspects of the work, for the hunches, the timing, the intuitive outguessing of the animal; and the practical animal trainers, with vast individual experience, but with their own superstitious behaviors, people who usually were unable to sort the useful from the merely traditional in their shaping recipes, and who had a tendency to explain far too much on the basis of the personalities of the animals and the magnetic personality of the trainer himself. Two vast camps, and almost no communication between them.

At Sea Life Park, we had a foot in each camp. With Ron's manual, and scientists coming and going whom I could quiz about details of learning theories, we had a firm scientific footing. With the practical necessities of mounting ten trained animal shows a day, and varying those shows all the time, we had firm footing in the practical camp.

Somewhere between the two camps, new truths, new understandings, still remain to be discovered. It seemed to me I could sense these truths, or at least the questions that might lead to them, most clearly when we were playing the Training Game. What's "smart"? What's "dumb"? Why does one "love" one animal and not another? Why—oh, why indeed—does the animal love the trainer? At what point, and why, does the artificial communication system of operant conditioning begin to give way to some genuine social communication, to that feeling that trainers call rapport? It is a golden feeling when the trainer really begins to feel as if he *is* reading the animal's mind, or when the animal begins to respond to the trainer's voice and emotions, something we take for granted in a horse or dog but have to work to earn with the more alien porpoise. It is really an eerie thrill when the animal turns the training system around and uses it to communicate with you.

People love to ask porpoise trainers about "communication." I usually brush the question aside by answering that I can communicate just fine with a whistle and a bucket of fish. I really saw nothing, in years of watching, to suggest that porpoises have an abstract language or are in any way more than nice bright animals. Two-way communication, however: that, through training, we built. Communing might be a better word.

I recall walking up to Ocean Science Theater with David Alices while the show was just coming to a close. Ahead of us we could see a junior trainer standing on the elevated platform giving Makua the signal for the high-rise. We could also see Makua lolling around underneath the platform, looking up first with one eye and then the other, acting as if he'd never heard of the high jump. From 50 feet down the path, David yelled "Makua!" in tones of wrath. The animal took one startled look through the glass in our direction and immediately dove, got up speed, and jumped 18 feet to the trainer's hand. We had no punishments or threats to use—it was just that Makua knew David, and he knew David expected disciplined obedience, and he answered David's voice by obeying the junior trainer.

A psychologist, Ron Schusterman, told me once of a porpoise of his that had learned to make a series of correct choices, pressing one of two paddles, in return for a fish from a feeding machine. One day she made a couple of correct responses and then suddenly made a long series of 100 percent wrong choices, apparently deliberately. Ron was baffled, until he looked in the feeding machine. The fish had been left there too long and were dried out and inedible. The porpoise was using the training situation to communicate this fact. As soon as the fish were replaced, she went back to a perfect performance.

I have myself seen porpoises "misbehave" to get a message across: an animal refusing to go out the gate, opening its mouth, and "saying," in porpoise body English, "Hey, Randy, before we go to work, take a look. I've got a piece of wire stuck in my back teeth—take it out, will you?"

I have seen an animal test the training situation to ask and answer its own questions. After we had established the double whale jump in Whaler's Cove, with Makapuu and Olelo crossing the line in opposite directions, I turned my attention to other things, and the jump began to deteriorate. Olelo took to jumping a second or two after Makapuu, so that Makapuu was landing before Olelo was in the air. The trainers called for help. The behavior was on a sound cue, and I decided that I might use this to correct Olelo; I anticipated that it might take days, or even weeks, to get the behavior cleaned up.

We had a short training session between shows. Jennie, David, Diane, and I put up the line, and the girls got the whales stationed and attentive. I turned the sound cue on. The whales headed for the rope. Makapuu jumped first, and as she left the water I turned the cue off and her trainer blew the whistle. Then Olelo jumped. No whistle. When the animals came back to the *Essex*, Makapuu got a fish but Olelo got none.

Again I turned the cue on. This time Olelo hurried. For the first time in days she cleared the rope exactly when Makapuu did; they both heard the whistle at the peak of the jump, and they both got lots of fish.

Hurray. I turned the cue on again. Makapuu jumped first. I turned the cue off as Olelo started her leap, late. No whistle, no fish for her.

Fourth try. I turned the cue on, and Olelo did an unprecedented thing: she switched around to Makapuu's side and jumped in unison, but beside Makapuu, instead of crossing from the opposite way. Again, she got no fish.

Fifth try: Olelo went from her own side, *almost* but not quite simultaneously with Makapuu. She was in the air before the cue went off, and in the air when the whistle blew, but just a shade late. Feeling slightly shady myself, I gave Makapuu her usual two-pound reward and gave Olelo one tiny small smelt. Olelo physically *startled* and looked me in the eye.

Sixth try: the cue went on. Olelo hustled obviously, matched Makapuu's jump precisely, got a whistle and a huge reward, and performed perfectly from then on. She had been trying the scientific method on us, deliberately testing the exact nature of the rules. Her testing, in about ten minutes of work, gave her the answers she needed. That's communication.

One of the most poetic moments of communication through training that I ever shared with an animal occurred with a new *Steno*, Malia, in a straightforward operant conditioning context; a fleeting event, and yet real enough so that I later felt justified in including it in a scientific paper:

A trainer was reinforcing a Rough-toothed Porpoise for leaping, and the animal was offering the response readily. In the course of work the animal happened to make an interesting noise which the trainer also reinforced. The animal repeated the noise several times, and the trainer became more interested and stopped reinforcing leaps to reinforce the sound.

That was an error. This animal had not yet had any experience of failing to be reinforced for something it had learned to offer in expectation of reward. After several unreinforced leaps the animal exhibited anger, refused to come to the trainer for fish, went to the far side of the tank and stayed there. It refused all food for the next two days. Physical examination showed no sign of illness. On the third day it volunteered a leap and accepted food. The trainer reinforced subsequent leaps and then established a stimulus control that leaping would be reinforced only when the trainer's hand was lifted. The animal began to show response to this new criterion, leaping when the hand was raised and waiting when it was lowered, and in one of these waiting periods it made the noise. The trainer immediately reinforced the noise and then raised the hand, elicited a jump, and reinforced that. Possibly the porpoise recognized this sequence as clarifying the rules governing when leaping would be reinforced as opposed to noisemaking. It approached the trainer and stroked the trainer's arm gently and repeatedly with its pectoral fin, a gesture very frequent between porpoises but extremely rare from porpoise to human, and in the next ten minutes not only demonstrated correct response to the "leap" stimulus but acquired some reliability of response to a different hand signal for "make noise."[*]

---

[*] Karen Pryor, "Behavior and Learning in Whales and Porpoises," *Die Naturwissenschaften*, 60 (1973), 412–420.

Malia, beautiful Malia, fresh-caught and still very green and shy, had used a porpoise gesture to communicate something like the following: "Okay, stupid, I understand what you're driving at now, and I forgive you." I had no way of communicating back what I felt like, which was like bursting into tears.

K. K. Kaumanua turned into "a great handsome red-furred dog with noble mien and plumy tail, nothing at all like the original Hawaiian curs." Nana the pilot whale holds one end of a flower lei while Nancy Kim signals and Akamai jumps.

6. BIRD BRAINS AND OTTER CONFUSION

In the middle of Sea Life Park stood the ruins of some ancient Hawaiian huts. We reconstructed an ancient Hawaiian village there, as a sort of museum exhibit among the trees we had left standing in the center of our land. Soon the exhibit was completed, gracefully embellished with displays and signs and a borrowed collection of Hawaiian artifacts. It lacked life, however. We decided to install some of the animals that the ancient Hawaiians brought with them on canoes: a dog or two, pigs, and Hawaiian chickens or junglefowl. A wild Hawaiian rat, now rather rare, also hitchhiked on those ancient voyages, but I never could get anyone interested in exhibiting rats.

Visiting the neighboring island of Molokai I spotted a typical Hawaiian "poi" dog under a fisherman's house: a dun-colored, potbellied, whip-tailed homely puppy, which changed hands for an exorbitant $5 and became our official Hawaiian dog. We named him after a mythical Hawaiian politician, K. K. Kaumanua. Unfortunately, with a good worming and lots of tender care K. K. grew into a great handsome red-furred dog with noble mien and plumy tail, nothing at all like the original Hawaiian curs; but he served the purpose.

Then we got a couple of cute little wild black piglets from the Honolulu Zoo and acquired some authentic junglefowl from original wild stock still living in the forests of Kauai. Once we had all these new animals around, the trainers began itching to teach them things. The dog quickly learned to ride in the canoe at Whaler's Cove and to perform several stunts such as tying up the canoe when it landed by looping a rope over a stake. I'm afraid the only thing that impressed the audience was the moment in the show when each porpoise got a fish and then the dog got one too and gulped it down whole with obvious relish. I don't know why this was amazing. Dogs like fish, and they don't care about bones and fins, but the audience always exclaimed.

The little junglefowl were attractive, if skittish, and we thought it might be nice to incorporate them and the two piglets into some kind of subsidiary show in the Hawaiian Village. We went to a good deal of trouble and expense to install loudspeakers, to develop a narration about Hawaiian life, and to draw people into the village between porpoise shows. Theatrically, it was a bust; after seeing the whales and porpoises work, no one was much interested in looking at pigs and chickens. From a training standpoint, however, it was a lot of fun.

Wela Wallwork and Nancy Kim were the two smart swimmer-narrators who began working with the junglefowl. Wela taught four little roosters to sit in the branches of the trees in the Hawaiian Village. Then she could call them, one by one, by name, and by name each rooster would fly to her outstretched arms. Nancy taught two hens to help her sort flowers to make leis. She set them down by a basket of three colors of plastic flowers. One hen quickly pulled out all the red flowers, and another the white ones, leaving the pink flowers in the basket. One or two roosters learned to crow when they were pointed at, and one of the hens learned a hilarious hula.

The pigs were more of a challenge. Pigs are supposed to be smart. We found them to be curiously handicapped by their own bodies and natures. A pig, for example, can learn to push something with its nose in just a few minutes; that is natural for pigs. On the other hand, to get a pig to carry something in its jaws seemed practically impossible: perhaps carrying things around is just not something pigs are programed to do.

Furthermore, pigs are terribly pigheaded. You can guide a pig ahead of you with a stick, but you can not, without great difficulty, make a pig walk beside you on a leash. Then there were things our pigs liked better than a food reward, such as lying in a shady place under a sprinkler. If the trainers took the pigs out of their pen to put on a little show with them, and the pigs saw a cool, wet place they would like to visit, it was goodbye show.

Worst of all, the pigs grew. In no time our cute little black piglets were 150-pound hogs, clean and handsome, if you like pigs, but hardly objects of interest for tourist cameras. We finally gave up trying to do trained shows with the pigs and chickens, and left them as an animated part of the museum display.

Nancy and Wela take their wild piglets for a stroll in Sea Life Park's Hawaiian village.

". . . the seals would 'kiss,' instantly, whenever she dropped the word 'moonlight' into her narration. . . ."

There is a native seal in the Hawaiian Islands, a very rare creature known as the Hawaiian monk seal. We obtained three of these animals over the years and kept them in a display pool near Whaler's Cove. They take exceptionally poorly to captivity; I know of only one individual that has ever lived in any zoo or aquarium for more than a few months. We had terrible problems with them: ulcers, feeding strikes, infections, worms; mostly, it seemed to me, they just moped to death. Finally we gave up on them and bought two California harbor seals, which look a lot like monk seals and which would be, we felt, company for monk seals if we ever acquired any again.

Another swimmer, Lehua Kelekolio, was responsible for the care and feeding of the harbor seals, and in due course taught them a remarkable number of behaviors with which to amuse onlookers: wearing leis, dancing the boogie, waving at children, and so on. Seals are not mobile like a sea lion; out of water they just squirm around like animated sacks of potatoes, and in the water they spend a lot of time floating around vertically with their heads sticking out like fat little buoys. They proved, however, to be extremely attentive and quick. They could see and hear very well, and they watched Lehua with acute attention. This enabled her to do what scientists call "disappearing the stimulus." She trained them, for example, to kiss each other on the nose; then she put the behavior under control of both a voice cue and a hand signal, and then spoke the word more and more softly, and made the hand signal smaller and smaller, until the seals would "kiss," instantly, whenever she dropped the word "moonlight" into her narration, or whenever she brought the tips of her index fingers together. No person watching or listening could have detected any signal at all. It is a device much used by circus trainers—for example, to make a lion roar at the trainer's wish, without any apparent command. It is also the way by which a fine horseman gets his mount to perform wonders without the rider's apparently moving a muscle himself.

A standing Sea Life Park rule of using only genuinely Hawaiian animals was broken when an animal dealer in California wrote me offering four Humboldt penguins at a modest price. These South American birds come from a temperate climate and would probably thrive in Hawaii. I persuaded the front office that it would be interesting to see penguins underwater at the Ocean Science Theater, and that I could make an informative narration comparing the evolution of penguins from land birds to water birds, to the evolution of porpoises from land animals to water animals. So the penguins arrived, and we established them in a pen on the deck of the Ocean Science Theater.

Penguins on dry land are awkward and pompous-looking,

but penguins underwater turned out to be indeed a fabulous sight. They are perfectly streamlined and swim around like little torpedoes by flapping their flipperlike wings. They can dive, U-turn at top speed, and jump out and shoot themselves across the surface of the water like miniature porpoises. We applied the spinner-training methods to training penguins, reinforcing all of them with the whistle and then throwing a bit of food to whichever one did the right thing.

Penguins are stupid, but they are active and greedy, and you can train any creature with those attributes. Our little flock soon learned to climb up a flight of steps and go down a slide into the water, to show off their jump across the water surface, and to dive through a hoop which we lowered halfway to the bottom of the tank. Actually, two of them learned to dive down and swim through the hoop, and two of them learned to fake the dive and get back up first and steal the honest penguins' fish.

"Penguins are stupid, but they are active and greedy, and you can train any creature with those attributes."

Since the audience could see what was going on very clearly, this never failed to amuse.

Our penguins also learned to scramble up a ramp and go back in their pen when it was time for them to leave the show tank. Sometimes, however, though they had a pool in their pen, they didn't want to go back, preferring to swim around and preen themselves in the larger show tank. Then we used a porpoise to chase them ashore.

This required absolutely no training at all. Every Ocean Science Theater porpoise adored chasing penguins and did it with gusto from the first experience. Penguins are much more maneuverable than porpoises, and could duck and reverse direction and thus avoid being bumped from below; but they are dumb. Sooner or later a penguin would stick his head up to get a breath. Then seemingly he forgot all about the porpoise, who would sneak up underneath him and boost him into the air. The penguins hated this, though it didn't harm them. Soon they all learned to rush for the gangplank whenever a trainer made a move to open one of the porpoise gates.

To our great surprise, when we'd had the penguins a year or so, one pair produced an egg and hatched and reared a chick. They have continued to do so yearly; at the time of writing the flock numbers eleven, good performers all.

One day another animal fancier wrote me, this time from Kuala Lumpur in Malaysia, offering me his pet half-grown river otter. After the success of the penguins, it was easy to get permission to try adding an otter to our underwater evolution demonstration. The otter arrived by air freight in fine shape, and we quickly ordered up another to keep her company.

What weird animals. At first we all loved them. They were gorgeous creatures, sleek, frisky, and amusing. They quickly learned to walk on a leash; their necks were so stout and muscular that they could back out of a collar at will, but a small harness, made for dogs, would hold them. They didn't care about being petted, but they loved to rub against a person in order to dry their fur. Any trainer could take the otters for a walk in the

Ingrid Kang and the otters.

Park and let visitors admire them. If the trainer sat down, the otters would climb in the trainer's lap and wriggle around with what looked like affection, but wasn't. Humans were just mobile bath towels to the otters.

We began thinking up things for them to do. Otters have clever little paws, almost like hands; they can, for instance, turn a doorknob (we found that out). They dive and swim marvelously, and see well both on the land and in the water. We could envision a dozen interesting things to train an otter to do underwater, such as packing and unpacking a picnic basket or playing a version of the old shell game.

There were, however, some obstacles to using the otters as performers. First, they were escape artists supreme. Hawaii state law said we *had* to keep them confined; but the only place we found that would hold them was an empty 10-foot-deep porpoise tank, with smooth cement walls. They could escape from any kind of cage or building. It was very difficult to work them at the Ocean Science Theater without having them get out of control and disappear over the edge of the building. They didn't want permanent freedom. They came back quite willingly. They just wanted the liberty to do as they pleased and go where they wished. "Help me catch the otters!" became a daily cry, and the task wasted a lot of everyone's time.

Second, otters are incredibly variable in their behavior. They seldom do the same thing twice in a row. Life for an otter is a constant search for novelty. It's amusing to watch, but it is not a trait that lends itself to five trained shows a day, six days a week, or even to one sensible training session.

I griped about it at lunch one day to Bill Weist and Dr. Leslie Squier, our visiting psychologists from Reed College. I'd been trying to train one otter to stand on a box, I told them. No problem getting the behavior; as soon as I put the box in the enclosure, the otter rushed over and climbed on top of it. She quickly understood that getting on the box earned her a bite of fish. *But.* As soon as she got the picture, she began testing the parameters. "Would you like me lying down on the box? What if I just put three feet on the box? Suppose I hang upside down from the edge of the box? Suppose I stand on it and look under it at the same time? How about if I put my front paws on it and bark?" For twenty minutes she offered me everything imaginable except just getting on the box and standing there. It was infuriating, and strangely exhausting. The otter would eat her fish and then run back to the box and present some new, fantastic variation and look at me expectantly (spitefully, even, I thought) while I struggled once more to decide if what she was doing fit my criteria or not.

My psychologist friends flatly refused to believe me; no

animal acts like that. If you reinforce a response, you strengthen the chance that the animal will repeat what it was doing when it was reinforced; you don't precipitate some kind of guessing game.

So I showed them. We all went down to the otter tank, and I took the other otter and attempted to get it to swim through a small hoop. I put the hoop in the water. The otter swam through it, twice. I reinforced it. Fine. The psychologists nodded. Then the otter did the following, looking up for a reward each time: swam through the hoop and stopped, leaving its tail on the other side. Swam through and caught the hoop with a back foot in passing, and carried it away. Lay in the hoop. Bit the hoop. *Backed* through the hoop. "See?" I said. "Otters are natural experimenters."

"Amazing," muttered Dr. Squier. "It takes me four years to get graduate students to think like that."

It was amazing, all right. It was also a big pain in the neck. Worse yet was the unpredictable temper of the otters. They chose enemies. (Victims might be a better word.) One of the assistant trainers who had never been near the otters hung his feet over their tank wall one day, watching the training, and an otter leaped up and bit him, lacerating his foot so badly he had to go to the hospital. A few weeks later, walking in the Park, that same otter spotted that same boy and took out after him and bit him badly again, on that same heel.

The trainers at Ocean Science Theater got bitten once or twice, and became afraid. The meaningless, unpremeditated nature of the attacks, and the speed and power with which otters move, suggested nightmarish possibilities. In bending over a nice, warm, lazy, lolling otter to put its harness on, one began to think seriously of how exposed one's throat was during the process.

We found that the damp air and wet cement in the pen we built for the otters at Ocean Science Theater was having harmful effects on their fur. Raw places appeared and got infected. Also the otters took to screaming for attention during the porpoise and penguin performances; the screams were unpleasant and so loud that they drowned out the narrator.

With funds to design and redesign an ideal otter training tank, with more patience, and with more skill, we might have done something amazing with the infuriating but beautiful beasts. But we had no funds, and we'd run out of patience. We gave up, and the otters went to the Honolulu Zoo, where they seemed quite happy.

I always enjoyed playing around with the training of odd sorts of animals; I would very much have liked us to have built an aquarium exhibit of trained fish and invertebrates. I could never get such an item incorporated into the master plan, but we did from time to time have a few aquariums in the training facility to play with. I taught a two-inch damsel fish to swim through a hoop in about ten minutes one afternoon. I taught a large hermit crab to yank on a string and ring a bell for his supper. David Alices, the maestro, taught a small octopus to climb onto his hand and be lifted from the water, and also trained it, *on command,* to turn upside down and squirt its siphon into the air, making an octopus fountain. The display possibilities in the training of "lower animals" are endless and, except for one aquarium in Japan, entirely unexploited as far as I know. Turtles, lobsters, minnows, virtually *anything* can be trained, if you can figure out how to reinforce it effectively and think of something interesting and appropriate for it to do. Dr. Larry Ames, at the University of Hawaii, developed a little device that measured a three-inch goldfish's daily dinner into eighty tiny portions. He used it to train discrimination experiments. Goldfish are not particularly zestful creatures, in my experience, but Larry's goldfish would almost leap from the water to get at their target buttons. It was a hilarious sight to me. To use the dog trainer's term, Larry had "happy-working" goldfish.

Dr. Roger Fouts, a nationally known authority on the training of chimpanzees, told me once that his secret desire in life was to find out if you could train blowflies to circle left and right on command. B. F. Skinner, the father of operant conditioning, let playfulness go to his head in a matter that he vows he will always regret: teaching two pigeons to play Ping-Pong. My favorite professorial training accomplishment of all, however, is one told to me by Dr. Richard Herrnstein, of Harvard, who in an idle moment trained a scallop, that lowly cousin of the clam, to clap its shell for a food reward.

The Hawaiian chain of islands consists not only of the five main islands usually shown on maps, but of a chain of reefs and rocks and islets extending nearly 2,000 miles westward of Honolulu all the way to Midway. Collectively known as the Leeward Islands, because they lie downwind of the main islands when the prevailing trade winds blow, these reefs and rocks are the home of a large portion of the natural wildlife of Hawaii, sea and land birds, green turtles, and the Hawaiian monk seal. Tap hoped to display a collection of this native fauna at one of the shallow pools he'd built in the Park. He hired a zoologist and ex-Navy pilot, Jim Kelly, to hitch a ride down to the Naval Base at Midway and the Coast Guard base at nearby Kure Island, and come back on a Navy plane with birds, turtles, and perhaps seals. Jim returned with several turtles, two monk seals, and a fine collection of birds: Laysan albatrosses or goony birds, turkey-sized black and white birds that drive the Navy crazy by nesting all over the runways on Midway Island; black-footed albatrosses (why called black-footed, I don't know; they are almost black all over); fairy terns, and tropic birds. We clipped the birds' wings, established them behind a wire fence around the Leeward Isles pool, and let the visitors watch the girls feeding the birds several times a day.

When spring came, Jim got the necessary state permits, went out to a sea bird rookery on Oahu, and collected several adult red-footed boobies, handsome black and white birds with blue bills and fetching pink feet. He also brought along a booby chick, with its nest and one of its parents, in the hope that the parent would go on raising the chick in the Park. Well, of course that didn't happen, so we took the chick up to the training facility and gave it a name, Manu ("bird"), and began raising it ourselves.

Manu was ridiculous. He looked like a snow-flocked basketball decorated with two black eyes and a sharp black beak. Slowly he feathered out into the dark-brown plumage that red-footed boobies wear in their first year. He was very tame and comical. We did not have the heart to clip his wings. We let the feathers grow, and we let him fly away.

He didn't fly away. He stayed. As soon as he could fly well enough to land on the *Essex* rigging without falling off (which took a month), he started hanging around bumming fish from the trainers at show time and would even contribute to the show by catching a tossed fish in midair. He stayed with us all winter long.

The next spring, when it was baby booby time again out in the rookery, we collected fifteen baby boobies and hand-raised them all. We let go all of our adult birds, including the albatrosses and the rest. Why should we have trapped, grounded birds, no matter how interesting, on display when we could have free-flying birds? The albatrosses, I'm sure, when their wing feathers grew out, went home to Midway, no journey at all for an albatross. The adult boobies we had been keeping with clipped wings went back to the rookery, and the rest of the birds disappeared, no doubt to their various homes. The new booby chicks grew, feathered out, and flew—but not away. They went out to sea and fished when the weather was good. When the weather was bad, they hung around the Leeward Isles pool and cadged food from the trainers. Many of them learned to catch fish on the wing, a pretty sight for the photographers, especially when a lissome Hawaiian girl in a bikini was tossing the fish.

In their second summer, that bunch turned brown-and-white-streaked, and Manu, now in his third summer, achieved the full adult plumage of his species, snowy white with black wing tips, pink feet, and his brown bill now sky blue. He picked a wife from among the two-year-old birds, and they set up house-keeping in a bush by the path to Whaler's Cove, made a typically

A red-footed booby and her chick, in their nest a few feet from passing crowds in Sea Life Park.

messy, flimsy booby nest, and to our joy and astonishment raised
a chick, six feet from the passing public.

This was a bit of a zoological triumph. All wide-ranging sea
birds, around the world, nest in traditional colonies, in traditional
locations. Sometimes each nest site is preordained down to the
last inch. Nobody, as far as we knew, had ever got a true sea
bird to breed in captivity, or indeed anywhere but in its traditional colony. We began to hope that we could establish a new
breeding colony at the Leeward Isles pool that would perpetuate
itself from year to year.

Indeed, that is what happened. Although some birds disappeared over the winters, each year we always ended up with
several adult birds which paired off and nested and raised young,
right in Sea Life Park. The fuzzy babies were a cameraman's
delight, and the rich display of bird behavior, courting, aggressive displays, nest building, and so on was fascinating for animal
lovers.

Why these untransplantable birds settled down at Sea Life
Park so nicely, we were at first at a loss to explain. The answer
came by accident. One day I was called to the ticket office to meet
a furious gentleman who announced that he was the federal wildlife officer and that we were holding a lot of his birds illegally
and were no doubt subject to fine or imprisonment or both.

Now what? It seemed that in the past year, all the wild sea
birds of Hawaii, which had always been under state protection,
had also come under federal protection. This man, Eugene
Kridler, had been transferred to Hawaii to see that they got it.

We had our state permits. No one had told us about federal
permits, but then no one had told Kridler about us, either, and
he was very upset.

We walked down to the Leeward Isles Pool together, and Mr.
Kridler informed me that all the birds there would have to be
released. I pointed helplessly at the white adults and the brown-
streaked yearlings and two-year-olds that were flying in great
banking circles over our heads. "They *are* released."

Well, then they would have to be banded. They already wore state bands on their legs, and some had colored plastic bands as well which Ingrid Kang and I were using to try to differentiate individuals by sight. I was quite agreeable to catching the birds—they were very tame—and putting federal bands on them too. The federal official began to see his way toward issuing us a federal permit to cover the situation. Peace seemed to be restored.

Then I realized I would have to confess that we had a new batch of fifteen chicks in the training facility, which were being hand-raised until they were feathered out enough to go out in the weather and be displayed at Leeward Isles. We went back and looked at them. It was a new shock for our new federal man. His urge was to say that we should return them to the wilds at once, but we both realized there was no chance that their parents would take them on again. They had to be hand-raised.

We compromised. The babies would not be put on exhibit until the correct permits had come through, which might take several weeks.

As a result, the babies did not move to the Leeward Isles exhibit as early as usual. Two of them began to fly before they left the training facility. When we did move the chicks, we spread them around the park, two at Ocean Science Theater, two on the hut on the Island of Whaler's Cove, and so on. As these birds began to take wing, we learned what it probably was that pinned them to their traditional nest site for life. It was not a question of where the bird was raised, but of where it happened to be when it learned to fly. It was as if our birds made a map of their world, with X marking "home," during their first couple of weeks on the wing. The birds that first flew from the training facility or the Ocean Science Theater could be found anywhere, in the *Essex* rigging, at Leeward Isles, out at sea— until breeding season rolled around again. Then they returned to the very spot in which they first took wing and did their best to entice a mate to that site and start to raise young.

There were no bushes in the training facility, and boobies nest in bushes, so those birds were unsuccessful. The birds at Ocean Science Theater were even worse off. It seemed (I'm not sure) to be only the males who were site-imprinted in this way. Probably even now, if you go to Sea Life Park in February, you can witness those two original birds flying in and out under the Ocean Science Theater roof, followed just as far as the edge of the tank by females which they are trying, unsuccessfully, to charm into setting up housekeeping on their "home" spot, a totally unsuitable pipe railing.

I never got tired of watching the boobies soaring around the park. They are magnificent fliers. It always seemed to me to be at least theoretically possible to train individual birds to offer aerial behaviors on purpose: to hover, to dive, to do wing-overs, perhaps even barrel rolls, and other aerobatics that came naturally to them. Sometimes a bird would scratch its head with one foot while flying along, and that was funny to see and would have been nice to catch. The practical problems were insuperable, however, the primary one being that we never developed a permanent way of marking and distinguishing individual birds in flight, in order to know whom to reinforce for what.

We did achieve a little training on the ground. Some birds learned to spread their wings on command, or to hop on a trainer's arm and be carried around and photographed. Some group training also occurred. The birds learned when they would be fed during the Whaler's Cove show and when they wouldn't. As a result, after the opening of the show there became established a magic moment when most of the birds that happened to be in the Park that day launched themselves into the air and swooped in a counterclockwise circle over the canoe, catching fish from the swimmer's hand. Then, when the girl landed her canoe on the island, the birds lined up and buzzed her, single file, for more fish tossed into the air. After that the birds would retire to their pool or to the rigging of the *Essex*.

They are a nuisance, no doubt. They spatter the *Essex* and an occasional visitor with generous, fishy gouts of bird lime.

". . . when the girl landed her canoe on the island, the birds lined up and buzzed her, single file, for more fish tossed into the air."

They can peck, not dangerously, but hard enough to draw blood. Every trainer who raised or hand-fed boobies has little peck scars on his or her hands. Gaylord Dillingham, a student working at the Park one summer, went down in Park history for a party entertainment that he called "The Bird Feeding Hula," in which he mimed, in Hawaiian hula gestures, all the discomforts of that task, from trying to get feathers off your fishy hands to ducking the wicked pecks. Still, the stunning beauty of the boobies on the wing makes them a wonderful exhibit, and to a biologist that unique breeding colony is worth any amount of trouble.

146

7. RESEARCH AND RESEARCHERS

In 1968 Ken Norris took leave of absence from the University of California and moved his family to Hawaii permanently, right next door to us, while he took over the directorship of the Oceanic Institute. The Institute had by then constructed a generous two-story laboratory building, porpoise tanks, a library, and a staff. All of us who knew the Norrises were delighted.

Ken and Phyllis Norris are two of the cheeriest, roundest, warmest, liveliest, dearest companions in the world. They have four interesting children, and their house, wherever they happen to be living, is full of music, guppies, pillows, coffee cups, ringing telephones, students, plants, birds—both in and out of cages—lethargic cats that leave the birds alone, barking dogs, and carpentry projects.

Phyllis is a marine botanist. Ken is an international authority on cetaceans, on lizards, on desert ecology, and a few other things, but he doesn't act like a world-foremost anything: the barefoot biologist. He is capable of putting on a tie and going to Washington and coming back with money; he has a wide-ranging and penetrating intellect and is much consulted in areas where science and government cross paths. He is also capable of considerable beer drinking and guitar playing, and is a marvelous and painless teacher who has inspired dozens of students to take up careers in the natural sciences.

Ken is a craftsman and an artist with an original and humorous turn of mind. The Norris house in Hawaii featured a stairway railing made from the curving rib of a sperm whale (try to get a building permit for that!) and a huge assemblage portrait of the harbor of Santiago, Chile, made by Ken and his children entirely of flotsam and jetsam picked up from the edges of that harbor.

On long summer visits to Hawaii, previous to moving over, Ken had accomplished a number of research projects with porpoises. Once he was permanently on the premises, his main task was running the Institute, but he continued his research on details of cetacean sonar production and on observations of a school of wild spinning porpoises on the "Big Island," the neighbor island of Hawaii.

Surely cetaceans are among the hardest of mammals to observe in the wild. One can sit on a mountain and follow the daily lives of a herd of elk through binoculars. One can trail elephants, or befriend wild chimpanzees, like the remarkable Jane Goodall, or make one's own den next to a wolf's den, like Farley Mowat. One can camp out on the guano and experiment with sea bird chicks like Niko Tinbergen, or label individuals in a troop of army ants and observe the behavior of each one, like T. C. Schneirla. But porpoises are largely invisible, and they are always on the move. No boat or swimmer can stay with them long, and any boat that comes among them disturbs their normal routine, distorting the very thing one wishes to observe undistorted. How can one get an honest picture of their lives and ways?

There are at least thirty species of porpoises in the world. Some live in limited areas, like Hawaii's spinners, a subgroup which seems to be found only along the coasts of the Hawaiian Islands. Some, like kikos, are found all over the Pacific Ocean; some, like *Stenos*, may range nearly worldwide. The slow accumulation of field notes brings information. Georges's careful recordings of every sighting he made suggest that around Hawaii the bottlenoses travel in schools of from three or four up to twenty individuals, and that these schools either live well out to sea or are just passing through our area when we see them. Spinners, on the other hand, live in schools of sixty or more and have particular territories which they patrol and in which they stay. One school "owns" the east coast of Oahu, another the north coast, and a third is normally seen off Waikiki. Hawaii, Maui, Kauai, and Molokai presumably have their own schools too.

Georges Gilbert knew at a glance which school he was in when the *Imua* ran across spinners. Indeed, there were some recognizable differences in these populations; for example, some schools tended to have slightly longer rostrums than others, or more teeth, on the average—a tiresome discovery for the taxonomists, since tooth counts are used to differentiate species on the premise that this is a fixed characteristic within species.

For an observer less familiar than Georges with the animals, identifying a particular previously seen school is nearly impossible, and indeed it may be difficult even to identify the species. Fishermen and sailors see a lot of porpoises, but one rolling back and triangular fin looks much like another. One cannot hope for fishermen's sightings to read: "approx. 40 *Tursiops gilli* at latitude xx and longitude xx, xx hour and date"; all they can give you is: "Sighted large porpoises, sighted small porpoises, some had some markings on the sides." Stranded or harpooned individuals often offer the only positive proof that a given species may be found in given waters. Most of our knowledge of distribution and occurrence of species comes from the evidence of dead specimens, painstakingly accumulated by museums.

The residential habits of our Hawaiian spinners offered Ken Norris some possibilities for field observation of the daily lives of porpoises. There were a number of possible approaches. One could catch and tag several individuals in a school and then return them to the school. The presence of the tags would confirm repeated observations of the same school and might give an idea of its daily movements. One might also be able to gather some knowledge of the relationship of tagged individuals to each other and to others in the school.

One could put a radio beacon on a single individual and track the school in this way. William Evans, in California, was successful in doing this with a school of Pacific white-sided porpoises, *Lagaenorhynchus obliquidens*. He found them feeding nightly along certain ledges about 100 fathoms or 600 feet down. Ken Norris and his team found that our Hawaiian spinners also traveled out to about the 100-fathom line. Here they dove to the bottom to feed on deep-sea squid and other organisms, the so-called deep scattering layer, made up of creatures which rise nightly from the great depths to be met by the porpoises 100 fathoms down.

The most promising approach in Hawaii seemed to be to find a school of porpoises that routinely came in close to land, at some place where it would be possible to observe them. Georges had noticed the frequent presence of a group of spinners in a little bay on the Kona Coast of the island of Hawaii, Kealakekua Bay—the spot where Captain James Cook, western discoverer of Hawaii, was killed. Captain Cook reported porpoises in this bay, as did Mark Twain and many other observers. Kealakekua Bay, an underwater state park and wildlife preserve, is ringed by high cliffs which would make good observation points. Ken set up an experimental program which ran for three summers, with observers stationed on shore, on the clifftops, and on boats. He followed the porpoises in a small, semisubmerged viewing chamber, recorded their sounds, and crossed their paths whenever possible at sea. He found a definite daily pattern. More often than not, the animals came into the bay at midmorning to cruise and rest in the sandy shallows, and then went out again around twilight to feed along the coast. Many individuals were identified by scars and marks and seen over and over again. Many observations scientists had made in Whaler's Cove—about sleep habits, for example, and social structure of subgroups—were at least tentatively confirmed.

The full story of Ken's observations of what he calls "Captain Cook's Porpoises" belongs to him (*The Porpoise Watcher*, by

Kenneth S. Norris, W. W. Norton and Co., Inc., N.Y., N.Y., 1974).
I saw them, under the auspices of Ken's experiment, one
memorable time.

From my journal: Undated [summer of 1970]

Ingrid and I flew to the Big Island this weekend to see the porpoises.
Westward was anchored in Kealakekua Bay, looking as beautiful as a
travel ad, full of Ken's students and Tap's guests, a floating hotel. [The
Westward was a 100-foot schooner that was being used as a research
vessel by the Oceanic Institute.] We had the forward starboard cabin,
very nice. Ken was absent; his assistants Tom Dohl and Dave Bryant
in charge. When we got there, Tom and his team were already up on
the cliff, observing. The skiff came to the dock to meet us. As we
made for the *Westward,* across the bay, we passed the porpoises,
cruising quietly, and three or four came over and rode the bows of
the skiff; we could almost touch them.

The *Westward* was a long way from the animals, so after lunch
Ingrid and I asked Dave Bryant if we could take the little rubber
boat and go close to them. He said okay. We didn't want to disturb
them, but it was a heaven-sent chance to see close-up the animals we
know so well.

Our plan was to coast alongside the slowly moving school, about
twenty feet from them, far enough away so they wouldn't be annoyed,
and then to put on a face plate, hold onto a rope, slip overboard, and
be towed behind the little rubber boat at the porpoises' speed, two or
three knots. We thought we could see more, that way, than from Ken's
bulky semisubmarine. We would be free to turn our heads all about,
and we would be minimally disturbing to the animals, provided we
used our experienced judgment of their "escape distance" and didn't
crowd them. Tap's guest Jack Rubel kindly offered to run the outboard
for us.

Ingrid went in first, stayed until she was chilled, and came up
thrilled speechless. I went in then, while Ingrid told Jack where to
drive the boat.

From the skiff I had been able to see the backs of four or five
animals, fairly near by, and a few more traveling slowly beyond those.
I thought that was the school; about twenty porpoises. Once in the
water, I saw I'd had it all wrong. The school was not a layer of
animals, scattered across the surface, but a three-dimensional pod,

extending, in groups of two or three, layered below each other, from the surface all the way down, fifty feet or more, to the silvery, sandy sea floor. There were rank upon rank of animals, before me, beside me, below me, beyond me, maybe sixty or eighty of them, cruising tranquilly, holding flippers, and looking at me with their gentle, merry little eyes.

An occasional animal amused itself by dashing down to the sea floor, turning sharply, and stirring up a great puff of white sand. The water was gently cool, like a breeze on a hot day, and the porpoises were gray and dun and silver, with the white sand reflecting turquoise light off their pale undersides.

Once I saw a pair of animals peel off for a wild, looping flight together, "holding hands." How often I've seen this in Whaler's Cove, the animals racing in circles and figure eights, but now, how much more beautiful, because in three dimensions: great fifty-foot parabolas from the glittering surface down to the white, glowing sand, back up again, and off into the dim distance and back. Turquoise and silver animals in a turquoise and silver world, a weightless world of three dimensions, in which everyone can fly. And all around me the whispering, twittering voices of the spinners, music of an unutterable tranquillity.

That was the one glimpse, for Ingrid and me, of our beloved spinners in their hitherto unimagined wild beauty. We got greedy and decided to go overboard together, and our driver, who gallantly refused to take a turn overboard, was used to horses, not porpoises. Without a spinner-sensitive trainer in the boat to guide him, he tended to go too close to the animals, to cut across their path, and to barge through them. We soon had the school disturbed and awakened, spinning, flipping, and scattering in every direction. When Ingrid and I realized what had happened, we went back to the *Westward* and left the porpoises alone, but too late. The animals, aroused, gathered themselves and went out to sea, thus putting an end to the day's observations.

Things were not too tranquil for me when Ken's assistant Tom Dohl came down from the observation point on the cliff, raging about the little rubber boat that had spoiled the day's data collection. Ingrid and I were apologetic, but unrepentant. That glimpse was worth earning a scolding.

Probably the world's most famous porpoise researcher, at least in the eyes of the public, is John Lilly, whose provocative book *Man and Dolphin* has implanted forever, as far as I can see, the general impression that porpoises can talk and might be smarter than people. One of my first tasks, after the shows settled down, was to write to other porpoise studiers asking for copies of their scientific papers, a customary procedure in the academic world. One of the first I wrote to was Dr. Lilly. He wrote back from Florida with the welcome news that he intended to pay us a visit. We were all delighted; the training staff was most curious to meet him, and since he had worked only with the Atlantic bottlenose porpoise, *Tursiops truncatus,* we wanted to see what he thought of our spinners and other exotic species. I took an hour off one morning and shaped Makua's "aloha" squawk into a semblance of "Hello, Dr. Lilly," a sophomoric jest which no one but me thought was funny.

John arrived on a sunny morning, toured the Park with me, and set up his tape player and some tapes he'd brought with him in the training facility. John is a handsome, intense, articulate man with piercing blue eyes, a playful imagination, and a great deal of charm. We immediately started a running argument about porpoise language. I am a disciple of Konrad Lorenz, the German biologist who with others established that many behavior patterns are inherited and can be studied as products of evolution, as clear-cut and measurable as fin shape or feather patterns. Thus even communicative behavior is usually inherited, innate rather than learned. Animals communicate extensively with one another, by sound, gesture, scent, and so on; one of Lorenz's followers identified 87 meaningful and consistent sounds in the vocabulary of chickens. Animal signals, however, do not refer to facts or objects, like human language, but to emotions and states of being. They are given spontaneously and understood innately; a porpoise whistle is in my opinion probably much closer to a human frown, or sigh, or giggle, than to a human word.

Because porpoises have almost no facial expression, and in fact in dark or cloudy water can hardly see each other anyway, much of the emotional expression which in other animals is expressed

visually—by a wagging tail or a raised crest or bared teeth—
might in the porpoise be expressed sonically. I was willing to
concede that much, and that therefore the porpoise repertoire of
specifically meaningful sound signals might be very rich; but I
was not willing to concede that there could or should be more
information in porpoise whistles than in the sounds and gestures
of any other highly social animal—say, Lorenz's Greylag geese or
a pack of timberwolves. And as for native intelligence, porpoises
were obviously bright, but they could do some dumb things too.

So, the disagreement between John and me flamed at once:
I said they were dumb animals, in both senses of the word, and
he denied that. But John's ideas, though they smacked to me of
mysticism, were often provocative. We walked down to Whaler's
Cove. John dropped his nifty little portable hydrophone in the
water, and we listened to the incessant trilling and fluting chatter
of the spinners. I said, "Wouldn't it be funny if it turned out to
be music?" and John said with asperity, "Of course it's music."
He wasn't kidding, and I think maybe he was right; I've been
thinking about that remark ever since.

If I wouldn't concede that porpoises might or must have a
secret language, perhaps I would concede that one could teach
a porpoise to talk our language. That evening we gathered in the
training facility and Lilly told us his story. A porpoise named
Elvar had been trained, in Lilly's laboratory in Miami, to start
to talk. He vocalized in the air, through his blowhole—we have
already seen how that can be established. He was presented with
a series of nonsense syllables, which he was required to imitate.
The lab team did bring the animal to the point where he could
not only repeat learned sequences, but could repeat new sequences correctly, at least capturing the intervals and rhythm
patterns with recognizable accuracy. From my standpoint, the
animal had been trained to respond to the criterion "Mimic what
you hear," which is a very sophisticated rule to understand, and
a nice piece of training, but no more. Elvar, however, had done
one rather startling thing; he had taken to initiating training sessions by offering a semblance of the trainer's usual first words:

"All right, let's go." You could hear that on the tape quite clearly. This was intriguing, and one could surmise that from there Elvar might proceed to imitating other useful human words ("Polly want a cracker"—"Elvar want a fish"), but as far as I know he never did.

What about the innate porpoise whistles? We wanted to know. We knew the "meaning" of the angry "bark" bottlenoses sometimes give, and we thought we understood one or two other whistles. Porpoises and our small whales seemed to have at least one whistle in common, the sound trainers refer to as the "distress call," a rising and falling whistle from middle C to high C back to C. The distress call is given loud and clear, and it meant enough to us so that if we heard it we dropped whatever we were doing and ran to see what was wrong.

John knew a good deal about that and other frequently heard whistles. He was the only person I've ever met who could imitate such whistles well enough to be understood by the animals. To prove it he took us down to Whaler's Cove and whistled a loud "distress call." The spinners instantly bunched into a tight little pack, dove to the bottom of the pool, and circled down there at great speed, in obvious terror. I was extremely impressed by this; John dismissed it as a parlor trick.

John's real purpose in visiting us was to see if we might provide a home for Gregory Bateson. Bateson, a distinguished anthropologist, psychologist, and philosopher, had been working in Lilly's lab in the Virgin Islands, pursuing studies in nonverbal communication. Now funds had run out, and the lab was being closed. Bateson had a federal grant that supported him; what he needed was free access to porpoises, to continue his observational work. Lilly felt strongly that Bateson was important and that his work was important—strongly enough to travel to Hawaii at his own expense to try to convince us to shelter this man. We agreed to do it.

We were, over the next few years, to do a great many exciting things at the Park and its related facilities. It may well be, however, that the most important thing we ever did was to look after Gregory Bateson. Tap agreed to give him lab room and later found funds to support him. Gregory and his wife, Lois, came to us that fall and stayed for eight years. Gregory was able to continue his own work; and as a dividend he influenced us all.

Gregory Bateson became our resident guru. He taught us to think, one by one, or to try to think. He taught no facts, no theories, no history, no narrative (although he could tell some pretty funny stories in New Guinea pidgin). He taught, rather, by example and by conundrum, like a Zen master. Many people found it disconcerting.

One might meet Gregory on a sunny path en route to his office and have a conversation like the following.

Karen (carrying a bucket of fish): Good morning, Gregory.

Gregory (He is a huge elderly man in old trousers, a faded shirt, and the world's oldest sneakers. He stoops, squints, and smiles with an air of surprised pleasure at running into a friend): Good morning, Karen.

Karen (sets down the bucket, hoping he has more to say today).

Gregory: You know, I've been thinking.

Karen (attentive silence, not doubting it).

Gregory: If you had been born with two hands on your left arm, would both of them be left hands? Or would one of them be a right hand?

Karen (after a pause for consideration of a brand-new puzzle): I don't know.

Gregory: Hmmm (nods, smiles, and ambles on).

Gregory's question of the moment might be whether alcoholism is a religion or what a cat really means by "Meow." Some people felt a little stupid in this circumstance. Gregory was talking, they were listening, what he said seemed to make sense, and yet it sounded like nonsense, too. If you pride yourself on being educated and intelligent it can be humiliating to participate in a conversation that keeps skidding uncontrollably in the direction of Alice in Wonderland.

Gregory's formal areas of expertise included cybernetics, anthropology (he was Margaret Mead's first husband), ethology (the Lorenz approach to behavior), primitive art, and psychiatry. He is probably best known as the formulator of the double-bind theory of schizophrenia, which, briefly, suggests that schizophrenia arises when a child's parents keep him constantly in a state of "damned if you do and damned if you don't" by sending him double messages, telling him one thing and meaning another.

People who were outstanding in any one of Gregory's fields tended to brand him a dilettante, because how could he possibly know all about their field and still have time left over, which they did not have, to know all about several other fields too? Besides, you couldn't understand a thing he said.

I had no illusions that I "should" understand Gregory's thinking, or that I needed to look smart and impress him, so I enjoyed the odd fecundity of his imagination without trying to make it make sense.

After a year or two of encounters—meetings on sidewalks, lunch with Gregory at the Galley, a glass of sherry at the Batesons' in the evening, I began to realize that everything Gregory said was related to everything else he said. If you just listened long enough, that three-handed person would crop up again, and that dedicated alcoholic, and that noisy cat. As Gregory went around and around, some kind of nonverbal picture emerged concerning thinking and communication itself.

In fact all of Gregory's speculations came back to the problem of communication, of messages that loop back and change what went before, of the true circular nature of what we wrongly think of as a straight-line business. False communication made the schizophrenic. Bilateral symmetry was a piece of genetic communication, full of loops and feedback, with its messages most visible when one went astray—hence the three-handed question. Porpoise communication was nonverbal and "loopy," with built-in feedback. It was all a piece of the same thing, it was all Gregory's message, and to drive it home he *gave* his message in loops and parallels and circles. Those of us who liked to listen to him were all changed; we became a little loopy too, no doubt. Ken Norris and I agree, for example, that we no longer try so often to force things into straight lines, to separate thoughts about a bit of information from thoughts about its context, to dedicate ourselves to single aims and single lines of reasoning.

John Lilly had put Gregory on our doorstep to continue his observations of porpoises. For quite a while Gregory spent early mornings with his students, below decks on the *Essex*, watching the spinners and recording their behavior. He learned a lot that had not been understood before: the meanings of many body postures and gestures, the nature of the porpoise pecking order, and the fact that it is beautifully displayed when the animals sleep. Our school dozed while sculling in a wide, constant, circular course. The dominant animals swam not in front of the others, but above them. They got to breathe first, and they had the shortest distance to rise to breathe. The other animals swam in layers beneath them. So, in our school, first Kahili and his lady took a breath, and then the next rank of animals would rise through or behind them and breathe, and then the lowest, both physically and socially, surfaced, breathed, and sank down again to their poorer neighborhood at the bottom of the school.

There really was quite a lot of status-seeking fighting in the school too, mostly among the males, who would ram each other amidships, sometimes knocking each other right into the air, and occasionally leaving terrible bruises which formed lumpy scars. Sex play, too, was very much related to status questions; Gregory identified a behavior he called "beak-genital propulsion," in which a subordinate animal would put its rostrum against the genital area of a superior animal and push that animal all around the pool, giving it an apparently pleasurable free ride.

Gregory began to feel that he had seen all he wanted to see of the porpoises and that it was time to start writing a new book. I clinched the matter for him with an incredibly stupid mistake. Lei had died, tragically, tangled in a length of rope, an irresistible toy, that someone let fall into the tank overnight. She was the only animal that wore a lei during the not very colorful hula, and it was hard to train another one to do so when they were all full of fish from doing five shows a day. I decreed that Haole, the tamest of the spinners, would be moved to the training facility and quickly taught, in solitude, to put on a lei.

I didn't think of Gregory. When he came to observe the school one morning, Haole was gone. Lei's death disturbed only Kahili, but Haole's absence changed the whole social structure of the school. All the patterns Gregory had been painstakingly coming to understand broke down, while the animals re-sorted themselves and built a new pecking order. To add to my embarrassment, Haole was so upset at being taken from the others that he refused to eat and couldn't be trained at all. We shamefacedly returned him to Whaler's Cove after a few days, but it was too late. The old order had changed, Haole had to make a new place for himself, and Gregory did not care to start making his charts all over again.

Tap immediately started hunting for funds to build a large porpoise pool for the Institute, where a scientist would not have his work disturbed by the necessities of public performances. The pool was eventually built, and we called it Bateson's Bay. Gregory was very pleasant about the whole thing; however, he laid direct observation aside and spent most of the rest of his time at the Institute working on a book, a collection of essays called *Steps to an Ecology of Mind* (Chandler Publishing Co., 1972). It's a charming book: the cat, the drunkard, and the three-handed man are there. The introduction alone is worth the price of admission, especially if you happen to be wrestling, yourself, with the conflict between the various mind-expanding approaches to life and Western, linear rationality. It is not exactly a linear book; the arguments come and go, like the Cheshire cat, words fading away, leaving only Gregory's smile.

Gregory has always despised Skinnerian theory and operant conditioning with an almost religious intensity. He has always hated the thought of bending creatures to one's will, especially if those creatures happened to be human (in spite of the fact that Gregory goes around bending people to his will all the time). The fact that operant conditioning *works* makes it even more infuriating to him. I always found Gregory's stand unbecoming to the scientist in him, but perfectly acceptable in the philosopher, who may hate the fact that the sky is blue, if he wishes.

Ingrid Kang, in an effort to share our view of things with Gregory, once persuaded him to be the "animal" in a round of the Training Game. She picked something simple: get Gregory to sit on a chair. Gregory was very cooperative, but he turned out to be, as a subject, exactly like an otter: as soon as he recognized that earning a reinforcement had something to do with the chair, he did forty or fifty different things with that chair: everything except sit in it. A case of the biter bit, all right; after twenty minutes Ingrid gave up in disgust, and Gregory, who truly had not been trying to flummox her on purpose, continued to despise and disbelieve in operant conditioning.

One of the things Gregory needed while studying the spinners was some way of hearing directionally underwater. We hear directionally in the air; if three telephones are on a desk, and one rings, you can generally tell which one to pick up. Our ears, however, can't tell which way a sound is coming from in the water; it seems to be all around you. Our hydrophones have the same problem. Thus it was impossible, when a porpoise whistled, to tell which animal was making the sound. This made it very difficult to connect the animals' sounds with the animals' activities.

This problem brought Wayne Batteau into our lives. Wayne was an acoustics expert, operating out of Boston, who had tremendous inventive talents and a wackily playful imagination which led him to produce all sorts of wonderful technical toys. He was a bug-eyed, black-haired, effervescent person who looked a bit like a Kewpie doll. Much of Wayne's work was done for the research arm of the Navy, under another highly imaginative scientist, Dr. William McLean, who also sponsored a lot of our porpoise research. (Bill McLean invented the Sidewinder missile, which like a rattlesnake homes in on the heat of its target rather than on its noise or movement. He built the first Sidewinder largely in his own garage, using, among other things, parts from his wife's washing machine.)

Wayne had decided that what Gregory needed to hear with underwater was ears. Our directional hearing largely depends upon the fact that we have highly convoluted external ears, or "pinnae." Sound coming in bounces around on all those little bumps and ridges, and we learn by experience how it bounces in our own ears, in relationship to the source of the sound. You can check this out easily. Shut your eyes and have someone jingle a bunch of keys in different parts of the room; you will be able to point right to the sound. Now shut your eyes and with your

Wayne Batteau, Gregory Bateson, and trainer Bob Ballard prepare to install Wayne's "Ears" in Whaler's Cove.

fingers bend your ears forward a bit, distorting the pattern of bumps and ridges; it will be *much* harder, maybe impossible, to locate the jingling keys accurately.

Sound travels five times faster in water than in air. To compensate for this, Wayne made a pair of human pinnae out of steel and plastic, five times bigger and five times farther apart than our ears on our heads. These had hydrophones installed in them and were lowered into the water while Gregory and his students, inside the *Essex*, listened through the Ears via earphones. I have heard physicists pish-tush this arrangement, but in truth Gregory felt that it gave him quite a bit of directional hearing, with practice, and he discovered, among other things, that sometimes what sounds like one porpoise whistle to us is actually made by two or more animals, either in chorus or alternately, one picking up where the other leaves off.

Wayne's equipment, like all electronic gear, often needed repair, and so the Ears and various other projects often brought him to Hawaii. I loved Wayne's visits; he never arrived without a new toy or game. Once he brought a beautiful plexiglass box with two fluids in it, one transparent, one blue. By tilting the box you could make waves between the fluids, everything from a ripple on a mill pond to storm surf that crested and broke in miniature fury like a hurricane. Similar items are now on the market, but I have never seen one as perfect, as easy to make good waves in, as Wayne's. Another time, he brought a porpoise toy, a little flying saucer that could be controlled in the water by sound cues. The object was to see if a porpoise could "drive" it around the tank by whistling at it. We tried it out with one of the bottlenoses. Wayne was too impatient to have the porpoise trained for the job first; I think he hoped the porpoise would get the idea spontaneously, which indeed might have happened. Before it did happen, however, the gadget zoomed into a wall of the tank and had to go home to Boston for repairs.

Sometimes Wayne's new present to us was a game, such as "Little-known questions to famous answers." Example: "Dr.

Livingstone, I presume." Question: "What is your full name, Dr. Presume?"

The best Batteau toy of all was a device developed by a New Zealand acoustician for enabling people to see, like porpoises, with sound. It consisted of a Martian-looking headset, bristling with antennae, and a sort of suitcase you could carry around; I later saw an improved version reduced to a pair of spectacles and a pocket-sized energy pack. This device made noises in your ears which, like sonar, were broadcast in front of you, echoed back off surrounding surfaces, and were rebroadcast into your ears. The farther away they went, the higher the pitch. The texture of what they bounced off was reflected in the texture of the sound. Thus, if you put the device on and walked around a room, you could "hear" the couch: zumm-zumm-zumm; the walls, harder and farther away, zang-zang-zang; the windows, zink-zink-zink; the open door, zeeeeeeeeee. We all tried it out at a dinner party one night. In no time even small children could walk briskly around the room "seeing" with their ears, and people were fighting to try it and saying things like "Let me hear the mirror." It took concentration, but almost no intellectual effort; you could do it spontaneously. It was like a new sense, like hearing a color or smelling lights. For a moment, we could all feel *truly* like porpoises.

I wish I knew what happened to this invention. The last word I had on it was that it had been offered to a school for the blind but rejected on the grounds that none of the instructors would know how to teach people to use it.

Wayne's principal experiment in Hawaii was a long effort to teach porpoises to talk. Since human noises are hard for porpoises to make, and porpoise noises are hard for humans to hear, he built a device, a "translator," which turned human words into porpoiselike whistles. There was to be another translator which pushed porpoise whistles into humanoid sounds, but that, to my knowledge, was never built.

Randy Lewis left Sea Life Park and became Wayne's trainer

on this project, first at the Navy porpoise facilities in California, then in Hawaii at University of Hawaii facilities and at the Oceanic Institute. Peter Markie, one of Wayne's associates, also trained the animals. Peter and Randy performed some incredible feats of training, in my opinion. They developed a set of verbal commands, heard by their pair of porpoises underwater as porpoisoid whistles, for several simple behaviors, such as batting a ball, swimming through a hoop, and jumping. Then the porpoises each learned their names, Maui and Puka, so that the trainer could say, "Maui, jump; Puka, hit ball" and each animal would obey correctly.

Then they developed a "go" signal. The trainer could tell Maui to hit the ball, and Maui would not leave until the trainer said "Okay." Thus you could signal, "Maui, ball—" and nothing more, and Maui would hang around, doing whatever he felt like, for up to a full minute, until he heard "Okay," whereupon he would go hit the ball. It made him awfully cross to have to wait, but he could do it.

Furthermore, Randy and Peter established a correction signal, "Negative!" a most useful training device. They could say "Puka, hoop, okay," and then, if Puka started toward the ball instead, the trainer could say, "Negative," and the porpoise would stop. Also, and I do think this shows intelligence on the part of the animal, they could say, "Puka, jump. Negative. Hoop. Okay," and Puka would go through the hoop instead of obeying the negated command.

The object of the experiment, of course, included getting the porpoises to make sounds themselves. While waiting for the second translator to be built, Peter and Randy installed a hydrophone, through which they could hear the porpoise whistles, and a sound spectrograph, which would draw the shape of the whistles as they were made on a roll of paper. Then, using their own ears to judge when the sound was more accurate than last time, a fiendishly difficult task, they trained Maui and Puka to duplicate, exactly, a number of the command signals. Thus the trainer could say, "Maui, ball, repeat: okay." The machine would issue four little whistles, one for each word, and instead of going out and hitting the ball, Maui would issue one faint whistle of his own, almost inaudible to me; yet you could see on the sonogram, the machine's drawings on a roll of graph paper, that Maui's whistle was a perfect repetition of the machine's whistle-signal for "ball."

I thought this was a superb job of training; but no more. I infuriated Wayne Batteau by arrogantly offering to repeat the whole experiment using colored flags, instead of sounds, as signals. Unfortunately, the porpoise-to-human sound translator was never built. The porpoises, equipped with that, might indeed have learned to give signals to the humans, and even to invent their own signals; perhaps it could have become a language. Since the machine worked best with vowel sounds, and the Hawaiian language is mostly vowel sounds, Hawaiian words were used for quite a few of the cues. We all agreed it would have been delightful if the first true talking porpoises spoke Hawaiian.

Wayne Batteau's tragic death in a drowning accident brought the experiment to an end. Soon after that Gregory remarked to me at lunch: "Have you heard about the people who are teaching chimpanzees to talk?"

"No," I said, in a voice laden with ennui—there have been a number of highly unsuccessful attempts to teach chimps to vocalize human words, which they seem physically incapable of doing.

"They're using Ameslan," Gregory said. "American Sign Language, the hand signal language deaf and dumb people use."

I was electrified. I knew at once it *had* to work. Here was something both chimpanzee and man could do equally well, make gestures; and both species could see and understand each other's gestures, too. No need for clumsy machinery. It was a workable two-way system.

The experiment has been a tremendous success and has become widely known. I visited the originators, Drs. Alan and Trixie Gardner, at the University of Nevada at the first opportunity, swapping a showing of films of my porpoises for an evening of their films and their conversation. I've also visited the original experimental animal, Washoe, who is now at the University of Oklahoma with one of the Gardners' students, Dr. Roger Fouts, and a host of other chimpanzees, all learning Ameslan like mad. The darned chimps *can* talk. Chatter, even. They invent words. They use sentences. They make jokes and call each other dirty names. They develop vocabularies of well over a hundred words. There seems to be no end to what they can accomplish. A variety of other experiments, using plastic symbols, computer push buttons, and other word substitutes, are under way now, revealing more and more completely the rather unnerving fact that animals, at least the great apes, are indeed capable of language.

I think the establishment of an artificial but mutually understandable two-way code might be possible with quite a variety of animals, given a *mode* of communication suitable both to the animal and to us. It is my own feeling that the truly elaborate communication between highly trained horses—some cowponies, for example—and their riders includes an arbitrary, mutually learned language based on touch. I think it would be nice to repeat some version of the now classic chimpanzee work with porpoises, just to show it could be done. One of the computer push-button systems could be used by a porpoise, no doubt. However, if one just wanted to show that "language" can be established in a totally nonhuman animal, in my opinion the animal of choice would be the elephant.

In 1966 I went on a lecture tour, talking about porpoises, which took me to Boston. There a Navy scientist friend, Bill Parker, offered to introduce me to B. F. Skinner, the man who discovered and founded the whole business of operant conditioning and behavior modification.

From my journal, April 22, 1966
Bill Parker and his girlfriend and I had breakfast, and then we met Skinner, who is the *last* thing I expected. He is said to be cold and reserved, but I found him a charming, jovial gnome, all warmth and interest. We saw the behavior labs, and I showed my porpoise movies

to Skinner and about ten other people, and they all loved them. Then we had lunch and drank ale; Skinner insisted on paying for lunch. Skinner was most amusing about the training errors in international relationships. Walked back across the Harvard campus, of which Skinner is immensely proud. He showed me the rare book collection at the Widener Library. I took a movie of him, and he gave me two of his books and some reprints, and I interviewed his handsome daughter, Debby, as a possible summer trainer. Skinner is planning to come to Honolulu to give a lecture this summer; all the more reason for Debby to come out.

The behavior labs are really weird. Two rooms of electronic relay systems, humming away, and a room of small boxes, each containing a rat or a pigeon, completely out of sight inside the box, with the training being done by the fantastically elaborate relay equipment. Then there are rooms of rats and pigeons that live in cages and are cared for by two bright, kind people, a middle-aged woman and a young man, who reminded me of a head nurse and a capable ward attendant at a hospital.

The graduate student plans his plan, builds his forest of relays, and comes in once a day to collect miles of computerized data. The head nurse and the ward attendant pick the subject animals, put them in the boxes, take them out again, see that their weights and food intake are right, and know more, I suspect, about operant conditioning than most of the grad students. The student never even sees the animal. What could be the fun of doing research like that? You might as well be working with nuts and bolts.

Amidst all this impersonal mechanization I was fascinated to notice that the two animal caretakers love the animals. They showed me particular rats that they considered touchingly brave about electric shock (brr!), and they handled the animals with great gentleness. The head nurse brought out her favorite pigeon for me to admire. Looked like any other pigeon to me, of course, but its cleverness in learning response patterns was so outstanding that she felt it was a very special individual, as indeed I have no doubt it was.

Perhaps the biggest payoff of that trip was Debby Skinner, who did come to Sea Life Park and proved to be a hard worker and an imaginative trainer. Debby was one of the babies who had been raised in Skinner's famous baby box, something the world thinks of as an inhuman prison, which it was not. In some cultures, babies spend all their waking hours and most of their sleeping hours in someone's lap or on someone's back. In our culture, though, babies spend a dreadful amount of time alone in their cribs, where they are bored, often wet, hot, or cold, and usually surrounded by constricting, uncomfortable clothing and bedding. All Skinner did was build a supercrib, in which the baby could be naked and yet at a comfortable temperature, with material beneath it through which urine could pass away, and with interesting things to look at and touch. Thus those hours which the baby had to spend in the crib would be comfortable, even amusing hours. Nothing wrong with that, in my opinion, and nothing wrong with Debby—she was a dream, and we had fun together.

My journal, Wednesday, August 30, 1966

Narrating OST [Ocean Science Theater], Debby Skinner training. OST birds are just starting to fly. One of them flew off the perch as I was narrating today, and I stuck out my arm and made it land on me in midflight. I went on talking while the bird flapped and teetered, trying to balance—it was a big surprise to the bird and the audience, and I didn't even break my sentence. Debby died laughing, and after the show we had a lot of fun tossing birds back and forth to each other and making them land on our arms, which they don't seem to mind doing.

Wednesday, September 14, 1966

Fred Skinner is here. Yesterday was amusing. He had fun training Keiki, and he enjoyed the training game which we played for his benefit. *Why* does Skinner reject all that is sensible in ethology, while Gregory and other ethologists reject all that is sensible in operant conditioning? I feel like a British barmaid with a fight on her hands, saying, "Gentlemen, gentlemen! *Please.*" I sounded Skinner out on various experiments, and he was interested in some of them. Deborah told me an amusing story, which she implied is apocryphal, but which sounded just like her Dad. Two of his students decided to shape a piece of behavior in their roommate by giving or withholding smiling and approval. They succeeded so well that they could elicit the be-

B. F. Skinner having fun training a porpoise.

havior of standing on a chair and doing a little dance, at will. Excited
by success, they invited Skinner to coffee in their room one night and
showed him the poor roommate, climbing in all innocence onto a
chair and shuffling about. "Very interesting," says Skinner, "but what
does it tell us about pigeons?"

A Skinner story which is not apocryphal is one he told me himself.
If strict behaviorists look down on the natural observers of behavior,
like Gregory, they look down even more on the humanistic psychologists (and the sentiment is returned). A major figure in humanistic psy-

chology, and a major detractor of the "inhuman" Skinnerian approach, was giving a lecture at Harvard. Some lecturers like to look out over the whole audience and talk into space (I do), and some like to pick one responsive face in the front and talk to that one. This doctor was of the second sort. Skinner had never met him but went to the lecture, sat down in front, looked very animated and interested, and got the psychologist talking toward him. Then, Skinner looked bored when the lecturer talked on love, but he brightened up and nodded every time the doctor made an aggressive or hostile gesture. "By the end of the lecture," Skinner said, "he was chopping the air like Hitler."

Fred Skinner's visit to the porpoises was fun all around, and we continued to keep in touch: "Dear Fred, I thoroughly agree with your point in this month's *Psychology Today* that creative behavior can be shaped. . . ." "Dear Karen, Thank you for the positive reinforcement. . . ," but this friendship was not the only chance the porpoises gave me to meet one of my intellectual heroes. Konrad Lorenz, Nobel laureate, and father of ethology, the study of the behavior of animals in their natural setting, came to the University of Hawaii to give some lectures and to collect reef fishes for his incredible aquariums back in Seeweisen, Germany. Lecturing might take me to Boston, but I couldn't foresee lecturing taking me to Germany, so I was thrilled at the possibility of meeting him. Fortunately, Lorenz was staying with friends of mine, and like everyone else, he liked porpoises, and so he came to Sea Life Park.

When I heard he had arrived, I hurried to the training facility and found a twinkly-eyed, white-bearded man, somewhat portly, looking very much like Santa Claus, surrounded by fascinated trainers. I rushed up, gushing my pleasure at meeting at last the author of my favorite book, *King Solomon's Ring*. Lorenz beamed kindly and said, "I wish I were a timber wolf, so I could respond to your greeting properly," and with one hand he gestured behind him, creating in imagination the merry sweep of a large, plumy, wagging tail.

It was my first glimpse of Konrad's knack for miming animals.

His lectures were greatly enlivened by this ability. He could become, with one hand or a thrust of the head, an angry goose, a mouse-hunting fox, a fainting butterfly fish. His ultimate accomplishment in this line for me was a fleeting instant during a lecture at the University of Hawaii in which, eyes crossed, arms tangled, legs wrapped around each other, he turned himself into a visible representation of the Einsteinian Universe.

Konrad spent a lot of time with Gregory Bateson at Sea Life Park and a full morning talking with the trainers in one of the conference rooms. We were illuminated by his deeply scientific and yet human approach to animal behavior. He spoke, for example, of his Greylag geese "falling in love," and one of the trainers said, respectfully, "Dr. Lorenz, how can you apply such a human expression to animals? Isn't that anthropomorphizing?"

Konrad said, "It is the accurate term for a real phenomenon for which there is no other name. I consider the term appropriate to any species, if that is in fact what they do." Then he told us that the most auspicious situation for this event was when two geese met which had known each other as youngsters but had been separated since then. "You know the feeling: are *you* the same little girl I used to see running around in pigtails and braces?" We laughed. "That's how I met my wife," Konrad added.

My journal, April 6, 1967

Konrad spent a couple of hours looking at Gregory's videotapes of the spinners. Then we went to Whaler's Cove to see the animals themselves, who were playing with a towel. Konrad watched them through the portholes and instantly began calling them by name: "Haole's got it. Now here comes Akamai. Oh, Moki's stolen the towel now." He had learned to identify the six animals by watching them on videotape. I was utterly astonished. I know the animals well, yet I have trouble telling them apart quickly when they're zooming around like that, and I can't even tell them at all on the blurry video machine!

I learned almost more from him, face to face, walking around the park, than I could stand in one dose. Reef fish behavior. Training. Play. Mimicry. "Conscious mimicry of something not in the animal's natural repertoire is extremely sophisticated—it is an example of what Gregory means by deutero-learning, or higher-order learning. Naturally you are not going to see this spontaneously, at least not often." Bravo, and also aha. Later I asked, "What do you do with the curious anecdotal material that interests you?" "Why, try to make it happen again." A simple idea, but one that had perplexed me. And when one of the students keeping him company sighed at having to do an experiment over from scratch to satisfy a professor: "*Never* feel unhappy about repeating your work to silence a critic. When I have repeated something I thought I understood well, that is when I have learned the most." Konrad also told me, "Take good care of Gregory. He is one of the world's few theoretical biologists, and important." (We are used to the idea of theoretical physicists, but this was a new and useful thought to me.)

Lorenz had done me the courtesy of dipping into the book on breast-feeding that I had written some years before, *Nursing Your Baby,* and he put his finger right on the problem that had caused me to write the book in the first place. "I think you are absolutely right that it is the break in tradition that interferes with this behavior. There is no overlapping of generations in the modern family, and thus no continuation of tradition." I remarked on my feeling that a woman "instinctively" expects to learn this traditional skill, nursing, from another woman, and that the behavior often breaks down because attempts are made to pass on the tradition via male doctors. "Of course, of course," Konrad said almost impatiently. "She trusts another woman." The concept of trust as an innate rather than strictly learned condition surprised me and yet rang wonderfully true to me.

Konrad's visits enabled us to look at our animals and their curious ways much more open-mindedly, still making no false assumptions, hopefully, still trying to avoid reading human thoughts into animal reactions, but at least avoiding, without shame, the reverse sin of what Joseph Wood Krutch calls "mechanomorphism," ruthlessly reducing all the animals' behavior to that of a machinelike automaton, counting for nothing if it cannot be measured, a hampering but definitely fashionable error.

On the last day of his stay in Hawaii, Konrad invited me out to Coconut Island to see the fishes he was taking back to Germany. I took him a present of a few little fishes he had admired in our Reef Tank, which one of the divers had netted out for me. We went collecting on the reef, Konrad and I, and I was more hindrance than help, stirring up mud with my flippers and getting water in my mask at inopportune times, but Konrad was kindness itself. He has a gift for making one feel cherished, but also a gift for making one feel abashed for a foolish or un-thought-out remark. He also has a gift for teaching, in all directions, all the time.

My journal, April 9, 1967

Lester, the Coconut Island fish collector, ran me back to the dock in his boat, and I was able to repay him for the service by repeating all the nice things Lorenz had said about him. He responded with heartfelt comments about how much he had learned from Lorenz. "You

Konrad Lorenz and a Greylag goose. *Henrich Westphal*

know, I see these fish all my life. I see them doing things, but I never thought, before now, *what* are they *doing?* Konrad made all the ocean look new to me."

Lorenz's visit had an unusual personal dividend for me. My father, Philip Wylie, had just written a book, *The Magic Animal,* which sprang partly from Lorenz's work, and I sent Konrad a copy and introduced them, as it were, by mail. Phil, warmed by Konrad's response, urged him to come and visit the next time he was in the States, never expecting that the invitation would be accepted. It was, however, and the upshot was that Konrad and his wife, Gretl, spent two very happy weeks with Phil and Ricky Wylie at the Lerner Marine Laboratory in Bimini, in the Bahamas, watching fishes and swapping stories. The friendship, maintained thereafter by correspondence, brought my father enormous joy and pleasure in the brief remaining years of his life for which I shall always be grateful. It was another gift, in a roundabout way, from the porpoises.

8. OPEN OCEAN WORK

In 1963 and 1964 the Navy was interested in how fast a porpoise could swim. By calculating the amount of power a porpoise should be able to put out, and the amount of water resistance pressing against an object shaped like a porpoise, Navy engineers came up with a theoretical top speed somewhere between 15 and 18 knots, or under 20 miles per hour. It seemed, however, that porpoises out in the ocean were being observed traveling much faster than the laws of nature allowed. Porpoises had been seen, time and time again, swimming alongside Navy destroyers that were going 30 to 35 knots. The animals could keep up with the ships, and officers and sailors often vowed they had seen them pass from the stern to the bow and take off ahead of the ship while the destroyer was fully under way.

If porpoises could truly swim at speeds of up to 35 knots, then they presumably knew something about the laws of hydro-dynamics which the Navy didn't know, and would like to find out. The first question to be answered was: How fast can a porpoise really swim, all by itself?

The staff of the Naval Ordnance Testing Station (NOTS) in California, working with hydrodynamicist Dr. Thomas Lang, had run various tests with trained porpoises in small and large tanks, but had not come up with anything very exciting in the way of speed. Ken Norris got together with Dr. Lang and decided to hold some speed trials in Hawaii, in the summer of 1964, with an animal from Sea Life Park. On March 24, Georges captured what we were to learn is the nearly ideal training subject: a male, three-quarters-grown bottlenose porpoise. A "teenaged" bottlenose is a gregarious, curious, relatively fearless animal. He is not silly and hysterical, like little Lei, the kiko. He also does not have the weighty questions of prestige that preoccupy an adult porpoise like Makua. Our new youngster, named Keiki (Hawaiian for "child"), absolutely loved the training facility and all the things that went on there, and we absolutely loved Keiki. I recall a Marineland trainer passing through and blanching with envy as Keiki practically climbed in his lap and looked in his pockets out of sheer porpoise gregariousness. "That is the perfect animal," the trainer said. "He'll do anything you ask of him." We were to ask a lot of Keiki.

Ken wanted to use Keiki for swimming speed tests. One conjecture was that the NOTS animals had not moved very fast because they were hampered by the confines of a tank. The University of Hawaii maintained a laboratory at Coconut Island, in Kaneohe Bay, about 10 miles north of Sea Life Park. Alongside that island there was a long, narrow, man-made enclosure of sea water which made a nice runway. It could be netted off, across its narrow mouth, so that an animal within it could not escape to the bay. It was hundreds of feet long, at least 50 feet wide, and about 10 feet deep—surely big enough to give a porpoise a sense of freedom. Ken gave us instructions as to how he wanted Keiki trained, and we started getting the young animal ready for a sojourn at Coconut Island.

One of the nice things about Keiki was that he didn't care who trained him; he liked everybody. I whistle-conditioned him, Dottie hand-tamed him, David taught him to come when he was called with an underwater buzzer, and Ken Norris himself taught Keiki to swim onto a stretcher and allow himself to be lifted from the water so he could be easily transported. We all had a hand in the first few weeks of training at Coconut Island. Various students and offspring of Ken Norris participated, too.

The basic plan was to induce Keiki to sprint, on a starting signal, from one end of a marked course to the other, while someone timed him with a stopwatch. This turned out to be inadequate. For subsequent experiments, Ken laid out a line of buoys along the course, and Tom Lang provided a carefully calibrated movie camera, which, from a height, could be used to photograph each run. Thus speed could be calculated more accurately than with a stopwatch; the buoys provided fixed reference points for the camera, and by examining the film frame by frame one could ascertain exactly how fast Keiki was going between any two buoys, over any part of the course.

There were training problems. Keiki liked to sprint at about 11 or 12 knots, but it was difficult to induce him to go faster, and the various methods tried, such as offering greater rewards for more speed, or withholding reward for less speed, sometimes confused and discouraged him. Dottie, David, and I all played around with the problem, without much success, and Ken finally sent for Ron Turner, the author of our training manual. What shaping recipes Ron used, I don't know, but he did achieve sprints of 16.1 knots, rather impressive, in the light of later events, but much less than Tom and Ken were hoping for at the time.

Ron went back to California, and Ken continued working at Coconut Island with Keiki. He had a skiff with an outboard, which Keiki enjoyed following up and down the lagoon. I happened to be there, with several other people, on the day when it occurred to all of us to try taking Keiki out into the bay. Maybe in open water, with a fast boat to follow, Keiki could be coaxed into higher speeds.

At that time nobody, as far as I know, had ever taken a tame porpoise deliberately out to sea, with the idea of getting it back. There was every chance that the porpoise, like a fish or any other wild animal, would simply take off for parts unknown as soon as it was free. Still, our hunch was that Keiki would not leave. Ken has described what happened then in his book, *The Porpoise Watcher: A Naturalist's Experiences with Porpoises and Whales:*°

. . . Karen, Ted, Matt, Susie and I piled into a big work skiff, set up the recall console on a thwart, pulled back the barrier net and called Keiki. He hesitatingly came around the net, like a dog invited into a house where he's not been welcome. We putted slowly toward the entrance channel with Keiki following along behind, dutifully coming to the speaker when we switched on the recall signal. Once the skiff was in the lagoon entrance, Keiki became perceptibly more nervous. He hung farther behind, and when we called him, he reluctantly came, but quickly retreated again into the lagoon. I stopped the engine and recalled him until he seemed to have gained a little confidence. Then we started the engine again and moved slowly out into open Kaneohe Bay.

Keiki followed us until we were three or four hundred yards from the lagoon, and then bolted suddenly, diving below the surface and out of sight. We looked anxiously in all directions. No Keiki, for dozens of seconds. A horrible sinking feeling assailed me as I thought we had lost our friendly Keiki with whom we had worked so long and happily. Then Ted and Matt spotted him, plunging swiftly along close to the reef edge, but beyond the lagoon entrance which he seemed to have sought. A glance at his lunging flight told me that he was terror-stricken. I had no idea if he could hear our signal through those hundreds of yards of water. I pushed the switch, and he stopped as if struck by a stone, turned, and came plodding back to us. When he arrived at the underwater speaker, blowing hard, his jaws were actually chattering and the whites of his eyes were showing. We knew that these signs were evidence of fear, just as they are in humans. Keiki was terrified, but he had come back to us.

"No more for today," I said with finality. We turned and gingerly led Keiki back into the lagoon. Once inside he raced the length in a long gambol and circled with us in the confines of his cage, as delighted as we to be in his home again.

° New York: W. W. Norton and Co., Inc. 1974. Pp. 142–143.

Back at the dock, we celebrated by dancing up and down and toasting Keiki in orange pop. Ken now wanted to try speed trials in the open sea. If an animal would stay with you, and not run away, there were a lot of other things that could be accomplished besides speed trials. And it could be done, it *could* be done!

Back at the Naval Ordnance Testing Station in California, people were also experimenting with the possibility of releasing a trained porpoise at sea, and about the time that we made this first excursion with Keiki, they briefly released a trained animal which was harnessed and tethered to a small float. Their animal was less fearful than Keiki, but considerably inhibited by her tether. Nevertheless she made no attempt to escape; and they too saw a vast range of possibilities in this fact.

The speed trials with Keiki were then continued in open water, using a longer run and a very fast boat to lure him on with. Georges and Leo set up a buoy line inside of Rabbit Island, the volcanic rock sticking up just offshore Sea Life Park. There was a lot of loose talk about working "in the lee" of Rabbit Island, but in truth Rabbit Island didn't have much lee. It was rough out there. A large cage of chain link had been constructed for Keiki, a cage which would give him plenty of room to maneuver, to avoid being cut or scraped against its walls in the surging waves. Again a calibrated camera was set up, on the steep flanks of Rabbit Island, to film each run. Tom Lang, the Navy hydrodynamicist who had inspired the experiment, a tall, slow-speaking, genial man, flew in from California to run the camera himself.

Half the fun of being a scientist is being able to put down your chalk and your slide rule and do something once in a while like flying to Hawaii and playing with porpoises. I'm not sure how much fun it was to spend every day all day perched on the sun-scalded upper slopes of Rabbit Island among the noisy sea birds and the guano, peering through a viewfinder and listening to us down below over the walkie-talkie having the *real* fun; but

Tom was cheerful about it, and his presence guaranteed the accurate filming without which the whole elaborate job would be wasted.

Besides Tom's team, on the first day, we had Georges and Leo, a news photographer and an underwater photographer, Ken, of course, and myself. I was the trainer for a week of experimentation in open waters, one of the most entertaining and at the same time one of the most exhausting weeks I ever spent.

Keiki seemed glad to see us, and none the worse for his first night at sea. We tied our skiff to the cage, where it pitched and tossed remorselessly all day, an uneasy place to be parked. The photographers promptly got seasick, poor creatures. I'm prone to seasickness, too, especially in a small anchored boat that reeks of motor fumes, but I had fortified myself with Bonine, a pill for motion sickness which works for me, and besides, the situation was too exciting to leave me time for queasiness. Ken grabbed the bucket of fish and jumped overboard in his clothes and swam to the cage to see Keiki. Keiki frolicked around him and accepted some fish, answered the recall buzzer when we hung it in various parts of the cage, and seemed ready to go to work.

Keiki was having no trouble avoiding the rasping wire walls of the cage, in spite of surging seas. That was not true for us; in a couple of days we were all a mass of skinned knuckles and scraped knees and bruises and scratches. Clothing was some protection, but not much; clothing did protect against the sun, however. The water was so warm that it really didn't matter if you went in and out all day in your clothes, and wet or dry, a long-sleeved shirt and slacks and a hat were useful. Suntans are very nice to have, but even if you are tan already, two or three days of working at sea in Hawaii, without protection, can put you in the hospital. As it was, I got a ferocious sunburn on my lip which took weeks to heal, because putting the whistle in and out of my mouth all day wiped off whatever sunburn cream I had remembered to put on.

Leo came up in the speedboat, towing the recall apparatus; I climbed aboard, with whistle and fish, and Ken signaled for

Keiki to be let out of the cage. Down went the side of the cage, and out dashed a new Keiki, a confident, happy Keiki, a Keiki who seemed to understand very well what was going on. He paid a call to Dr. Norris, who was hanging on the outside of the cage whooping greetings and encouragements. Then, when I turned on the recall, Keiki came roaring over to the speedboat and stuck his nose obediently in the speaker. He investigated the underwater photographer, who had recovered from his seasickness, as usually happens, as soon as he got *in* the water instead of *on* it.

We started the motor and, towing the signaling speaker, headed off down the line of floats, Keiki following, for the first of many, many runs. Here is part of Ken Norris's account:

Throughout these tests the porpoise remained near one of the small craft, even in the absence of the recall signal, and never strayed farther than about 90 meters. The operation became quite routine after the first day, and little attention was given to holding the animal close to the skiff with the recall signal. The porpoise re-entered the floating cage upon hearing the recall signal (with the portable speaker hooked over the rear of the cage) and allowed us to close the door without any attempt to rush from the cage.*

We found that Keiki loved chasing the speedboat, much as a dog enjoys chasing a car. He would come bounding through the waves to join us as soon as we gunned the motor. Sometimes he ran at the bow, and sometimes he overtook us and ran ahead, but mostly he took up a position behind us and to one side, right in the boat's curling wake, leaping with glorious grace from wave crest to wave crest. It was a heart-catching sight, this wild, graceful animal, completely free, accompanying us by choice with such evident joy at top speed through the blue waves.

But what was that top speed? The boat's speedometer sometimes read 20 knots, and when Keiki overtook us at that speed, Georges and Leo and I would cheer and pound each other on the back and give Keiki all kinds of extra fish at the end of the

* Kenneth S. Norris, "Trained Porpoise Released in the Open Sea," *Science,* 147, No. 3661, Feb. 26, 1965, 1058–1060.

Widely reprinted (it made the cover of *Science,* among other things), this joyous photograph of Keiki, utterly free in the open sea, eagerly pursuing his trainer's boat. *Camera Hawaii*

run. In that rough water, 20 knots on the speedometer seemed very fast indeed. The boat stood on its tail and leaped from wave to wave. I had to stand up during the runs, hanging on fiercely with one hand, crouched and braced for balance, eyes on Keiki, whistle in my teeth, and one free hand on the recall button. It was grueling.

A couple of training problems remained. It was obvious that Keiki was getting some assistance from the boat's wake and bow wave. He almost always stationed himself where the water movement caused by the boat would lend him additional forward momentum. Furthermore, there was no way to make him keep up with us if he didn't care to. Much as he loved to chase the boat, when it got too far ahead of him he just turned around and went back to his cage. He knew we were coming back.

After a week, when we thought we had done all we could, we went back to the Park. Keiki had thinned down considerably, in spite of the fact that he was eating much more at sea than he normally ate in the training tanks. For him, as for us, it had been lots of fun but lots of hard work.

We were in for a shock when the results came in from analysis of the film. Keiki's top speed, whatever our speedometer read, had been 13.1 knots—and then only for 10 seconds. Most of the time he was doing less than 11 knots, and he really had stayed with the boat indefinitely only at speeds of 6 knots or lower.

Back to the drawing boards. Tom Lang speculated that maybe the porpoises that chase destroyers are some other, faster species than the stockily built bottlenose. Kikos, for example. I was convinced that some other training system was needed, one in which the animal could be induced to increase its speed by small increments and in some way that would be clear-cut to the animal, with one single condition to be met and to be reinforced. We began to think out a joint project for the following summer, when Tom would be free to come to Hawaii again.

The following summer, Tom Lang and I decided to use kikos for the new speed trials. At least, they *looked* faster than bottlenoses. Because kikos hate solitude, we used two at once, a pair

of males named Haina and Nuha. We confined them in the long
channel at Coconut Island; no need to go out to sea, we felt, as
long as we had enough room for a respectable sprint.

To make the training situation clear to the animals, I wanted
to use a moving target system like the electric bunny which grey-
hounds chase at a dog racing track. This was a tricky design
problem. We needed some way to pull a target through the
water, at an exact, steady speed which could be increased by
small, accurately measurable increments. Ernie Simmerer, de-
signer of the *Essex* and an imaginative engineer who had finally
created for the Ocean Science Theater some truly porpoise-proof
gates, among other ingenuities, came up with a machine that
could do the job. It was an electric-powered winch, rheostat-
controlled, which could reel in a line at any speed from 2 miles
an hour to 35 miles an hour. The speed could be increased at
any rate you wished, on a continuous dial. Furthermore, the
machine had a beautiful advantage, the need for which I had
not foreseen: you could stop the target dead in the water at any
speed, without having the winch free-wheel and tangle up the
line; it was absolutely backlash-proof. This meant that if the
animals dawdled or fell behind, you could reproach them by
stopping the target before the run was finished, with the same
effect as turning off a sound cue. Incidentally, when this happened, the animals quit swimming and just coasted for 30 or 40
feet to a halt. That habit gave Tom Lang some extremely interesting film data on "drag," the resistance of the animal's body to
the water. They appeared to be as well designed as the very
best torpedoes.

We described our project in a later report:

The first phase of training consisted of rewarding the animals for
entering and leaving their pen, following the work boat, progressing
down the unfamiliar lagoon to the barrier net, and for passing near
and under a cork-buoyed line used to mark the race course. The
animals had previously been conditioned to the food-reward system
and habituated to swimmers, boats, and a lagoon situation. Next, the
animals were rewarded for touching a floating or towed lure, and then

for overtaking a moving lure reeled toward or away from the boat by a fishing pole. During this phase of training one animal became fouled in the monofilament line and had to be caught and cut free. Both animals evinced caution and fear of the line thereafter, but not of the lure.

When the animals had learned to track the lure, a plastic finish line was positioned at a depth of 1 m and the animals were rewarded if they crossed the line simultaneously with the moving lure. If they fell behind before crossing the finish line, they were not rewarded. After a run, an assistant in the boat retrieved the lure and returned it to the starting point. The porpoises generally swam near the boat and positioned for another run.

During runs, the trainer stood on the camera platform near the finish line, from which he could observe and direct by walkie-talkie radio the operators of boat and winch. Run lengths were varied and lure speeds were gradually increased over a period of several weeks. Both animals were rewarded for each satisfactory run, although the larger and dominant animal was often closer to the lure. . . .

Once speeds of 6 to 8 m/sec had been established, the animals appeared disinterested in participating in slower runs.[*]

In fact, Haina and Nuha really seemed to enjoy racing the lure. By about 15 knots, near Keiki's apparent top speed, Haina and Nuha could still keep up with the target with ease. They couldn't accelerate from a standing start as fast as the winch did, so we established a behavior chain. The animals circled as the assistant in the dinghy held the target in the air. They came up behind the boat and, at a gesture from the assistant, took off, sprinting, ahead of the target. He tossed the target in the water, the winch turned on, the target raced, catching up to the porpoises, and the animals paced it to the finish line. If they crossed the line with the target, the trainer from the camera tower blew his whistle and threw a bunch of fish to them.

The animals grew discouraged if they made more than three unrewarded runs, or if the reward was not ample. The work was hard, and one or two fish were simply not worth it. It was neces-

---

[*] Thomas G. Lang and Karen Pryor, "Hydrodynamic Performance of Porpoises (*Stenella attenuata*)," *Science,* 152 (1966), 531–533.

sary to raise the criteria slowly, and to keep a high level of successful runs. There could not be too many runs in a day, either, because the animals got full.

When we reached a speed of 20 knots, it certainly looked as if the animals were going all out. None of us had ever seen porpoises hurtling through the water with such a flurry of tail beats. Still, at 20 knots they soon learned to catch the target on every single run. Not until 21 knots did their performance begin to falter. We got two or three runs of 22 knots, but between 21 and 22 knots the animals often failed to catch the target. We ran them at these speeds for nearly three weeks, until I was satisfied that the animals were failing, not because they weren't trying hard, but because we were indeed in their top range, their Olympic effort, their panic speed.

This was in fact somewhat more speed than the laws of hydrodynamics and power output seemed to allow. However, Tom Lang calculated that for short distances, a porpoise could put out more power than the human beings and horses on which previous power output estimations had been based. Maximum power output puts the muscles into oxygen debt; you burn up all your fuel and then some, and it is necessary to rest before doing it again, as our porpoises indeed had to do. A porpoise, however, can go farther before getting into oxygen debt than a terrestrial animal: the porpoise's heart is twice as large in proportion to body weight as a man's, the blood volume is larger, and the hemoglobin count, the number of cells in the blood which carry oxygen around, is higher. The porpoise stores more oxygen. He can, for a brief period, work harder than a terrestrial animal, producing a remarkable level of power output. Tom calculated that the so-called true porpoises, the genera *Phocoena* and *Phocoenoides,* which have hearts four times as big, proportionally, as land animals, and twice the blood volume, could probably sprint even faster than our kikos, though there is a point of no return involved; each small increase in speed requires a large increase in power output.

But how about those destroyer captains who vowed that porpoises "swam circles around the ship" at 35 knots? Thinking of Keiki and the speedboat, and looking at films of porpoises running on the bows of ships, we could see what was happening. The animals that pace destroyers are actually surfing on the bow wave and the stern wave of the ship. Cocking their tails into the pressure of the wave, they hurtle along without swimming at all, getting a free ride at whatever speed the ship is going. By adding their own speed to this they can sprint from the stern wave to the bow wave, or spurt ahead of the ship momentarily; but most of the time they are coasting, like a surfer or a skier. No wonder they think it's fun, and hasten to the bows of any ship passing through their piece of ocean.

One can see, too, at sea, that a school of porpoises never overtakes a ship from the rear. They come in at a tangent, intercepting the ship before it gets to them, and catching their free ride until the ship has gone farther than they wish to go. It's a worldwide porpoise sport, probably divided up somewhat by species. I doubt if it's often *Tursiops* on the bow of a destroyer: they no doubt prefer 20-knot fishing boats, while a 35-knot Navy vessel is more to the liking of thrill-seeking *Phocoenoides;* but in any case what the seamen are seeing is not super porpoise speed, but normal porpoise speed boosted by the speed of their own vessel.

The need to intercept a ship at a tangent is probably why Herman Melville described porpoises as always appearing "from the breezy billows to windward." A power boat may be going in any direction, relative to the wind, but a sailing boat, such as the whalers Melville traveled on, is usually traveling with the wind or at an angle to it. To intercept a sailboat, one would naturally prefer to head for it with the wind (and the waves) coming from behind one, to help one along. No wonder that to Melville the porpoises were "the lads that always live before the wind."

I couldn't help wondering where porpoises had learned this game of running on the bows of ships. Porpoises have been swimming in the oceans for seven to ten million years, but they've had human ships to play with only for the last few thousand. Yet nearly all porpoises, in every ocean, catch rides for fun from passing ships; and they were doing it on the bows of Greek triremes and prehistoric Tahitian canoes, as soon as those seacraft appeared. What did they do for fun before ships were invented?

Ken Norris made a field observation one day that suggests the answer. He saw a humpback whale hurrying along the coast of the island of Hawaii, unavoidably making a wave in front of itself; playing in that bow wave was a flock of bottlenose porpoises. The whale didn't seem to be enjoying it much: Ken said it looked like a horse being bothered by flies around its head; however, there was nothing much the whale could do about it, and the porpoises were having a fine time.

Meanwhile, both Ken and the U.S. Navy had become interested in another problem. How deep can a porpoise dive? How long can it stay down? And what happens to its lungs and internal organs when it dives? Doesn't the pressure collapse its lungs? How can whales stay down an hour, and go to enormous depths, as we know they do from finding sperm whales entangled in submarine cables 3,600 feet down? How come they don't get the bends, or nitrogen narcosis, or even—at great depths—oxygen poisoning, as human divers do?

One way to start answering these questions would be to train a porpoise to dive, and then to take it out in the deep waters around Hawaii to start studying its diving capabilities. Ken obtained another Navy grant to begin work with a diving porpoise. His coinvestigator on this project was Howard Baldwin, from the Sensory Systems Laboratory in Arizona, whose job it would be to design and construct equipment: the electronic dive target and the instruments worn by the animal for measuring heart rates and other data.

Ken wanted a *Steno* for this project, on the hunch that the peculiar build of a *Steno* suggests that it is designed for deep diving. We settled on Pono.

Now that the ice had been broken on open ocean training, I wanted other trainers to have a chance to do some. Dottie, by reason of both skill and seniority, was the logical choice. Dottie began devoting much of her time to Pono.

One perplexing problem was how to attach instruments to a porpoise. The animal would need to wear some kind of harness. Harnesses for any kind of animal must meet the same basic requirements. A harness must be comfortable and sturdy. It must fit well. If the harness is loose, or tends to shift, it will chafe the animal. And if the harness is to carry a load, such as an instrument pack, it must keep that load positioned properly and out of the animal's way.

We were finding it very hard to invent a harness for a porpoise. The animal is streamlined and slippery. There seemed to be no fixed place at which you could anchor the harness. A ring or band around the neck would hold the front end, but a porpoise tapers so quickly that a second band, around the middle, tended to shift forwards and backwards, no matter how snugly buckled, and so did anything aft of the dorsal fin.

Furthermore, we discovered that as the animal swam and flexed, all the harness parts loosened and tightened and shifted. And when the animal dove, even a few feet, its body seemed to compress, so that the snuggest harness became loose.

Attaching anything to the pectoral fins was out; the delicate axilla area, the "armpit," chafed raw immediately. Any strap that abutted on the back edge of the dorsal fin, where the fin tapers down to an eighth of an inch or less in thickness, also caused immediate trouble.

It seemed such a simple task, designing a harness. Our inability to do it made me feel extraordinarily stupid, until I sat down one night at home with one of my Welsh ponies' harnesses in my lap and really looked at it.

A horse or pony harness has six major components: bridle, belly band, traces, crupper, breeching, and reins. Each of these components is made up of multiple parts. The belly band alone, which basically does nothing but go around the animal's middle and keep everything else in place, has a back strap, a padded saddle that keeps pressure off the animal's backbone, a girth that can be detached from either side, shaft loops to carry the buggy shafts, "tie downs" to keep the shafts from going up in the air, terrets, or rings, for the reins to pass through, a D ring for the crupper (which goes to one fixed point, the animal's tail, and keeps everything from sliding forward), and a hook for the overcheck, which goes to another fixed point, the bridle on the animal's head.

A belly band, then, consists of about twenty pieces of leather and a minimum of eight buckles, as well as other kinds of hardware. In the whole harness there are about a hundred and fifty separate elements. Every single item is absolutely essential if the harness is to fit and work correctly. The size, shape, strength,

Pono's harness was comfortable for her, but difficult to put on. Dottie and I struggle to reach the buckles while an assistant stands by with a smelt for Pono. *Camera Hawaii*

choice of materials, and method of attachment for each element is strictly dictated by its function.

Now, consider. The pony harness in my lap was fundamentally the same, in every particular except decoration, as the harnesses used to pull Egyptian chariots three thousand years ago. Presumably the evolution of harness design had been going on for quite a while before the days of Egyptian civilization, too.

Designing a horse harness, then, was not something some smart cave man went out and did in a morning. I finally realized we were not going to come up with the perfect harness for a porpoise overnight.

Navy trainer Bill Bailey paid us a visit. He had been in charge of the animal that they had released into open water in California, harnessed to a float. He had been struggling with harness design for some time. Bill's current harness had a narrow band well aft of the dorsal fin, held to the neck collar and a belly band by straps along the animal's flanks. It made sense to us. Also he recommended a material I had not thought of. Leather, of course, is useless in water. Rubber and elastic quickly lose their tensile strength. Rope chafes. Cloth rots. Bill was using the soft, strong nylon webbing of which parachute straps are made, which was easily available in surplus stores.

I got hold of some of that parachute line, and Phyllis Norris volunteered to work on the harness problem. She and Dottie, following the Navy design, made a harness for Pono that was satisfactory in many respects. Its only drawback was that it was hard to put on from the side of the tank; Dottie had to get in the water with a face plate on to get Pono's harness sitting right and buckled up securely.

I have since seen one very elegant solution to the problem of harnessing a porpoise, something I had not thought of at all. In Mike Nichols' film *Day of the Dolphin* the porpoises carried their equipment on a solid, molded plastic backpack that slipped over them and then fitted loosely, as we might wear a solid bracelet. The animals could swim rapidly and make high jumps, appearing to be quite unimpeded by the apparatus, and the smooth plastic chafed them no more than we are chafed by wearing a pair of sunglasses.

Before we took Pono out to sea Howard Baldwin made a quick trip to Hawaii to test his instruments, especially a pressure gauge and an electrocardiograph pickup with which he proposed to monitor a diving animal's heartbeat. I took him up to Ocean Science Theater to try the instruments out on Makua. I wasn't sure that Pono was ready yet to accept strange instruments, but I knew I could put a belly band around good old Makua, with Howard's black boxes attached, and that Makua would be patient in the matter, being an old pro by now.

Between shows we took Makua into the main tank, and I buckled Howard's strap around him, took it off, and rewarded him. No problem. Then we put one of Howard's instruments on the strap, and I called Makua over and started to buckle the strap around him again. Makua reared like a horse and plunged away to the far side of the tank and wouldn't come back. What!?!

"Maybe it's the signal," Howard ventured. What signal? Well, Dr. Baldwin hadn't realized I didn't know, but the instrument was making a very loud sound; it just happened to be a sound too high in frequency to be audible to human ears. It *was* audible to porpoise ears, however. Makua must have felt as if we were trying to tie a screaming air-raid siren around his middle.

Howard had also brought Pono's dive target, a lever on heavy cable which could be lowered from the side of a boat to the desired depth. Pono was supposed to swim down and press the lever, which would activate a buzzer telling the trainer that she had made the dive, and telling Pono that she had done right and would be rewarded. Dottie began working with Pono and the dive target in the training tanks.

About three weeks before the animal was scheduled to go offshore, it occurred to us that the work could be done just as well in front of audiences at Ocean Science Theater. Hoku had been ill, and Hoku and Kiko were, I felt, due for a rest. We

"Pono showed her behavior of gliding through hoops, part of an experiment in measuring the drag, or water resistance, on her body." *Camera Hawaii*

brought them back to the training facility and took both Pono and Keiki into Sea Life Park.

With Pono and Keiki in the Ocean Science Theater, the show took on great meaning. These were actual research animals, and the tasks they performed in front of audiences were for a purpose. One could come back every few days—and some people did—to see for oneself that the animals were making progress.

Pono showed her behavior of gliding through hoops, part of an experiment in measuring the drag, or water resistance, on her body. Keiki learned to wear blindfolds for some of Ken's future sonar research projects. Both animals obeyed the recall and swam onto a stretcher on command. Pono dove to her buzzer target near the tank floor. Dottie got into the water during each and every show and put Pono's instrumentation harness on the animal.

Randy and Dottie did some wonderful shows in which they switched positions in the middle, Randy training and Dottie narrating, and then Dottie training and Randy narrating. It showed the audiences as nothing else could that these girls were doing something real, and that they really knew what they were doing.

Ken was happy, too. At first, perhaps, he worried that his research animals were being exploited for commercial purposes and that things would be said over the mike which weren't quite true. But we were all scrupulously careful in our narrations, and it soon became apparent that five daily shows meant five daily training sessions, instead of the two sessions which were all we could manage in the hectic and crowded training facility. The animals were coming along very fast.

The actual experiment with Pono has been charmingly described by Ken Norris in *The Porpoise Watcher*. I was a bystander, not really involved. However, I was an acutely interested bystander, and felt considerable responsibility for whatever occurred. My daily journals for the period that Pono went to

"Dottie got into the water in each and every show and put Pono's instrumentation harness on the animal." *Camera Hawaii*

sea were concerned with almost nothing but the diving experiment then taking place:

October 5, 1964

Ken is getting ready to take Pono offshore tomorrow. I do not have much faith in Howard Baldwin's instruments, which the animal is supposed to wear. They break down constantly in the Ocean Science Theater, so how are they going to work offshore? It's a tense moment, taking Pono out. Are we going to lose her? Will she work? The harness has been elaborated. It's hard to put on and hard for Pono to wear. I feel Ken rushes these things a bit—or maybe we trainers take too much time and go too slowly! However, Ken has been very generous, allowing us to use Keiki and Pono in the shows, and after all, the whole Keiki experiment was a great success. We are all full of doubts at the beginning of one of these things, I suppose.

The Lillys are here. William Schevill [an authority on cetaceans from Woods Hole] will be here this weekend. We'll have nearly all of porpoisedom under one roof.

October 6, 1964

Pono went to Pokai Bay today. She'll work one day at boatside in the harbor, and then move out to sea. Quite a contingent here to watch the experiment. Howard Baldwin is back, plus Gregory Bateson, and also John Lilly and Bill Schevill. Bill Schevill's erudite wit keeps us all amused. Lilly came in wearing a pair of loud plaid shorts today and Bill said, "Look, John's reticulate!" [a biological term meaning "having a networklike pattern"].

The Lillys annoyed me fantastically today by failing to stay and see the Whaler's Cove show. Imagine! And she had never seen spinners, either. She had laundry to do, so they walked away. Maybe she doesn't like porpoises!

October 7, 1964

Pono went offshore today, very successfully. She was timid and anxious to stay near Dottie, obeyed the recall, dove to the dive target alongside the *Imua*, which was anchored in the harbor, and wasn't frightened by the other boats, though she followed one once and had to be called back. She amused herself in between experiments by retrieving beer cans and grapefruit rinds off the bottom. Ken is absolutely in love with her.

Howard's equipment broke, and parts have to be flown in from the mainland.

Thursday, October 8, 1964

Mae was sick today and Dottie still offshore, so I did ten shows again, narrating five at Whaler's Cove and training five at Ocean Science Theater. So short-handed that Randy Lewis had to go get my kids from school.

Maybe I should have gone out with Pono myself, after all. They lost her today. She became wilder when they got out to sea, and when a lot of little sharks appeared around the dive target, she disappeared, and was last seen breaching a mile away. I think maybe they took her too fast—they got over 40 dives and 125 feet of depth. Also she was making a lot of dives off cue, not waiting for the signal, so they spent time at sea trying to extinguish off-cue diving, which was *not* the ticket, in my opinion. [This should have been done in earlier training, and I should have anticipated the need for it.]

Dottie dreadfully upset and in tears, and will go out with the recall equipment to search for Pono tomorrow. Rats. I was going to take the day off.

2 A.M.

Tossed and turned thinking about Pono. I think had I been there I would have raised a contrary voice now and then, even in front of Lilly and Schevill. Still, this would not necessarily have prevented Pono from leaving. I daresay Dottie stood up for the trainer's viewpoint, anyway. I wonder what made Pono leave? Are *Steno*s just plain wild? Did something happen? The animal followed the *Imua* nicely, but gave signs of nervousness from the moment they hit deep water.

Friday, October 9, 1964

Best news of the day: Pono was seen by a fishing boat off Pokai Bay and came alongside it for five minutes. Ken and Jim Kelly going out tomorrow to search for her again.

Ken and Jim spent two more days looking for Pono. Then Dottie and Howard Baldwin continued the search, but without results.

What did happen to Pono? Careful reconstruction of the circumstances suggested that the low-frequency buzzer, which was her dive target, attracted sharks, and Pono panicked. Porpoises certainly have trouble with sharks; in any wild school many animals show crescent-shaped scars and missing bits of fins and flukes that suggest shark bites. Presumably porpoises can outrun sharks or defend themselves against a single shark by ganging up and ramming it; there are a few fishermen's eyewitness accounts of such events. But a lonely porpoise, surrounded by sharks, would be in real trouble. Here is Ken Norris's scientific account:

Finally Pono refused to dive again and began rapidly circling ahead of the boat, slapping the water sporadically with both her flippers and her flukes, signs of agitation well known to porpoise trainers. Some of these sorties took her long distances from the boat. At this time we noticed three small sharks circling close around the buzzer. . . . We made preparations to hoist Pono and hauled in the diving apparatus, but she refused to come in to the recall speaker, and continued to swim rapidly near us in an agitated manner. Finally, she turned directly out to sea and was gone. As we turned the *Imua* in pursuit we saw the dorsal fin and tailtip of a large shark (about 4 meters total length) coming directly towards the place where the *Imua* had been drifting.*

Four meters! That's a heck of a big shark: as long as two tall men standing on each other's shoulders, and considerably heavier than the two men would be. No wonder Pono was frightened. Luckily she was not wearing any harness when she left, and there seemed to be no reason why she could not go happily back to her wild ways.

Georges, from then on, always loaded Pono's recall equipment on the *Imua* when they were on that side of the Island. Once, months later, they were passing through a school of *Stenos*, and Georges, Leo, and Ken, who happened to be aboard, thought they spotted Pono in the school. It seems unlikely, but then *Stenos*, with all their scars and scrapes, are often rather easy to identify individually, and all the men were skilled observers.

* Kenneth S. Norris, "Open Ocean Diving Test with a Trained Porpoise," *Deep Sea Research*, 12 (1965), 505–509.

They quickly idled the boat, dropped the recall speaker, and turned on the sound. The animal they thought was Pono peeled out of the group, came over to the boat, and stuck its nose in the speaker, as Pono was trained to do. They had no whistle or fish ready with which to reward her, and before they could come up with any plan of action, the porpoise rejoined the school and was gone.

The following summer Ken elected to try another series of diving experiments with a *Steno*. I decided to do the training myself. I had been distressed and had blamed myself that Pono had gone to sea without being fully trained. It seemed to me that a more elaborate training program, properly established, might reduce the chances of the animal going AWOL. Also, if things did go wrong, no one else would have to take the responsibility, and at least I would have the satisfaction of knowing that I had taken every precaution *I* could think of.

Howard Baldwin came up with a new kind of dive target, a hoop with an electric eye in it, through which the animal would swim. No buzzer to attract sharks, just a light beam—which, when broken, would tell us on deck that the animal had gone through the hoop and which would trigger a high-frequency tone to tell the animal that its work was done correctly. We chose our male *Steno*, Kai, for this project, a rather aggressive animal but a sharp worker. In addition, we taught all the things that Kai needed to know to another *Steno,* a little female named Hou ("happy"). If Kai did run off, Hou could replace him.

Ken had scheduled ten days of work at Pokai Bay, the quiet little harbor from whence Pono's work had been done. It was a good two-hour drive from his house, from my house, and from Sea Life Park. Tap was on the mainland, raising money for new projects, so the Norrises and I decided to eliminate the driving time by moving our families to Pokai Bay for the duration of the experiment. I located a delightful teenager, Claudia Collins, to stay with my children while I was offshore during the day, and we rented apartments in an inexpensive motel by the beach.

From underwater, Kai's cage with Kai inside it, the hull of the *Imua,* and the hoop, which Kai was trained to dive through, ready to be lowered deeper and deeper. *Oceanic Institute photo*

Besides four Pryors, and Claudia, and six Norrises, and Georges and Leo, who lived on the boat, there were two assistant trainers, Blair Irvine and Bob Ballard, Howard Baldwin (complete with tool kit and spare parts), and two people from *Life* magazine, writer Marge Byers and photographer Henry Groshinsky.

The children overlapped agreeably in ages and settled down to a blissful week of water play and sand castles, consuming record amounts of tuna fish and peanut butter and falling soundly asleep at twilight in nice, sandy beds, to the sound of wavelets lapping the sea walls, the creaking and slatting of fishing boats in the harbor, and distant voices and laughter from campers and fishermen around the bay.

The grownups overlapped agreeably in age and experience, too. It was a joyful hiatus for me. The constant human problems that beset me daily at Sea Life Park were all absent. There was no juggling for status, no conflict about job duties, no budgets, no anger, no flirtations, no conflicting or unrealistic memos handed down from above, just one interesting job to do and a bunch of people who knew how to go about it. How restful!

Every morning we putt-putted out to the *Imua*, at anchor among the fleet, and to Kai, in a nice little portable cage Ken had designed, resting alongside. The *Imua* upped anchor, and we proceeded slowly out into the calm summer sea (calm because it was in the lee of the whole big island of Oahu), until very shortly we were in waters 1,000 feet deep or more. We towed Kai alongside in his cage. Sensible Kai maintained his place in the middle of the cage by swimming at the pace of the ship, a task which in no way taxed him.

We ran tests in bunches of ten or fifteen dives, paying strict attention to maintaining the behavior chain I had developed. First Bob Ballard got into the cage and put Kai's harness on him. Then we opened the gate, and I put a lever into the water. When Kai pressed the lever, he got a sound cue to dive. Thus, if he was anxious to start work, he would hang around begging me for the lever, rather than wearing himself out making unscheduled dives.

When the lever tone went on, Kai dove down to the hoop which hung beneath the *Imua*, passed through it, broke the light beam, got his return signal, came up, got his fish, and went back into his cage. Making him go back in his cage before he dove again was another device for controlling his behavior. Besides, we figured that if sharks did show up, we could shut Kai in the cage and guarantee his safety.

Henry Groshinsky had been assigned to get underwater pictures of this business for a *Life* story. Henry knew how to scuba-dive, but he was worried about sharks, especially after hearing the story of Pono, who had taken flight in the same piece of ocean. Naturally we all made him miserable with elaborate farewells and prayers for his safety every time he suited up and went overboard, and we reassured him by saying that while sharks are common in Hawaii, shark attacks are rather rare, and then telling him about every shark attack in recorded history.

In fact, we never saw a shark on this trip. If they'd been

there, we'd have seen them. The water was so fabulously clear that week that you could see about 200 feet in every direction. We all had a swim or two overboard to take a look at this transparency, the ocean deeply dimming blue below and all around, and from underwater the whole of the *Imua*'s hull as visible, almost, as if she were hanging in air. Georges and Leo kept a sharp eye on the photographer every minute he was in the water, and a scanning eye on the sea all around us. Had they ever seen a shark, any rapid banging on metal, perhaps by hitting a wrench against Kai's cage, would have sent divers a clanging alarm and brought them in to safety.

In the late afternoon each day, when Kai was getting full of fish, we shut him back in the cage and went home to harbor. Sometimes Phylly and I cooked dinner. More often the grownups went to a tiny Japanese restaurant catering mostly to commercial fishermen, where our little group of eight or ten took up half the tables. We ate miso soup and sashimi and sukiyaki and yakitori and huge bowls of rice, and drank quarts of Japanese beer. In the calm, starry evenings we sat around by the beach and played the guitar and listened to Ken Norris tell porpoise tales, and to Marge and Henry tell stories, funny or thrilling or sad, of their life working for *Life*.

For two nights there was a huge run of young aweoweo in Pokai Bay. These were little bright-red fish about three inches long, good eating and excellent bait. Georges invited all the children out to the *Imua* after dark to catch aweoweo for him to use from the freezer when he needed bait to collect fish for the reef tank.

There seemed to be one aweoweo in every cubic foot of water from the surface to the bottom of the bay, and from one side of the bay to the other. Using tiny hooks and short bamboo poles the children caught fish as fast as the grownups could bait hooks and as long as the children could stay awake, little scarlet aweoweo by the bucketful. All around us in the darkness, from the dock and from other ships, Japanese and Hawaiian families drank beer in the light of gas lanterns and caught aweoweo too, and the laughter of their children floated over the water and mingled with the laughter and shouts of ours.

Country communities in Hawaii are so polite. As with Pono, the summer before, people came by to look at the porpoise, but they never bothered the animal or us, just looked, smiled, nodded to us, and went away again. The fishermen chatted with Georges over the radio during the day, but no boat ever disturbed our work by coming to sightsee, and no crowds of curiosity seekers ever invaded our peaceful days and nights.

By the fifth day, we had discarded the various harnesses we were asking Kai to wear. Howard had the data he needed, I suppose; as trainer all I cared about was that there was no more harness requirement. We did try one more experiment; we had Kai diving reliably to depths of about 150 feet, and Ken wanted to know if his lungs collapsed at that depth. People die if their lungs are collapsed by pressure, but porpoises have rather flexible ribs and it seemed as if this might be something that happened to them all the time, harmlessly.

Ken decided that we could tell if it happened by making a strap that tightened as the animal went down, and then stretched again as the animal came up, leaving a hook on a ratchet to show how much tightening had taken place. We went to the Pokai Bay dime store and stocked up on the necessaries, and then Ken and I had fun sitting on the deck of the *Imua* making a scientific instrument out of a plastic ruler, two measuring spoons, a hacksaw blade, some wide elastic, and dental floss. It worked pretty well, too, in that the animal did grow narrow in diameter as it went down, and the spoons did slip and hook onto the sawteeth; the only problem was that we assumed the animal would become about four inches less in circumference, and apparently he grew much smaller than that. Our fine instrument indicated a change, but the change was so much larger than the shrinking capacity of the elastic, stretched tight at the beginning of the dive, that the whole thing just fell out of place and Kai invariably came up with it no longer snug around his middle, but flapping uselessly around his tail.

Even though no harness was now required for data collection purposes, I felt that Kai should wear something. I knew that a horse wearing a halter may be easy to catch in a pasture, whereas the same horse without a halter feels freer and may not let you get close to him. Kai therefore was making his dives wearing a soft nylon collar around his neck.

We worked late, that fifth day. Kai, like our other porpoises when working hard, needed time between dives to catch his breath. He never took a big breath before a dive, but after coming up he would circle, breathing repeatedly, before he would obey the recall and go back in his cage to begin the cycle for the next dive.

He was doing this, circling and breathing, off the *Imua's* port side, as usual, when he suddenly changed his pattern and circled the whole ship. He looked at the hoop, at the cage, and at us; and then he took off, headed for the horizon, leaping and chasing flying fish ahead of him as he went, a wild animal who had suddenly chosen to be free.

No one was upset. Kai had made nearly three hundred dives, over five days, with perfect discipline and reliability. Training techniques alone, I felt, could do no more. Kai had earned his freedom. What made him take off, we'll never know. He showed no signs of fear. Did he hear the distant whistling of his old school? Did he feel differently because twilight was coming on, and *Stenos* are perhaps naturally nocturnal? Whatever it was, our only concern was that the neck collar he was still wearing would give him trouble. Hopefully, it soon rotted and fell off; just possibly, some other *Steno* removed it; I wouldn't put it past that clever breed.

Ken and Howard had learned quite a few things from Kai's dives. We had also all discovered that diving for depth is not a behavior that can be accomplished overnight. Kai rebelled every time we lowered the hoop more than a few feet deeper than the previous dive. We had had to go one slow fathom (6 feet) at a time. It might have taken months to get Kai to show us what we suspected he was capable of, dives of 600 feet or more; and Ken's budget didn't stretch to months of ship time.

"He looked at the hoop, at the cage, and at us; and then he took off, headed for the horizon, leaping and chasing flying fish ahead of him as he went, a wild animal who had suddenly chosen to be free." *Camera Hawaii*

We fetched little Hou from the Park the next day and spent two days at sea with her. She was not as sensible or as ambitious as Kai. She would not, for example, swim along while the cage was under tow; she just let herself be washed helplessly against the back wall, so that we had to go to and from the dive site with Hou on the deck of the *Imua*. She did confirm some of the observations that had been made with Kai, relating to time needed for recovery between dives and other physiological matters. On the second day, she caught a cold and didn't feel up to working, so we closed down the experiment and went back to Sea Life Park. As so often happens in science, we didn't get the results we set out to get, but we got some answers, including a few we hadn't expected, and we set the path for future work.

The Office of Naval Research, which had sponsored this work, continued deep-diving experiments of its own, using an Atlantic bottlenose porpoise named Tuffy. Their trainers, like us, found that Tuffy would not respond if the criteria were made more severe too rapidly. They told me that Tuffy hit plateaus in his training. He would go so deep, and then, for weeks, refuse to go any deeper. They had really begun to think that 125 feet down was his bottom depth, when one day he broke off from diving to a 125-foot target to go down to 200 feet to hobnob with a scuba diver working on the bottom. With great patience and persistence—Blair Irvine, who helped us with Kai, became one of their trainers on this project—they eventually got Tuffy diving reliably to 1,000 feet of depth, a formidable distance.

They also developed some free-swimming, trained, diving whales, using both pilot whales and true killer whales, with the purpose, I believe, of training the animals to locate and recover valuable items at great depths. These animals too, while not as easily controlled as bottlenoses, are said to have accomplished dives of well over 1,000 feet.

Ingrid Kang gives a spinner an antibiotic injection as two assistants try to hold the animal still.

9. HEADACHES

Running an oceanarium is not 100 percent pleasant excursions and fun with science. We had easily as many headaches as joys.

My most consuming problems, as curator, were human problems: fighting with the higher-ups for more pay for my people, or for ten or twenty dollars for paint or lumber; recognizing resentments in my staff before they flared into anger; getting rid of troublemakers. I think there is a biologically determined role in human society for The Troublemaker. It always seemed to me that as soon as I got rid of the Training Department's Official Malcontent, some previously cheerful person assumed the office. Even pleasant emotions could be a problem. It was baffling to discover how fast the day's work ran downhill when two trainers fell in love with each other.

Scientists, while they were our raison d'être, could be a headache to have around. Because of scientists the antibiotic injection that we gave to every newly captured animal was the source of some of the most venomous fights and bitterest moments of my years as head trainer at Sea Life Park. Scientists objected to it; they ranted and raved over it; they knew you don't give antibiotics for "no reason" to an animal which is fresh from the ocean and obviously healthy in every respect.

There *was* a reason. If a newly caught animal *didn't* get the shot, he died. Not tomorrow, not the next day, but perhaps in four or five days. Although our water was clean and our staff was healthy, there were almost inevitably enough human germs around to overwhelm the nonimmune newcomer. Protective antibiotics did not guarantee that you were out of trouble; the guarantee was that you would be in trouble without them.

The trainers had standing orders to administer long-acting broad-spectrum antibiotics on introduction. But I could not be on hand to oversee the arrival of every new animal. If I was absent, and Dr. Whoever was present when an animal that had just been collected for his research project came in, Dr. Whoever invariably threw a fit when he discovered the animal was about to get antibiotics. Standing orders or no standing orders, if a scientist was bringing all the force of an often formidable personality to bear on preventing "scattergun antibiotics," the trainers tended to obey him and skip the shot.

I tried issuing memos to new Institute staff members and to all visiting scientists. I tried stiffening the trainers' spines to resist. Nothing worked. Several times, indeed, the crucial shot was prevented by some bigwig who had nothing to do with the new animal, who was just a curious bystander during the introduction, but who felt he had to say "Stop! You can't give antibiotics for no reason!"

No matter how often I double-checked the records, no matter how many pep talks I gave to new trainers, over and over an animal slipped by me without getting its shots. The trainers were at a peculiar disadvantage, especially the younger ones; they caught hell on the spot if they gave the shot, and they caught hell from me if I found out they hadn't, so it was a question of which kind of hell to choose. More than once they agreed not to dose the animal, and then entered the dose on the records as having been given, to keep me and the vet off their backs.

I believe Ingrid Kang finally got ahead of the problem. Complete separation of Institute and Park facilities probably helped, too. But it was never solved entirely. How many, many animals died after this contretemps, this battle which was never won, this scientific hydra which kept rearing another head: perhaps forty, during my tenure. Ten years later, at somebody else's porpoise research facility, I saw five new animals die within a week while the trainers begged and pleaded to treat them with antibiotics on capture, and the head scientist (who had worked once at our Institute and should have known better) stood firm: "No scattergun antibiotics for *my* animals." It makes me sick.

Animals came, animals went. We tried to do our best for them. What always came, and never went, was an endless series of mechanical problems, first for me, then for David, later for Ingrid, problems so numerous and so infuriating that sometimes it took the joy out of the work.

The electronic cuing and public address systems, constantly exposed to dampness and salt air, were always giving trouble. It was bad enough when the cues stopped working. It was fatal to the shows when the PA systems leaked sound. Suddenly underwater sound cues would be blasting over the PA system, or an Ocean Science Theater narration would be mysteriously delivered at top volume into the Galley restaurant, or the Galley's piped-in music would suddenly swamp the narration at Whaler's Cove.

Bill Schevill calls scientific technicians "termites," because they work indoors and always look very pale. When things went wrong, we called one of these men. I grew to hate the sight of a "termite." It was infuriating that the very men who had built the system were often quite unable to fix it. We trainers felt like screaming when we were tearing our hair out over some new and exotic sound system aberration, and trying to figure out how to survive the next show in spite of it, while a laconic, slow-moving termite shook his head and chuckled, poked aimlessly around with his screwdriver, and suggested we wait and see if the trouble would go away spontaneously. Not until we got our own in-house termite, Wilbur Harvey, the seventeen-year-old genius son of one of the Institute scientists, did the sound system calm down and begin to be trustworthy.

The sound systems were a formidable headache in another way. They leaked electricity. In the first few months of operation, when every person on the staff was desperately overworked, it was very hard for me to get anyone in authority to pay attention to what seemed to me to be a potentially very hazardous situation. There were times, after a heavy rain, for instance, when a little film of electrical juice ran all over the ship *Essex*. Every railing, the deck, even the ropes and lines, would be a little prickly to the touch. Sometimes the mikes got hot. I remember standing in bare feet on wet cement at Ocean Science Theater narrating a show and tossing a slightly shocky microphone from hand to hand, like a hot potato, as I talked. We sometimes held the mike in a dry towel to make it usable at all. For a while the trainers kept a pair of rubber-handled pliers handy to throw switches that were too "live" to touch.

We finally had an accident. We were lowering the tank at Whaler's Cove on cleaning day, and Gary Anderson jumped into the water to listen to the underwater cue speakers and see if they were all working. Just as he swam up to a speaker, the water level dropped low enough so that the speaker was out of the water—and, I guess, ungrounded. Gary's wet hair brushed the speaker, and he got a shock that almost knocked him out. Lani jumped into the water and used her Junior Lifesaving training to get Gary, twice her size, to the edge of the pool. She and Chris got him out. He was unconscious by then, but breathing. We called the ambulance, and Gary got checked out and scolded by a doctor. The shock didn't seriously harm him, but it did prompt the front office into getting a safety engineer out and getting all our systems properly shielded and grounded, and into reacting with more speed when trainers complained about loose juice running around. Eventually we acquired wireless mikes, which have problems of their own but are at least safe. On the whole I think it was nothing but the luck of the ignorant that saved us from any serious disaster.

Salt water and salt wind got to everything. Planks and decks rotted. The chain that hoisted the training platform at Ocean Science Theater broke twice, dropping trainer, platform, fish bucket, and all into the water. We learned to inspect the chain ourselves for signs of weakness and to start a bitching and complaining campaign for a new chain *before* it was in danger of breaking.

Metal gates and props and railings dissolved, sometimes before one's eyes, sometimes invisibly. Once Ingrid Kang was training an Ocean Science Theater show in which a new assistant was closing the holding tank gate in a desultory manner, giving the porpoise plenty of time to change its plans and come back into the show tank. *"That's* not the way to close a gate," Ingrid said, very annoyed, knowing that from such small lapses in human discipline big lapses soon arise in porpoise behavior. She marched off to the training platform, snatched the gate handle, leaned into it to slam the gate briskly, and the handle broke off, dropping Ingrid neatly into the holding tank head first in front of several hundred interested people.

Often the maintenance problems were really due to human error, not to equipment failure. Once I was told that an Institute animal wasn't eating, and yet no one could find anything wrong with her. Would I take a look? I fed her myself, and indeed she wasn't eating. The fish I tossed her sank to the tank floor. Fallen fish should always be picked up immediately, since they rot quickly, and an animal that changes its mind later in the day and picks up a decomposing fish off the tank floor can get sick. We usually used a net to gather them, but since I was in a bathing suit, and the day was hot, I jumped in to pick them up myself—and was instantly blinded. That particular tank had an automatic chlorinating system to reduce the growth of scum on the walls. Someone had turned the drip rate up too much. Although there was no giveaway odor of chlorine, the chlorine level was so high that I not only couldn't keep my eyes open underwater, I couldn't bear to open them once I got out. I fumbled my way to the shower room and washed my eyes until

I could use them again, feeling the most profound sympathy for the poor animal who had been living for days in a chlorine solution strong enough to bleach laundry.

Uniforms were another exasperating problem. For a while, at Ocean Science Theater, we all wore white lab coats to give the show an air of authenticity. The coats were supplied by a laundry service. Of course trainers come in all sizes, but the laundry did not necessarily return the right size lab coats every time. Audiences would be treated to the sight of petite Dottie in a size 44 lab coat, sleeves rolled up in a bunch and hem flapping around her ankles, or, worse yet, of husky Chris in a 32, with the sleeves halfway up his arms and the hem well above his knees. When we switched to personal uniforms in pretty prints, the size problem was solved, but I never solved the problem of coming up with a uniform which at least 50 percent of the staff didn't loathe, despise, and feel silly in.

We were always needing things built or repaired—props, boxes to keep fish buckets in, hoists, ladders, temporary partitions in tanks. The Park budget was very tight, and most repairs tended to be made with a baling-wire-and-chewing-gum approach, which was understandable and therefore tolerable. It was maddening, though, when human error crept in. Once I frantically ordered a temporary partition for the long tank in the training facility, so I could separate two *Stenos* and enable a visiting scientist to get some work done with just one of them during his limited time in Hawaii. The partition was proudly installed two days later (a record time), but someone had measured the depth of the tank wrong. The partition stopped 18 inches above the tank floor, and the *Stenos*, delighted with something new to do, whisked back and forth underneath it with utter freedom and considerable gusto.

Once we had extremely expensive pipe gates designed and built for the holding area, in Whaler's Cove, behind the *Essex*. We wanted to separate the whales from the spinners at will, so we could train them more easily. We were joyful the day the gates were installed, until we discovered as the pool filled that the water surface was about two feet higher than the tops of the gates, and, again, all the animals—whales included—were having a high old time zooming back and forth over these new toys.

The porpoises and whales themselves, in their quests for entertainment, often created problems. One summer a fashion developed in the training tanks (I think Keiki started it) for leaning out over the tank wall and seeing how far you could balance without falling out. Several animals might be teetering on the tank edge at one time, and sometimes one or another did fall out. Nothing much happened to them, except maybe a cut or a scrape from the gravel around the tanks; but of course we had to run and pick them up and put them back in. Not a serious problem, if the animal that fell out was small, but if it was a 400-pound adult bottlenose, you had to find four strong people to get him back, and when it happened over and over again, the people got cross. We feared, too, that some animal would fall out at night or when no one was around and dry out, overheat, and die. We yelled at the porpoises, and rushed over and pushed them back in when we saw them teetering, but that just seemed to add to the enjoyment of what I'm sure the porpoises thought of as a hilariously funny game. Fortunately they eventually tired of it by themselves.

Smashing gates and partitions just for the fun of it was another tiresome porpoise pastime. Amiko, an Atlantic bottlenose at the Institute, was so dedicated to this that it was quite impossible to keep him or any other porpoise isolated if Amiko had access to the gates. Makua, at the Ocean Science Theater, separated from his neighbor Malia by a chain-link partition, broke into her tank over and over again by slipping his powerful flukes between the partition's pipe frame and the cement wall of the tank, and prying so hard that he sheared the bolts which held the partition to the walls. And he didn't even *like* Malia. We finally had to set the partition in a rim of cement blocks.

One of the niftiest animals we ever had was a baby false killer whale named Ola, a little male about two years old and about 8 feet long when captured. Ola became a performer at the Ocean

Science Theater. He was quite reliable and had wonderful, loud sonar clicks that you could hear right through the glass, even without amplification. He did like to entertain himself, however. One day Ola completely wrecked an entire show by upstaging us all with a game of his own invention. Ola was in his holding tank, at the back of the show tank, where Keiki was performing for the audience. A booby bird landed beside Ola's holding tank—hoping, no doubt, to find an unguarded fish bucket and steal a meal. Ola poked his head out at the bird, almost touching it. Boobies are incredibly unflappable; the bird did nothing. Ola then made a rush at bird, leaping out at it with his jaws open. He was a baby, but even so his toothy jaws were quite wide enough to consume a whole red-footed booby.

The bird looked bored and didn't move. I was watching Ola, as I narrated about Keiki. Now my narration faltered. The jaws-open rush had attracted most of the audience's attention too. Now Ola waved his tail at the bird. Nothing. He rushed around his tank in a circle and made waves which washed out over the imperturbable booby's feet. Nothing. Finally Ola ducked underwater, came up with his mouth full, and squirted about five gallons of water in a fanning spray through his teeth all over that bird. That was too much. The bird flapped into the air, shaking its head, and flew away. The trainer and myself and all the audience laughed hysterically, and there was no way to go back gracefully to whatever pontificating the regular show called for.

Ola was not stupid. One of the tokens people grab at as a sign of animal intelligence is cooperative behavior. Ola provided us with a dilly of an example. Keiki, who lived in the adjoining holding tank for a while, was Ola's favorite buddy. Keiki took to jumping into Ola's holding tank at night, making it difficult to separate the animals the next morning for show purposes. We tried raising the partition, but Keiki jumped it anyway. Finally Ernie Boerrigter jury-rigged a barrier, a wide plank laid over the partition, which overhung on Keiki's side and looked too formidable to jump. That worked for a few days, and then one morning Ingrid came to work and found one end of the plank in the water, and Keiki in Ola's tank. The plank was a 2 by 12, very heavy; it could not have fallen by accident. It seemed to us that some soft-minded trainer or maintenance man must have levered the plank aside and let the animals get together. Staff sentimentality often secretly overruled my fiercest dictums.

Anyway, it happened again. When it began happening not just at night but between shows, Ingrid decided to devote an hour to catching the culprit. She hid behind a post to watch after the Ocean Science Theater crowd left.

Ola was no jumper, but with his superior strength, he could brace his tail on the bottom of the tank, put his nose under the plank, and lever it off the partition, enabling Keiki to jump into Ola's tank, Ingrid watched them do it. From then on we bolted

Wicked Keiki keeps a low profile as he sneaks into Ola's tank when he thinks there are no people around.

the plank in place, but we let Ola and Keiki have playtime together in the main show tank as soon as the last show of the day
was ended. What interested me most about the episode was that
the animals knew it was illegal and made their moves clandes-
tinely, when there were no people in sight.

Porpoise games were often a nuisance. Porpoise aggression
was more than a nuisance. Porpoises do get angry, both with
people and with each other. They can cuff or ram a swimmer in
the water with dangerous force. Usually an angry porpoise gives
warning before it resorts to blows. Bottlenoses, both Atlantic and
Pacific, clap their jaws and give a sort of bark. The spinners, when
annoyed, would "buzz" a swimmer, zooming past uttering an
especially loud sonar blast, which you could both hear underwater
and seemingly feel in your bones; Randy Lewis said that it felt
like a dotted line going through you. If the swimmer did not leave
the water at this point, the animal on the next pass might strike
out with dorsal fin or tail. Akamai, the most jealous and temperamental of the spinners, gave me a ferocious bruise on the arm
once when I failed to respect his warning buzzes.

The false killer whale threat display consisted of swimming
head on and full tilt at the person in the water and stopping,
without seeming to slow down, 6 inches from the swimmer's solar
plexus. No one ever stayed in the water to see what the next
move would be after that. *Stenos* and bottlenoses also might
choose the solar plexus for a ramming attack. It is really hazardous to have the wind knocked out of you when you are swimming. After a couple of experiences the training staff unanimously
decided that no one would ever swim with any animal, no matter
how docile it appeared, unless someone else was available to
stand by and watch.

One of our bottlenoses, Apo, became so rough on swimmers
that she was downright dangerous. She was a brilliant performer,
and one of the stars of Whaler's Cove, but she was really malicious
to the girls who swam in the show, dashing up underneath them
hard enough to boost them in the air, or swinging around them

Apo, a Pacific bottlenose, a brilliant performer but a dangerous bully, very aggressive to human swimmers. This dog is a barkless wild dog from New Guinea, obedient but timid.

to hit them over the head with her tail flukes. We controlled her initially by training an "incompatible behavior." While the swimmer was in the water, Apo was given a chance to earn fish by pressing a lever. She could not do this and molest the swimmer simultaneously; the behaviors were incompatible.

Apo liked her lever and spent her energy defending it from other porpoises, but the girls were still nervous, and we finally built Apo a private pen where she could be confined until the swimmer's part of the show was over.

Porpoises and whales seldom bite aggressively. They rake each other with their open mouths in play, leaving curious parallel tracks of tooth marks, but I've never known one animal to bite down and puncture another porpoise. Several human beings got bitten over the years, but usually in rather curious circumstances that had, I felt, nothing to do with hostility. Wela, Makua's companion at the Ocean Science Theater, bit me once. A photographer was taking a picture of Wela jumping up to take a fish from my hand. Just as she came up, the photographer said something. I turned my head and forgot to let the fish drop. Wela's mouth closed on my hand, and a couple of teeth sank in; I still have the scar. Wela was hideously embarrassed, as a dog might be if it bit you accidentally. She retreated to the bottom of the tank, jammed her nose in a corner, and refused to come back until I got in the water and petted her into accepting my forgiveness.

Once a month it was our custom to lower the water at Whaler's Cove and catch and weigh each spinner. These delicate animals needed close watching, medically. A weight loss of three or four pounds was often the first sign of poor health. Makapuu, the false killer whale, objected to this procedure. Once, when one of the boys caught and lifted Haole, Makapuu's favorite spinner, the whale sculled through the shallow water and grabbed the boy by the leg. Her intention, I think, was to pull him away from Haole, not to hurt him; but her huge teeth sank in, and he had puncture wounds that had to be stitched up. Another time, a junior trainer dived into Whaler's Cove to retrieve a fish bucket from the bottom. Olelo, the other whale, had been playing with the bucket and did not wish to lose it. Instead of removing the bucket from the boy, however, she took the boy's head in her mouth and removed him from the bucket to the tank edge. Her lower teeth lacerated his ear, and he too had to be sewn up, not to mention calmed down.

Perhaps because Ola was only a baby false killer whale, he never showed any signs of temper, and for a couple of years we swam and played with him without a thought. Then we developed a section in the Ocean Science Theater in which an animal and a human diver worked together. Ola was taught this work. We had several divers, some of them with no training experience.

We didn't know that one of these men was afraid of Ola and was surreptitiously expressing this fear, between shows, by teasing Ola in the holding tank.

One day when Ola was working with that diver, he put his nose in the small of the man's back and pinned him to the tank floor. Of course the diver had scuba gear on, so he wasn't going to drown, but he could not get away, either. For five minutes the trainers wheedled and commanded Ola, tempted him with fish, tried to alarm him with loud sound cues. Finally Ola decided he'd made his point and let the diver go. But we never quite dared use Ola with a diver or swimmer again, and the divers themselves refused to work if we didn't give that part of the show to some other beast.

I have never worked with *Orcinus orca,* the great true killer whale that is such a spectacular attraction at many mainland oceanariums. The trainers who do work with them seem to treat them with the same thoughtful respect we accorded to our whales. Oceanariums are understandably rather close-mouthed about any

Ola, the young false killer whale, pushing a diver in the Ocean Science Theater.

difficulties they do have with these animals. It was my guess that their whales would be, on the whole, trustworthy; that accidents, when they happened, were in the nature of Olelo's biting to get her bucket back. One famous incident occurred at San Diego's Sea World, unfortunately right in front of network TV cameras, so that we saw it on the evening news the next day even in Hawaii. A killer whale, accustomed to being ridden by a male diver clad in a black wet suit, was mounted by lovely Anne Eckis, a female diver, in a bikini. The animal perhaps became aware of the novelty of this; it shook Anne off, and grabbed her by one of those long white legs, biting her in the process. Luckily she wasn't seriously injured. The Sea Life Park trainers exchanged a good deal of sarcastic laughter around the coffee machine the next morning, everyone having seen the incident, and everyone agreeing that the last thing you should ever do is surprise a whale in any way. I still thought the animal to be basically safe. I have since heard, however, from a lady tiger trainer who saw it happen, of at least one killer whale which launched an unprovoked attack on a favorite trainer, in normal circumstances, savaged him very badly, and nearly killed him. So—if you see a killer whale, admire him. But don't fall in the water.

In general, aggressive whales and porpoises "pull their punches." Equipped with lethal power, they hold back. Peter Markie, Wayne Batteau's trainer, told me that he once accidentally kicked an animal rather hard as he was climbing out of the training tank. The next morning when Peter got into the water the same animal swatted him, just once, with a blow equal to Peter's kick. Peter thought of it as a typical example of porpoise politesse.

I wrote in regard to another trainer's experience:

One gains the impression that the porpoise is a firm, fair disciplinarian, exhibiting just as much aggression as will suit its purpose, and no more. A female Rough-toothed porpoise [a *Steno*] was kept in a tank alone with her calf, and frequently solicited stroking from her trainer. The calf occasionally situated itself between mother and trainer while the mother was being stroked. When the calf was approximately a month old, the trainer in this situation one day stroked the calf. The mother swung her tail from the water, reached up and out, and struck the trainer a sharp but not damaging blow across the shoulders, and then, with no further apparent fear or anger, continued to solicit stroking for herself. As if to say, "Here now—don't you dare touch my baby."[*]

VIPs were another hassle. Dignitaries coming through Sea Life Park were always handled personally if possible by Tap or me— often by me, since Tap traveled a great deal. In the midst of a busy day, conducting a group of dignitaries through the Park could be something I did almost unconsciously. I had the deplorable habit of answering all the usual questions, seeming to be listening and talking to the visitors, while my mind was working on how to get the spinners to spin higher or whether the maintenance men had noticed the rust on the Ocean Science Theater railings yet. Glancing through my journal, I can see that in October of 1965 I gave a personal tour of the Park to the president of the Philippines, his wife, Mr. and Mrs. Angier Biddle Duke, and six Secret Service men. I must have done so; I wrote it down; but I don't remember it at all.

It was certainly discourteous to be so abstracted, and I have been embarrassed more than once in the years since by being effusively greeted by some stranger, who thanks me again for the fascinating day or half-hour spent with me at the Park, and then feels unavoidably discomfited when it becomes apparent that I don't remember the day or the person at all.

Some VIPs I remember. One morning I got a message summoning me to the Galley for lunch to help Tap with a VIP group. I washed the fish scales off my hands, trotted up there, and found myself sitting through a long, chatty lunch with Thor Heyerdahl, the dashing author of *Kontiki,* on my left, and astronaut Scott Carpenter, equally dashing, on my right, both

[*] Karen Pryor, "Learning and Behavior in Whales and Porpoises," *Die Naturwissenschaften,* 60 (1973), 412–420.

of them being very attentive and gallant. I remember that, all right.

Henry Luce and Clare Boothe Luce, new residents of Hawaii, came to Sea Life Park one day. Tap and I (I at least full of curiosity) took them around. Henry looked like your average tycoon, to me: silent and dyspeptic. At numerous dinner parties over the ensuing years I don't recall his uttering a word, save once an exclamation of surprise when a pet bird of Clare's landed on his bald head. Clare looked exactly like an arctic falcon I once had the pleasure of meeting: pale, fragile, strong, with huge dark eyes fixed on the horizon, a fierce, ephemeral, solitary creature of great beauty. The Luces enjoyed the Park, and their visit was profitable for us. *Life* magazine did several stories on our projects over the years.

One time the visitor of the day was the Archbishop of Canterbury. I had to set secretaries to phoning around until they found someone who knew how to address an archbishop ("Your Grace").

Once I found myself with a genuine king as a guest, Leopold, former king of Belgium, and very nice he was, too, quite easy to talk to, though I had a hard time saying "Your Majesty" without giggling. While we were waiting for lunch at the Galley I absent-mindedly sat down on the steps, something quite forbidden, I suppose, in the presence of royalty. King Leopold glanced at me with surprise and immediately sat down on the floor— gracefully, but with an air of never having done it before in his life.

I took a governor of California through the Park in the pouring rain, and he got his trousers wet and was displeased. I took one of Lyndon Johnson's daughters around (I failed to record which one). She chewed gum and flirted with her Secret Service men. I let Art Linkletter swim with the spinners, and he thrashed and cheered, and scared them all. We did a TV special with Arthur Godfrey, and a number of his radio shows.

One day, when I was rushing home from the Park to the children, late as usual and vowing that nothing and nobody could hold me up any longer, I was stopped as I drove out of the parking lot by our public-relations man, frantically waving his arms. Now what?! Not a VIP in sight. I stepped out of the car, heartily annoyed, and down from the sky came a helicopter, which whack-whacked to a halt in front of me, opened its doors, and disgorged Perry Mason. Actor Raymond Burr must have wondered a little why half of his welcoming committee of two was leaning on the other half, laughing hysterically.

Directors and curators of other zoos and aquariums always got special treatment, so I was not surprised to find a message in my box one morning asking me to take care of a member of the board of directors of the London Zoo, who wished to have his picture taken with a porpoise.

I met him at the gate house. He was an enchanting old Englishman named Sir Malcolm. By the time we'd got through the Reef Tank I was so amused by Sir Malcolm's nonstop, nonsensical, witty chatter and his zest for everything that I took him to the Ocean Science Theater and let him swim with Wela, an unheard-of privilege for someone not on the staff. Our photographer took a picture of the man, with Wela smiling in his arms. Sir Malcolm used it on his Christmas card that year.

Wela adored Sir Malcolm, as far as I could tell, and so did I. His annual winter visits to Hawaii became something I looked forward to, since he always came and swam with Wela, often took me (and Tap, if he was available) to lunch or dinner, and brightened my day with some of the silliest conversation I have ever enjoyed. He had a penetrating mind, and would occasionally lay aside frivolity (not for too long) to pursue with avid interest some question of porpoise intelligence or behavior, and I enjoyed that, too.

Somehow it never seemed important to ask Malcolm what he did for a living. In fact he dressed so elegantly and took such long vacations that I assumed he did nothing for a living.

I believe I knew him for two or three years before I really understood that he was Sir Malcolm Sargeant, conductor of the London Philharmonic. There followed some illuminating and thrilling times of listening to and talking about music. My fondest recollection, though, is of the first time I persuaded Malcolm to go swimming with the spinners instead of with his old girlfriend, Wela.

As he stood waist deep in the shallows of Whaler's Cove, the little spinners came drifting over, sleek and dainty, gazing at him curiously with their soft dark eyes. Malcolm was a tactful, graceful man in his movements, and so the spinners were not afraid of him. In moments he had them all pressing around him, swimming into his arms and begging him to swim away with them. He looked up, suffused with delight, and remarked to me, "It's like finding out there really *are* fairies at the bottom of the garden!"

Interruptions; visitors, delightful or otherwise; maintenance problems; money problems; human problems. These of course are the headaches that beset anyone who has to be a boss. When I read *1000 Nights at the Opera*, Rudolph Bing's autobiography about managing the Metropolitan Opera, I found myself laughing sympathetically on every page. He was lucky! At least the Met wasn't half underwater.

One of the most nightmarish and yet funniest episodes of my tenure at the Park began as an innocent experiment. Ingrid and I became interested in token reinforcements, which means giving the subject, instead of food, some object which it can use in exchange for food later on. Chimpanzees had proven well able to accept this concept, and would work hard, pressing levers, for instance, for tokens which they could later put in a sort of slot machine (the "Chimpomat") to buy grapes. Money, of course, is a token reinforcement, and we people have grown accustomed to working for that. The concept of other sorts of tokens, combined with operant conditioning techniques, had just caught hold in the world of psychiatry, and tokens were being used in mental hospitals, in prisons, with disturbed children and juvenile delinquents, and in all sorts of ways.

We thought it would be fun to establish a token reinforcement system with a porpoise. Furthermore, it seemed like a worth-while thing to show at the Ocean Science Theater.

I scoured my favorite prop-hunting grounds for a usable token. It had to be something easy to see, that is, bright-colored, something that was waterproof and preferably floating, something small enough to handle but too big for the porpoise to swallow. When I had a new requirement like this, rather than trying to make something, I had learned to go to the waterfront stores in Honolulu: the ship's chandlers, the fishing supply stores, and the yachtsmen's and divers' shops.

Sure enough, I found just the thing: towline floats. Designed to keep a water skier's towline on the surface, they were brilliant fluorescent red plastic objects about 4 inches long and 2½ inches in diameter, light, durable, waterproof, and buoyant.

We chose to train Keiki in token reinforcement, since he was always so quick to learn new things and since he was then in-stalled at the Ocean Science Theater. First we taught him to pick up a float and bring it in and swap it for a fish. Then we taught him to put his float in a basket. When that behavior was shaped, we taught him to put two or three floats in a basket; then we dumped the basket, and Keiki brought the floats in one at a time and "bought" his fish. For Keiki's convenience, we put the basket upside down in the water. Instead of dropping the floats in, from the top, he swam underneath and released them, and they floated up and stuck in the upside-down basket. Buoyancy is a handy aspect of objects in water, a fact which is often forgotten or overlooked, we are so used to thinking terrestrially.

Once the behavior was well established, we put it in the show. We would ask Keiki to do something—jump over the trainer's arm, perhaps—and then reward him, not with a fish, but with a token, which he in turn put into his porpoise piggy bank, the basket. Then we'd cue him for another behavior, until he had earned four or five tokens. Then we dumped the basket, and Keiki retrieved his tokens one by one and went to the trainer and bought his fish.

It was amusing and provocative; we could imagine that in due course one could run a whole show without using fish at all until the animal was back in the holding tank, which would be dramatic and mysterious. The willingness of porpoises to work for tokens would be very useful, too, working with divers in the open sea. Divers are reluctant to swim about in sharky waters with a pocketful of dead fish on their person.

Keiki did not particularly enjoy having his reinforcement delayed. Perhaps it would have been wiser to bring another animal along with token reinforcements from the very beginning of training, so that it would be accepted as a matter of course. Keiki developed an unfortunate habit, when he got tired of tokens, of reinforcing himself by regurgitating three or four fish he'd had at some previous meal and eating them up again. It was an odd sight at best; if the fish had been down in his stomach long enough to get partially digested, it was a disgusting sight.

Worse things yet were in store for us. One day Keiki was returning a float to Ingrid. Whether it is true, as the trainer's assistant said, that Malia—who happened to be in the tank—bit Keiki in the tail, I don't know; but in any case he gave a start—and swallowed his token.

With his great regurgitating skill we hoped he would throw it up again. But he couldn't, though he tried. In a few hours we realized Keiki was in serious trouble. He looked and acted uncomfortable, and he wouldn't eat. What *were* we going to do? Darling Keiki, our pioneering famous Keiki, could hardly be allowed to die as an object lesson to Karen to choose bigger tokens next time!

Surgical removal seemed the only answer. However, at that time, surgery on a porpoise was almost unheard of. The problems did not lie in making an incision and causing it to heal, but in anesthetizing a porpoise.

Unlike all other mammals, in which breathing is a function of the central nervous system and carried on quite unconsciously, a porpoise breathes only on purpose. In order to take a breath, he must first swim up to the surface and get his blowhole into the air; so he has to think about it. Consequently, if you render a porpoise truly unconscious, he stops breathing. Which is fatal. Yet you can hardly hope to have him survive surgery if he is not anesthetized.

Doctors have devices called respirators which can breathe for a deeply unconscious human being. Human beings, however, turn over something like a quarter of the air in their lungs with each breath, whereas a porpoise exchanges almost all the air in his lungs on each blow. A human respirator would not really be up to the job.

On the day Keiki swallowed his float, there was only one person in the country currently involved in porpoise surgery: Sam Ridgeway, D.V.M., the Navy's vet at Point Mugu in California. Our vet, Al Takayama (and a very good vet too), got on the phone with Sam. Sam agreed that the likelihood of Keiki vomiting up the float was very small, and that surgery seemed like the answer. He agreed to get on the next Navy plane to Honolulu, to bring with him a porpoise respirator he had just assembled, and to attempt the surgery himself.

While we waited for Sam, we did what we could to get ready. The first job was to load Keiki on a stretcher, take him to the hospital, and X-ray him. Porpoises, like cows, have two stomachs, and we needed to see which stomach the float had lodged in. A friendly M.D., cardiac expert Dr. David DeHay, arranged this for us, and also offered to come out to Sea Life Park with a portable electrocardiograph machine and help Sam by keeping track of Keiki's heartbeat during the operation.

The hospital X-ray technicians were matter-of-fact about X-raying Keiki, and Keiki took it calmly; I don't know what those human patients may have thought who saw a stretcher wheeling by with a porpoise on it.

The X-rays showed that the float was in the first stomach, or rumen. We rigged up our best stretcher with automobile safety belts every foot of its length, so we could utterly immobilize Keiki when the time came, and we put Keiki by himself in a training facility tank, where he moped around with a bellyache.

Sam got in late the next afternoon, and on the following morn-

"The first job was to load Keiki on a stretcher, take him to the hospital, and X-ray him." Pat Quealy, near right, directs the task.

ing we made ready for the operation. Keiki had not had a morsel of food in two days, and could not wait much longer. The stretcher was set up on a heavy table in the training facility. The respirator was set up. Dr. DeHay arrived with the EKG equipment.

Sam stood by the side of the tank and looked from Keiki to the X-ray films and back to Keiki. "You know what," he finally said to Al Takayama, "look at the position of this float. I think there's just a *chance* that we might be able to reach in and pull it out through his mouth."

The float would be too slippery to grab with any kind of tongs; it would have to be a person's hand that went in there. "That's an awfully long way to reach," Al said. Of course it was worth a try.

Out came the tape measures, and on Sam's instructions the trainers dashed around to find out who in the Park had the longest reach combined with the thinnest wrist. That person turned out to be Tap Pryor. So Keiki was strapped onto the stretcher, Tap scrubbed up like a surgeon, and the great attempt began.

The operating room team included trainers (me, David Alices, Pat Quealy, Bob Ballard, and Randy Lewis), scientists (acoustician Bill Evans and Ken Norris), three doctors (the two vets, Sam and Al, and the cardiologist), and a few other assistants and spectators. Bill Evans made a tape of the subsequent events, and here is what it says:

BILL EVANS: 17 July 1965. 1450 hours. *[Background sound: laughter, and a porpoise whistling repeatedly.]*

NAVY VET SAM RIDGEWAY: What'll we do if he coughs it up before the operation?

TAP PRYOR: Make him swallow it again.

SAM: Your lights all ready, Doc?

CARDIOLOGIST DR. DE HAY *[preparing to check out the EKG machine which will monitor Keiki's heart]:* Would you turn it on so I can get a reading? *[Murmuring conversation.]*

SAM: Okay, now, let's loosen the straps and turn the animal on his stomach. *[Keiki had been on his side, for greater comfort, until the last minute.]*

TRAINER DAVID ALICES: Do you need the bags now?

SAM: Yes, I need the sandbags now, three on each side. Now, let's turn him over. *[Small bags of sand are tucked against the animal's flanks to further immobilize him.]*

AL TAKAYAMA: Put them on each side.

TRAINER PAT QUEALY: Move him forward—the stretcher's made like this so his flippers can hang down.

SAM: Okay, let's pull him a little bit forward. That's good. Put the sandbags right next to his body.

KEIKI: Groan!

TRAINER BOB BALLARD: Okay, Keiki, that's what you think.

KEN NORRIS *[encouragingly]:* Come on, Keiki. . . .

SAM: Now, let's put the straps on. No, wait a minute.

DE HAY: EKG . . . *[passing over the wires, with their rubber-faced*

Tap begins to reach in.

pickup devices, which lead to the EKG machine. Sam dries a few skin areas and tapes the leads to Keiki's body.]

SAM: Okay, you want to give me your left arm lead?

DE HAY: I can't . . . wait a minute. Everybody, get your *hands* off the animal—I can't get a reading. Okay. If you're going to use one lead more, any place will do.

EVANS: I'm getting a very good record of the blow rate *[i.e., Keiki's breathing].*

KEIKI: Sigh.

SAM: Okay, you guys got your sprayers ready? His flukes are getting hot. *[Another problem in porpoise surgery: the animal must be kept wet and cool the whole time.]* Let's get this belt tightened.

FRANK HARVEY, SAM'S ASSISTANT: Let's see what the EKG is.

DE HAY: Okay, here we go. Okay, recordings are good. Hey! *[alarmed.]* Looks like a—oh-oh. . . . Oh. Somebody touched him—looked like a two-to-one heart block. Okay, you can touch him now.

SAM *[lifts the speculum, a device which fits between Keiki's jaws and can be screwed open to force his jaws apart]:* Okay, you guys, when I tell you, watch him, and we'll screw those screws down here. Each of you hold one side like this. *[Two trainers help pry Keiki's jaws apart and put the speculum in.]* Okay, Tap, are you ready now?

TAP *[begins to put his bare arm down Keiki's throat. His wrist passes down the throat, but his elbow can't get between the two parts of the speculum]:* I'm having a hard time going through the clamp.

SAM: How about his throat?

TAP: No, not so bad on the throat, the clamp; I can't turn my arm.

AL: How about lubricating it?

SAM: Take your arm out.

KEIKI: Gurgle. *[Some mineral oil is located, Tap's arm is greased, and the speculum is widened as far as it will go, forcing poor Keiki's jaws open another inch. Bill Evans offers to count off the seconds during the procedure, so that Sam can tell how long things go on and when to give Keiki a rest. Tap begins to reach in again.]*

EVANS: Six seconds, twelve . . . eighteen . . . twenty-four . . .

TAP: How's the heart?

SAM: Do you feel it? *[the rumen, or first stomach]*

TAP: I can feel the edge of it.

SAM: You feel that you got the tips of your fingers in?

TAP: My fingers, I believe, are in the rumen, the tips of 'em.

EVANS: Fifty . . .

SAM: You want to give an EKG now?

EVANS: Fifty-six . . .

DE HAY *[cutting in]:* No activity. No cardiac activity registered. *[Shocked silence in the room.]* There she goes, there she starts again. . . .

SAM: Let's go. Get out. I'm not sure. *[Tap pulls his arm out and wipes it with a towel.]*

TAP *[anxious]:* I feel that I got the tips of my fingers in. I felt some fairly smooth and fairly rough places, but, uh. . . .

SAM: Yes, that's it, that's the rumen, where it gets rough.

DE HAY: Your heart rate is considerably slower than it was originally. Her rate has been cut in half. *[Diving animals such as seals and porpoises are now known to respond to inhibition of breathing by slowing the heart down, and while Tap's arm was down his throat,*

Keiki either would not or could not breathe. The doctors wait until the heart returns to normal, and Sam decides to try to give Tap more room by discarding the speculum and holding Keiki's jaws apart manually.]

SAM: Let's get two towels.

AL: You got a couple of sheets? Or towels?

DAVID: Towels, yuh, we got towels. *[It would probably be impossible to run an oceanarium without towels; towels are as vital as the fish freezer. The vets roll two towels into soft, thick ropes and lay them between Keiki's jaws. Four husky men pull the animal's jaws apart, two holding down on the ends of one towel, two pulling up on the ends of the other.]*

KEN NORRIS *[panting from his end of one towel]*: Hold tight, let's be careful, now.

TAP: Going in.

EVANS: Five . . . ten . . .

TAP: Okay. I got my fingers on it!

EVANS: Fifteen . . .

DE HAY: EKG running *no* cardiac activity! *[Shocked gasps from the trainers.]*

EVANS: Twenty . . .

SAM: No cardiac?

TAP: I've got it. I'm coming out with it. Okay, pull! *[He tries to pull his hand, with the float in it, back through Keiki's throat, but cannot. Al Takayama tries to slip his hand in alongside to help.]* You got it? Pull!

RANDY LEWIS: Keiki, open your *mouth!*

TAP: It's right there, Doc, can you get your hand in there?

SAM: Help him pull, you guys, grab his waist! *[The nearest man grabs Tap's waist, and the next man grabs his waist, and all three men pull frantically.]*

DE HAY: Cardiac activity resumed.

KEIKI: COUGH! *[The three men stumble backwards, Tap's arm flies up, and the slippery red float leaps from his hand and goes bouncing across the floor.]*

FLOAT: Plink, plink, plink.

ALL: *[cheers, screaming, clapping, laughter]*

RANDY: Is his heart going?

DE HAY: Heart is beating.

SAM: Stop touching him! [*Everyone is patting Keiki.*] Let's look at his heart.

DE HAY [*crossly*]: How many people have their hands on him *now?* . . . Okay, heart is back to normal pattern now.

KEN [*to Tap*]: You know you're in the oceanarium business now.

KEN NORRIS'S ASSISTANT, KEN BLOOM: You get the Golden Rumen award.

SAM: Keiki? How was that, boy?

TAP: He didn't even taste it.

SAM: Okay, let's throw him back in the tank and give him some chow. . . .

Three minutes later:

EVANS: The time is now 1538. The object came out at 1535. They have now released Keiki in the tank, and he's swimming around. . . .

SPECTATOR [*to Tap*]: I thought it wasn't going to come out. Are you a nervous wreck?

EVANS: Keiki is taking food; he's eating now.

Keiki was quite unharmed by his misadventures and went back to the show a couple of days later. We switched to round plywood disk tokens which were quite impossible to swallow. We made them of two colors, so that there could be two values of token, one worth two fish and one worth six fish. Sure enough, Keiki always fetched the six-fish tokens first.

Fishing down an animal's throat turned out to be a very useful technique. Animals in captivity are always swallowing indigestible objects: leaves, paper, things visitors throw in the tank. When we thought an animal had a problem of this kind—and the vet could often tell from changes in the blood—we strapped it down and cleaned it out, and thus saved or prolonged many an animal's life.

10. THE CREATIVE PORPOISE

Ingrid and I decided one day that the show at the Ocean Science Theater was getting a little too good, a little too slick, a little too polished. The animals knew the routine perfectly; the narrators, including myself, were slipping into rote narration; there were no mistakes. Consequently there were none of those interesting moments when no one, including the trainer, knew what would happen next, when the audience could see people struggling and thinking hard and could sense the animal as a real being and not just as a spectacle.

It was time for me to "shoot the show down," as Randy Lewis put it, by introducing something new and undeveloped. We decided to show audiences the first steps in training a porpoise: reinforcing some spontaneous action until the animal began repeating it on purpose, until it became conditioned.

We chose Malia, the *Steno,* for this demonstration. In the first show of the day, as Ingrid let Malia into the holding tank, I explained to the audience what we were going to do and then fell silent, to let them watch. Malia swam around for a while, waiting to be given a cue. After two or three minutes, she slapped her tail impatiently, and Ingrid reinforced that. Then Malia swam around again; nothing happened, she slapped her tail again in annoyance, and Ingrid reinforced it again. That of course was enough for Malia; she got the message and slapped, ate her fish, slapped, ate, slapped repeatedly. In less than three minutes she was motorboating around the tank pounding her tail on the water, and the audience burst into uproarious applause.

Very nice; very convincing. When the next show began, we again explained that we were going to show the audience how we catch new behavior, and we let Malia into the tank. She swam around for a bit and, getting no cues, began to slap her tail. Ingrid and I exchanged glances across the tank and shook our heads. We realized simultaneously that we had already conditioned this behavior. Therefore we could not reinforce it now, because it was no longer an example of unconditioned behavior. We would have to wait for Malia to show us something else.

Malia slapped her tail for a while, and then, getting mad when this brought no results, she breached, throwing herself into the air and coming down sidewise to slap the water with her body. Ingrid reinforced that, and Malia immediately began breaching repeatedly, tail-slapping in between at first. When the tail slaps disappeared and she was just breaching, the new audience was as pleased as the first audience had been. Something real had happened, and they understood it.

So we went on, for a couple of days, reinforcing head slaps, swimming upside down, rising out of the water, porpoising, and once in a while picking up something that had been reinforced earlier and had then not been seen for several shows, such as the tail slap again. By the third day, however, we ran into a new problem: in fourteen shows, even when a behavior was occasionally used over again, we had picked up and conditioned almost every clear-cut action Malia normally engaged in. We were running out of things to choose. We cheated a little by shaping one or two behaviors, by reinforcing a nose raised in the air until we had shaped a backwards tail walk, for example. Still, it was hard to find something new each time, and we had one or two rather difficult shows in which Malia went on and on crashing around the tank offering one behavior after another, all well conditioned, and we could find nothing new to reinforce.

Malia solved the problem. On the last show of the third day, we let her out of the holding tank, and she swam around waiting for a cue. When she got no cues, instead of launching herself into a series of repetitions of old behavior, she suddenly got up a good head of steam, rolled over on her back, stuck her tail in the air, and coasted about 15 feet with her tail out: "Look, Ma, no hands!" It was a ridiculous sight. Ingrid, I, the training assistant, and six hundred people from Indiana roared with laughter. Ingrid reinforced the behavior, and Malia repeated it a dozen times, each time coasting farther and looking funnier.

I told Gregory about this that evening, and he got very excited and wanted to see for himself. The next morning he was at Ocean Science for the first show. This time Malia began with her tail-out coasting; when it didn't work, she tried a few other familiar things, and then precipitously threw herself into the air backwards and made a beautiful arching leap *upside down*, reentering the water with hardly a splash. Gregory was delighted, Ingrid was delighted, and so was I. Malia had again done what I suspected she might: invented a novel behavior.

She went on, show after show, producing new and astonishing responses. She spun in the air like a spinner. She swam upside down, drawing lines in the film of silt on the tank floor with her dorsal fin. She revolved on her long axis underwater like a corkscrew. She thought of things to do spontaneously that we could never have imagined, and that we would have found very difficult to arrive at by shaping.

Gregory was fascinated. Malia seemed to have learned the criterion: "Only things which have not been previously reinforced are reinforceable." She was deliberately coming up with something new, not in every session, but more often than not. Sometimes she was very excited when she saw us in the mornings. Ingrid and I had the unscientific feeling that she sat in her holding tank all night thinking up stuff and rushed into the first show with an air of: "Wait till you see *this* one!"

Malia "precipitously threw herself into the air backwards and made a beautiful arching leap *upside down. . . .*"

Gregory felt that this was an example of higher-order learning, of combining facts to learn a principle; he called it deutero-learning. He urged me to repeat the experiment with another animal, to record the events so that the moment of understanding could be pinpointed, and to publish the results as a scientific paper.

Bill McLean and the Office of Naval Research showed an interest in this project, dignified as it was by Gregory's interest and approval; so Ingrid and I began to figure out how to do it. We knew we could take another porpoise, preferably another *Steno,* and put it through the same experiences and probably come up with the same results. The question was how to record what was happening.

A complete sound film of every training session would be ideal, but there were two drawbacks. First, it was far, far too expensive. Second, a movie camera holds only 400 feet of film, at best, enough for twelve minutes. Either we would have to interrupt the sessions to suit the photographer or the photographer would inevitably be reloading his camera whenever something really interesting took place.

We decided to run the experiment at the Ocean Science Theater, because there we could watch both below and above water at once. We thought of using videotape, which is cheaper and much longer-running than film, but we were told that the light was not bright enough at the Ocean Science Theater. And the events were too numerous and complicated to use an event recorder.

Taped verbal descriptions seemed to be the practical choice. However, we would have to have more than one observer, since a single observer could not always see both above and below the water at once. Ingrid and I had missed some of Malia's good ideas because we had both been watching from above the surface.

We decided to use three people: the trainer, a narrator-observer above the water, and another narrator-observer out in the audience space, watching through the glass. Our electronics termite confirmed that he could supply us with microphones and record all three voices on a single tape. Furthermore, he would give us earphones so we could hear each other and chat back and forth over our mikes instead of having to yell across the tank or communicate, as Ingrid and I were in the habit of doing, by body language.

The termite worked out what such a setup would cost. Not too much. Also, since the Navy would be paying cash money for the experiment, I could afford to hire some skilled people to act as observers. Dr. Leonard Diamond, at the University of Hawaii, put me in touch with two of his graduate students in psychology, Dick Haag and Joe O'Reilly, who were willing to do the job. In addition to acting as observers, they would analyze the tapes and perform any statistical or other specialized work which might be needed for publication of our results.

Malia, of course, was not a suitable subject. She was sophisticated in the matter now; and what we wanted to pin down was the process of arriving at that sophistication. We chose another *Steno*, Hou, who had been living at the training facility. We moved Hou to the Ocean Science Theater to share Malia's holding tank and to be our experimental subject.

We worked out a schedule that suited all of us and started to work, usually running two or three short training sessions with Hou in the mornings before Sea Life Park opened to the public. It might have been fun, of course, to do the experiment in front of the public, but the business of setting up the tape recorder, keeping records, and so on was so time-consuming that the work really did not lend itself to show use.

Although we could not afford to film all of every session, the Navy very much wanted to make a short documentary film of the experiment, so we had a small allotment in the budget for a cameraman. We tried to get a little movie footage of each re-inforced behavior, even if it meant having an extra training session, just for the photographer, in which some previously chosen response would be reinforced again. Whether these review sessions would be bad or good for Hou's learning processes, we had no way of telling. Malia, however, had been exposed to occasional

Hou was "easily discouraged, and . . . she developed a pattern of circling, porpoising, circling, porpoising, over and over again. . . ."

review sessions, and it had not diverted her from arriving at the concept of newness, so we trusted it wouldn't harm Hou.

Hou was a very different individual from Malia. She was much more easily discouraged, and in the first few sessions she developed a pattern of circling, porpoising, circling, porpoising, over and over again, offering no other behaviors, hung up in a superstitious pattern that could go on for many long minutes. We found we had to interrupt this pattern in various ways to get the animal working again. We tried shaping a few behaviors: beaching, or coming partway out of the water onto the cement platform beside the tank; a tail wave; swimming on the tank floor. Sometimes we interrupted Hou's endless circling and porpoising by giving her a couple of fish "for nothing," without the whistle, reinforcing no particular action, but lifting her spirits and inspiring her to try her luck again. Hou was so placid in disposition that we never saw any of the anger signals, such as tail slaps and breaching, which had been Malia's first response to frustration. Her available repertoire of frequently occurring actions was slim indeed.

The first fourteen sessions followed the same pattern, as revealed in the following excerpt from a scientific article:

Hou began each session with the behavior that had been reinforced in the previous session. Occasionally this behavior was chosen for reinforcement when the trainer felt it had not been strongly established in the previous session. If the first response was not reinforced, Hou ran through its [sic] repertoire of responses reinforced in previous sessions: breaching, porpoising, beaching, and swimming upsidedown. If no reinforcement was forthcoming, it took up the rigid pattern of porpoising, inverting, circling.[*]

In session 13 Hou did come up with something a little different, a pattern of swimming upside down, then right side up, then

[*] Karen Pryor, Richard Haag, and Joseph O'Reilly, "The Creative Porpoise: Training for Novel Behavior," *Journal of the Experimental Analysis of Behavior,* 12 (1969), 653–661. (I had to call Hou "it," not "she," in the final paper, since the journal we published in believes in saving "he" and "she" for human beings.)

upside down again, like Malia's corkscrew. She remembered this, after a weekend, and the trainers shaped it, extending it to five complete revolutions; but in session 14 nothing new happened, and Hou went back to her circling.

The next morning, as the experimenters set up their equipment, Hou was unusually active in the holding tank. It slapped its tail twice, and this was so unusual that the trainer reinforced the response in the holding tank. When session 15 began, Hou emitted the response reinforced in the previous session, of swimming near the bottom, and then the response previous to that, of the corkscrew, and then fell into the habitual circling and porpoising, with however the addition of a tailslap on re-entering the water. This slap was reinforced and the animal then combined slapping with breaching, and then began slapping disassociated from jumping; for the first time it emitted responses in all parts of the tank, rather than right in front of the trainer. The ten-minute session ended when 17 tailslaps had been reinforced, and other nonreinforced responses had dropped out.

Session 16 began after a ten-minute break. Hou became extremely active when the trainer appeared and immediately began offering twisting breaches, landing on its belly and its back. It also began somersaulting on its long axis in mid-air. The trainer began reinforcing the last, a "flip," common in the genus *Stenella* but not normally seen in *Steno,* and Hou became very active, swimming in figure eights [unprecedented] and leaping repeatedly. The flip occurred 44 times, intermingled with some of the previously reinforced responses and with three other responses that had not been seen before: an upsidedown tailslap, a sideswipe with the tail, and an aerial spin on the short axis of the body.*

Well, Hou got the picture. And when she finally caught on to what was happening, when she began to understand that what she had to do to get us to blow the whistle was to do something *new,* she really went wild. Although we were reinforcing only the flip, she offered other new responses too, and she repeated them all. She had been in the habit of offering two or three types of responses per session. Now in one session she offered us eight types of responses, four of which were completely new, and two

* *Ibid.*

of which, the flip and the spin, were elaborate and perfectly performed from the beginning. She gave 192 responses in that session, nearly nine per minute, compared to a previous rate of three or four per minute, and instead of slowing down, at the end of the session she went faster and faster, until she was in such a wild flurry of swipes, leaps, splashes, tail slaps, and careening around that she was outstripping our ability to describe what was going on, even with three of us talking at once. Ingrid stopped the session with a big jackpot of about thirty fish at once.

From then on, Hou was a changed animal. She showed us a lot of anger signals. She seldom went back to her stereotyped pattern of porpoising and circling. She came up with novelty after novelty, sinking head downwards, spitting water at the trainer, jumping upside down. We went back to old stuff for some filming sessions, but that didn't confuse her. By the thirtieth session she had offered a new behavior in six out of seven sessions consecutively, had calmed down to the point of giving us the reinforced response and *only* the reinforced response, once she heard the whistle, and had started two sessions with a novel response and no errors at all.

Well, it worked. But what was it? And how to tell the story? Gregory said it was an example of higher-order learning or deutero-learning. Dick and Joe went back to school and wrote a paper for their course with Dr. Diamond, describing what had happened and relating it to the scientific literature on higher orders of learning in animals. They set out to prove "scientifically" that Hou's responses were novel, and not just things *Stenos* do all the time, by making flashcards with drawings of each behavior and mailing them to all Sea Life Park trainers past or present who had ever worked with *Stenos* (no other oceanarium had ever had *Stenos*, so it had to be our people.) The trainers were asked to rank each behavior according to how often they had seen it. Some, such as the tail slap, were judged to be common occurrences, but no one had ever seen a *Steno* flip or spin or jump upside down or spontaneously spit water at the trainer. Dick and Joe could thus make pretty flute music for our reports about the statistical unlikelihood of these things occurring by accident.

Harry Harlow, the distinguished psychologist who is perhaps best known for his work with surrogate monkey mothers, visited Sea Life Park. I chatted with him about this experiment, and he thought the American Psychology Association might be willing to publish it in one of their journals. Okay!

Now it had to be written up. The typed manuscript of our taped voices ran to a hundred pages or more. Some clear-cut way had

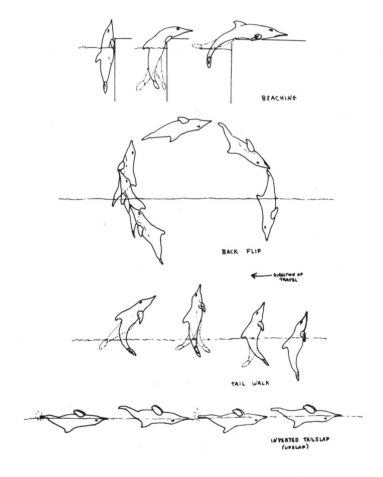

BEACHING

BACK FLIP

DIRECTION OF TRAVEL

TAIL WALK

INVERTED TAILSLAP
(UPSLAP)

Four of Dick and Joe's "flashcards" for Hou's behaviors during the "creative porpoise" experiment. *Oceanic Institute photo*

to be developed to show what had happened in each training session without resorting to space-consuming verbiage.

The standard method which operant conditioners use to record responses is a sort of graph called a cumulative record. Time intervals are marked out on the horizontal line, and the response count on the vertical line, and each response is a point on the graph, making a continuous slanting line showing how often and how fast the animal responded. That's all very well if you are dealing with a single response, lever pressing or key pecking, but how do you graph a session in which the animal does all kinds of different things all at once?

I racked my brains, pored over psychology books at the library, and asked every psychologist I knew to tell me the standard way for graphing sessions in which multiple response types were used. There seemed to be no standard way. Simplicity is vital in laboratory experiments, and no rat behaviorist would set up an experiment in which things got as complicated as in our training sessions. I had naïvely landed myself in the same situation as poor Hou; if I didn't come up with something new, no publication would result!

From my journal, May 17, 1966

Sitting in a San Francisco hotel. I think I know how to record Hou's sessions. Sit down with the tape transcript, *and* the tape, and a clock. Run the tape and mark the transcript at quarter-minute intervals. Underline each reinforced behavior. Then make a big graph, and take one behavior at a time and go through the written transcript and blip the graph in the appropriate quarter-minute section each time that response occurred. Using a different color for each response, go back to the beginning and make another set of blips—another line—on the same graph for each different response.

Joe and Dick understood and undertook this tedious task. They came up with thirty-two stunning graphs, each one showing every response and all the behaviors in a given training session. While they were at it, they cleaned up another loose end, the weakness implicit in judging a behavior by subjective observation. They ran a statistical examination of the three independent

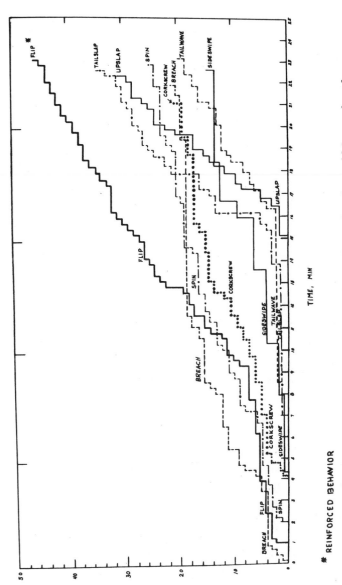

✳ REINFORCED BEHAVIOR

Our graph of the "Aha!" session in which Hou finally caught on that she could be reinforced only for new behavior. Each line represents one kind of behavior, each upward jig an individual response. Hou did eight kinds of things at once, four of which were brand new. *Oceanic Institute photo*

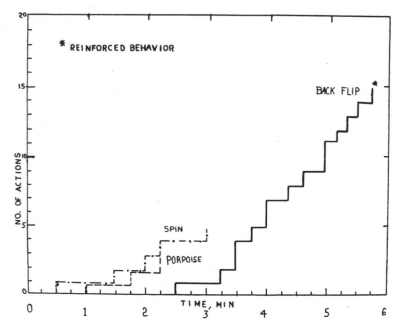

Session 31, a nice clean session. Hou offered a few spins and leaps, then presented a new invention which we called a backflip. She dropped the other behaviors at once when the backflip was reinforced.

observers' accounts of each behavior to see if we all agreed that we were seeing the same thing.

Always when something new occurred, the transcript indicated that we all saw it, that we all agreed that it was new, and that later, faced with Joe and Dick's little flashcards of each behavior, we all put the same name to it. They even went so far as to run the movies we took of each response a frame at a time, to compare them for accuracy to their flashcard cartoons of the actions. This laborious procedure provided scientifically palatable evidence that we were not just making the whole thing up, nor were we substituting opinion for fact.

With the graphs completed, we published a Navy report on the experiment, using Gregory's term, "Deutero-Learning in a Rough-toothed Dolphin" (the Navy prefers to call them all dolphins) and we helped a Navy film team make a short documentary on the subject. They made a dandy film, with the crucial graphs in glorious Technicolor, and a downright poetic ending speculating about the possibilities of man-porpoise interaction in which the porpoise was an equal, an initiator, not just an obedient subject, while the camera followed one of our male trainers romping with Hou in the water, both of them playing with joyful equality.

Still, neither our Navy report nor the Navy film seemed to me to state what I thought was interesting in the experiment. What, after all, was the point of this remarkable event? Yes, the animal learned a principle, instead of a single new response; but that happened every time an animal came to understand the concept of sound cues in general, as opposed to this known sound cue for that known behavior. Yes, the experiment suggested that one might think about getting more from a porpoise than simple conditioned behaviors. The change in Hou's "personality," from a docile, inactive animal to an active, observant animal full of initiative was a permanent change. (It was a useful change, too, and I was not surprised to learn that Navy trainers developed a technique, based on this experiment, of both refreshing an animal and extending its awareness and sophistication by having "play-times" between or after more stringent training sessions, in which all kinds of things could be reinforced, and from which, some-times, came new and useful responses.)

But what did *I* think about it? I mulled it over for about a year and then turned a little toolshed in the training facility into a writing room for myself. I pinned Dick and Joe's graphs up on the walls, in sequence, and stared at them for some days, writing thoughts and tearing them up. Somebody on our staff stole the electric typewriter out of my toolshed/office, and I sat without one and thought for a week, while the insurance people came up with funds for a new typewriter and management got me a lock for the door.

My thoughts kept turning to something my father had once seen. He had, in his backyard, a bird feeder which was designed to be inaccessible to squirrels. It hung from a branch by a string too thin for a squirrel to climb down, and it had a tippy conical roof which would tilt and dump the squirrel to the ground below if it should try to jump from the branch down to the feeder. One day my father watched a squirrel come out on the branch, look the feeder over, jump to the roof, and get tilted off to fall 6 or 8 feet to the ground. Again the squirrel tried it, and fell, and then again. On the fourth try he sat on the branch and looked at the feeder for a long time, and then leaned over and bit neatly through the string, dropping the whole apparatus to the ground, whereupon he ran down and helped himself to bird seed.

Originality. Rare, but real, in animals. Almost never observable in the laboratory situation. But here, with Malia and Hou, we had provoked originality, so that you could produce it at will, over and over again. What interested *me* was that the experiment showed a way to train for creativity.

At last I could write it up. It took months. My first draft was returned by the editors of the appropriate publication, *The Journal for Experimental Analysis of Behavior*, with ten pages of single-spaced criticisms and suggested corrections. Joe and Dick were appalled and feared we would never get the paper published. I, however, was so buoyed up by the general good sense of the critiques and by one commentator's kindly words, urging publication of "this elegant natural science account" that I went joyfully to work cleaning up the ambiguities and anthropomorphisms and other details the editors wished to have corrected. The paper was published, and caused a stir. It was excerpted, reprinted, or abridged in several other magazines. It was also anthologized in two textbooks, including one, to my private satisfaction, on experimental design (those blessed graphs).*

The work did *not*, in my opinion, go to show how smart porpoises are. Given the training, many, many species of animals show the same kind of development. The following summer, we had a go at using the same procedure, not with porpoises, but with pigeons. I coerced some of our summer students into build-

* Homer H. Johnson and Robert L. Solso, *Experimental Design in Psychology: A Case Approach*, Harper & Row, N.Y., N.Y., 1971.

ing a sort of Skinner Box and reinforcing pigeons for a different behavior every day. To quote from the final version of my research paper on the Hou experiment: "If a different, normally occurring action in a pigeon is reinforced each day for a series of days, until the normal repertoire (turning, pecking, flapping wings, etc.) is exhausted, the pigeon may come to emit novel responses difficult to produce even by shaping."

I'll say. Like lying on its back. Or standing with both feet on one wing. Or flying up into the air two inches and staying there.

The applications of this experiment—to schoolchildren, for instance—remain to be explored. Still to be investigated, too, is the interesting question of what makes one animal more creative than another. "Malia's novel responses, judged *in toto,* are more spectacular and 'imaginative' than Hou's." We're used to this differentiation in people; we call it imagination. Or creativity. Or talent. It interested me that it could show up so clearly in animals.

Another result for me was that my admiration for other researchers was most powerfully reinforced. The idea of this experiment and the execution of it were simple. We observed an interesting event, by serendipity. We had no doubts that we could re-create it, we did so, and the actual experiment was over in a couple of weeks. The conversion of our remarks into honest documentation which would stand close inspection was a much bigger job; it took Dick and Joe hundreds of hours. The interpretation of that documentation to arrive at the nuggets of truth therein took, literally, years, and seemed to me to be the hardest single task I'd ever undertaken. I think now with considerable awe of people like Ken Norris and Bill Schevill and Fred Skinner and Konrad Lorenz, chasing new ideas through project after project and publishing one sound paper after another all their lives.

Although the experiment was not about intelligence, per se, it did make me think about what intelligence is.

We Western humans love to put things in linear order. People were always asking Ingrid and me, "Is the porpoise smarter than a dog? As smart as a person? A chimpanzee?" People are always saying, "Cats are dumb." "Horses are stupid." "Pigs are smarter than goats." But what does that mean? Was Malia "smarter" than Hou? Is it intelligent to be "imaginative," or is "imaginative" something different? Because the circumstance produced "creative" animals, it made them look very "smart." How, then, do you explain those creative pigeons? Surely a pigeon is not "intelligent"?

Horses are supposed to be dumb. They rarely go in for problem solving, like that original squirrel, and yet I have seen a horse study a gate latch and then open the gate correctly on the first try. Horses, furthermore, have an incredible capacity for remembering. A highly schooled horse, such as a good cowpony or one of the famous Lippizaners of Vienna, knows literally hundreds of conditioned stimuli, singly and in combinations, and can use his learned behaviors to communicate his own ideas to his trainer, so that rider and animal seem to "read each other's minds," a sophistication resulting from extensive training. That is a kind of "deutero-learning" in itself. Are horses, then, stupid? Or do we ordinarily fail to press them to the level of showing "intelligence"? And is not that equine ability to retain vast quantities of firmly learned bits of information exactly what our school systems reward with "A" grades?

Cats are very rigid animals; they do things according to nature's program, which for them is very clear-cut. They are not given to problem solving. Yet cats are sharper than any animal I know, including porpoises, at learning by observation: at, for example, watching another cat jump through a hoop for a bit of food, and then doing likewise. The expression "copycat" is no accident. And mimicry, according to Konrad, is a sophisticated process.

It began to seem to me that "intelligence" is made up of a lot of different things: the ability to solve problems; the ability to learn and retain; the ability to observe; the willingness to be variable, a natural plasticity of behavior which is low in cats and high in otters and Gregory Bateson; beyond that, the presence or absence of courage, or persistence. These abilities or tendencies are meted out to different species and different individuals in different spoonfuls. There are individuals in any species that star in one or another aspect of intelligence, like my father's squirrel. How smart is a porpoise? I think, somehow, it's the wrong question.

Never mind. You still want to know. Well, if one must have a linear order, I favor the answer given by A. F. McBride and D. O. Hebb about thirty years ago, long before Lilly and Flipper and the porpoise mystique that captured the public fancy: "The porpoise in intelligence is between the dog and the chimpanzee, and nearer to the chimpanzee." When one thinks of Washoe and her brethren, that's quite a compliment.

There is a curious epilogue to the story of Malia and Hou. Both animals stayed in Ocean Science Theater from then on. They were both very active and imaginative. In fact they turned into big nuisances. They opened gates and let each other out all the time. Hou learned to jump the tank partitions. Malia developed an inconvenient habit of leaving the water and sliding around on the cement, rapping the trainers on their ankles to get attention. We had to put the behavior on cue to stop her from choosing to be terrestrial during the show.

In the show, each animal had her own repertoire of behaviors, and they performed separately, although they could watch each other through the gates. Malia did a training demonstration, showing off, on sound cues, several of the behaviors she herself had invented: the upside-down jump, the corkscrew, the "Look, Ma, no hands!" business of coasting with her tail in the air. She also jumped through a hoop 12 feet in the air. Hou wore blindfolds and evaded obstacles and retrieved three sinking rings on her rostrum, in a sonar demonstration. The training of the two animals did not overlap, except that Malia had been conditioned to accept blindfolds. She had never, however, been asked to do anything with them on.

Hou, being young, continued to grow, until she was almost as big as Malia. One day, Ingrid was training and I was narrating, and we ran into trouble from the beginning of the show. When

Malia's gate was opened, the animal came out and did every-thing she was asked to do—the back jump, the corkscrew, and the coasting with tail out—but in the wrong sequence, and with great agitation.

Something was wrong. Was the cue machine not working? When we got to the high hoop jump, she leaped toward it, in a frantic and disorganized way, but fell far short of the desired 12 feet. Usually, this would have called for firm measures: time outs, and insistence from the trainer. Ingrid, whose sensitivity for the animals is quite remarkable, decided to make a conces-sion and lower the hoop down to about 6 feet above the water, whereupon the animal leaped through it, without waiting for the signal.

What was going on? The animal was so nervous that we were both glad when her part of the show was over and we could put her back and open Hou's gate.

The second porpoise rushed out with an air of excitement. Ingrid had considerable difficulty getting her to accept the blindfolds. Twice they fell off, and the animal retrieved them from the tank floor. Finally the blindfolds were in place. She negotiated the maze of pipes we lowered in the tank by sonar and retrieved rings by sonar, but only one ring at a time, instead of the usual three. Again this animal seemed extremely nervous and excitable; one had the alarming sensation, as a trainer, that things were about to go completely to pieces. However, while everything was a little distorted, different from the usual pattern, we got through the show safely. I discussed the two animals' unusual nervousness with the audience over the mike, confessing myself at a loss to explain why they were upset and acting "funny," why Malia got her sound cues mixed up and Hou bucked the blindfolding. The show ended. Ingrid put the last animal back in the holding tank and then looked at me in utter astonishment. "Do you know what happened?"

"No."

"We got the animals mixed up. Someone put Malia in Hou's

holding tank and Hou in Malia's holding tank. They look so much alike now, I just never thought of that."

Hou had done Malia's part of the show, getting the cues confused but offering the behaviors so well that we didn't realize she didn't "know" them, and even managing the hoop jump, which normally takes weeks to train. Malia had done all Hou's blindfold stunts correctly, on the first try, nervously, but again well enough so that we thought it was Hou. I stopped the departing audience and told them what they had just seen; I'm not sure how many understood or believed it. I still hardly believe it myself.

11. THE DOMESTIC PORPOISE

Our open-ocean experiments filled us all with the profound conviction that porpoises could and would work for man in their natural environment, like a domestic animal. Never mind if Kai and Pono escaped, and Haina and Nuha were too chicken to go 10 feet beyond their accustomed terrain; Keiki had been very reliable, and if one could work at all, at sea, with the more difficult species, one could probably do wonders with good old *Tursiops*, the bottlenose.

One can theorize that every time man has moved into a new and alien environment, he has picked up at least one animal that lived in that environment, domesticated it, and put it to work doing things that man himself could not do in hostile terrain. The camel, for example, makes it possible for man to live in the desert; the sled dog makes it possible for man to live in the Arctic.

It has been thousands of years since any new animal has been domesticated: every working animal member of the human household, from the falcon to the yak, has been sharing man's life since before modern civilization began. But it has also been thousands of years since man had any new environments to move into. Now we were moving into the sea. Cousteau pioneered living on the sea floor; divers were working, building, mining, harvesting, underwater. What could be more reasonable than to take a creature who lives in this alien world already and bend him to our use? It almost seemed as if the porpoises, at home in the oceans long, long before man first stood upright, were hanging around waiting to be invited onto the human gravy train.

A porpoise can travel underwater infinitely more easily than we. With his sonar he can see where we cannot; with his acute hearing, find distant goals and targets where humans are lost and helpless. Drop something overboard? Send the porpoise. Lose something on the sea floor? A ship or a downed plane? Hunt for it with trained porpoises. Need to get fish into a net? Drive them with porpoise sheep dogs. Worried about sharks? Set up a porpoise-manned early warning system. Mislay a diver? Let the porpoise find him, like a seagoing St. Bernard. Porpoises might be able to guard a harbor, tow a tired swimmer, take photographs underwater, survey hostile coastlines. The speculations were endless, and exciting; and we all felt sure that if we put an animal into a domestic, working situation at sea, as a helper to man, the experience would suggest other possibilities that we couldn't even imagine. It was time to give it a try.

We began training a porpoise to be a domestic animal with Keiki in the Ocean Science Theater. The first task for which he seemed well suited was carrying tools and messages between a diver and the surface. When you're working on the bottom and need something you left in the boat, it's a nuisance to have to swim back for it; the porpoise could be a help there. When you're waiting in the boat, and you want your divers to move to another work area or come up for lunch or something, you have no way to tell them so, except by sending another man down. Again, the porpoise could replace the man.

We began by asking Keiki to carry small objects in his mouth— a flashlight, a monkey wrench—from one trainer to another across the surface of the tank. We soon found out that porpoises, like people, don't enjoy the feeling of a metal object against their teeth, and that therefore Keiki tended to drop metal tools.

This was easy to get round, not by clamping down on the discipline, but by putting a rope loop on the metal tools or by dropping metal objects into a net bag and letting him hold the bag.

When Keiki understood fetching and carrying, we put a scuba diver into the tank during the show, with a piece of underwater oil-drilling apparatus that he was supposed to be repairing. I wrote a narration entirely about the diver, and the problems and conveniences of working underwater, and the futuristic world of inner space. We never even mentioned the porpoise. It just slowly dawned on the audience that the diver, in the most casual way, was using the animal. The diver would whip out a plastic memo pad, write on it (you can write underwater with an ordinary child's crayon), rap on his air tank, hold the message over his shoulder without even looking, and the porpoise would zoom by, snatch the message, swim away to the trainer, hand over the message, pick up the requested tools, and drop them into the diver's hands. In addition to rapping on his air tank, the diver could call the porpoise with a cricket, one of those dime-store noisemakers kids have on Halloween. He could ask the porpoise to give him a hand by pulling on a line; he could of course send tools and equipment he was through with back to the surface; and after some training we managed to get Keiki to put his nose against a push-pad at the base of the diver's airtanks and propel the diver through the water by porpoise power.

It was an amusing show, and it was fun to hear the audience begin to buzz and rustle and murmur as people, listening to the narration going blithely on about saturation diving and buoyancy and water resistance, slowly realized for themselves what the porpoise was doing. Meanwhile we trainers were dying to have a chance to try the business at sea.

After our experiences with Pono and Kai, Ken Norris and I decided that any porpoise we released at sea should be tagged in some permanent way, so that if the animal took off and returned to a wild school, it could be recognized if it were ever spotted again. Scientists had devised various kinds of tags for whales and porpoises: plastic streamers that hook into the animal's flesh with a little barb, for example. None of these last very long, and none of them is comfortable for the animal.

In casual conversation with a State Fish and Game biologist one day, I found out that he was busy that summer tagging wild deer with a two-piece plastic tag that fitted through a hole punched in the animal's ear. The tags were virtually indestructible, bright-colored, and had a big, legible number on both sides. It seemed to me that we could put such a tag on a porpoise's dorsal fin, which at its trailing edge is no thicker than a deer's ear. The fin is relatively insensitive, too. Punching the hole might hurt for a moment, but it would be about like having your ears pierced for earrings—not too uncomfortable. Also the dorsal fin is the piece of the animal's anatomy that shows most above water. We ordered up some of the deer tags and planned to have a go with good old Keiki.

The Oceanic Institute was scheduled to start operating a two-man underwater chamber just offshore. That was going to be Keiki's chance to show off his stuff as a diver's assistant in the open sea. All at once, they seemed to be ready ahead of schedule, taking us porpoise types by surprise. Tap came home for dinner one night and grabbed up his diving gear and went out, full of excitement, to spend the night in the chamber (I wrote in my journal, "If there's one thing a normal woman disapproves of, it's Adventure!"). The next morning we pulled Keiki out of Ocean Science Theater, took him up to the training facility on a stretcher, punched a hole in his dorsal fin, and affixed a bright yellow tag.

We put Keiki in a tank so we could see if the tag swiveled easily as he swam. The tagging worked fine, and looked sort of cute. Bleeding was minimal, and Keiki didn't seem to be in any pain from the tag, although he certainly knew it was there. As soon as I stepped up and put a hand in the water to pat him, he swam over and laid his dorsal fin in my hand: "Karen, take a look, there seems to be something stuck to my dorsal fin!" All I could do, of course, was touch the tag, to show him I was aware of the problem, and then pat him sympathetically.

I guess he understood, because he seemed to ignore the tag from then on and never asked to have it taken off again.

We popped Keiki on a stretcher, took him down to the water, put him into a small boat, and drove out to the chamber site, where Kai's small cage was waiting alongside the barge which pumped air to the chamber. Pat Quealy got into a wet suit and scuba gear and dove in to be the trainer on the bottom. I stationed myself in a small boat to be the trainer at the surface. I was worried about Keiki's comfort in the small cage; he was quite a bit bigger than Kai; but he swirled around and around like an eel, maneuvering with no trouble.

We opened the gate and spent five or ten minutes reinforcing Keiki for going in and out of the cage. We'd never trained him with that particular cage, but we anticipated no problems, and had none.

Then Pat and Keiki and I went to work, sending messages and tools up and down, from boat to chamber, from chamber to boat, from diver to diver. Keiki was elated, full of porpoise joy; he leaped and bounded and dashed around us, like a happy dog being taken for a walk in the woods.

There were a number of divers in the water, including two cameramen who interested Keiki very much. He liked to swim over and look into the lenses of the cameras, particularly the movie camera, which made a whirring noise. Pat distributed a few smelt to each diver and to the men in the chamber—because of course when a porpoise brings you a message or a tool, you must tip the porter. We found that we could write a message for a specific diver, and Keiki would take it from person to person until he found the one who was willing to swap it for a fish. We also found that Keiki spontaneously obeyed a pointing finger. Pat could send him over to the chamber or up to me in the boat by pointing in the right direction. This was interesting, because it involved a concept animals usually don't grasp right away: "Go *away* from the pointing hand." It takes ages to train a dog to understand a point as a directional command.

It really was handy having Keiki along. Once, the men on the

"We also found that Keiki spontaneously obeyed a pointing finger." Near a large anchor, trainer Pat Quealy sends a tool to another diver via the porpoise. *Oceanic Institute photo*

barge wanted to be sure that the movie photographer got some particular shot underwater, and we sent the instructions via the porpoise. Once my sunglasses fell into the water as I bent over to give Keiki a tool. "Oh, Keiki, my sunglasses!" I exclaimed, without thinking, and he rolled under, caught them before they hit the bottom, and then surfaced and put them politely in my hand.

After Keiki had worked for a couple of hours and the fish supply was getting low (and consequently Keiki had to be getting full), we put him back in the cage. We were delighted with him; he'd done even better than we had hoped. The small boat came out and got Keiki, on the stretcher. We took him back to Sea Life Park, and he finished earning his day's rations performing in the last show at Ocean Science Theater.

Subsequently I put a domesticated porpoise into the ocean whenever I could get permission to do so. This was not often; a porpoise expedition involved man-hours and boat time, and those two things cost money. Without a good excuse to work the animal (*Life* photographers or network TV cameras were a good excuse), it was hard to pry an offshore day out of the budget. However, we did enough work to begin learning some of the limitations of working a porpoise. You could not ask the animal to carry much of a load. Anything you strapped on its body interfered with the streamlining of the animal and tired it badly. Even a five-pound weight was a real handicap. There was a great brouhaha in the newspapers that winter about the Navy training kamikaze porpoises to carry explosives and ram themselves into enemy submarines. In fact, that possible exploitation of the animal seemed to have been an invention of the reporter who wrote the story after seeing a Navy porpoise discriminate between copper and aluminum by sonar. He envisioned some kind of metal detection skill used for identification of enemy ships.

Knowing how small the maximum porpoise payload is, it seemed quite impossible to me that a porpoise could carry enough explosive to be used in this way, and equally impossible that a load-carrying porpoise could overtake a moving submarine. There are a lot of things to worry about concerning human misuse of marine animals, but that didn't seem to me to be one of them.

We found that the animal could not be trusted to work alone. Its well-being and its confidence depended on having a human being to direct it and associate with it. One probably could not, therefore, send a working porpoise out on its own for miles and miles. Search-and-rescue operations or salvage hunting or photographic missions were conceivable; but they would have to be done by a man-porpoise team. One could theoretically—we didn't try it—train one or more porpoises to patrol a fixed, known area and give warning of sharks or other danger, in the way guard dogs are trained to patrol inside a fence or to search department stores for intruders at night. Even so, to maintain the behavior there would have to be, we thought, a human trainer in the offing somewhere, as there has to be with dogs.

The Vietnam war was ablaze, and my thoughts turned to the use of porpoises in harbors to defend against underwater saboteurs. I knew it would be possible to train a porpoise to ram a target amidships. If that target were a human being, and underwater, the ramming would be debilitating, even fatal; and the saboteur, especially at night, would have no warning of the porpoise's silent, speedy approach. I felt sure the animal would have no sentimental feelings about ramming a human target he was trained to hit. A dog must be shaped to experience fear and anger if it is to attack a person. The porpoise would, I thought, deal its one swift blow quite impersonally.

I played with the idea of developing an "antipersonnel porpoise" in the Ocean Science Theater. Everyone was horrified, and Tap pointed out that such an animal might not be very safe to have around, once it was trained; so I filed the idea away.

There was another rather peculiar problem involved in putting such a display into our shows. The Navy was working more and more extensively with porpoises and other marine mammals, doing who knows what, most of it highly classified. Now, our Ocean Science Theater shows were based entirely on our own ideas; but then any trainer can have ideas, and chances were that some of our ideas were the same as some of the Navy's. I always thought the porpoise-powered diver was a case in point, judging by the way certain admirals frowned in annoyance when they watched it in our shows.

Working in the ocean, a trained porpoise gives a diver a tow up to the surface. *Oceanic Institute photo*

If we did accidentally show off something the Navy was developing, they could not very well tell us to *stop* publicly demonstrating the subject, because then we would know for *sure* what they were up to, and we didn't have the security clearance for that knowledge.

In fact I found it rather easy to tell what kinds of things the Navy was working on, whether we were doing them in shows or not, by speculating aloud at Navy cocktail parties as to what *I* would do, and watching to see which notions made the Navy types drop the shutters down in the back of their eyes and change the subject.

This was a dirty trick, of course, and some of our administrative people were angry with me for it. There were lucrative contracts to be had in the area of classified porpoise research, and I was blowing any chances we had to get them. Furthermore, we had a superior team of porpoise trainers, and perhaps it was our patriotic duty to engage in classified work.

I knew what my trainers would think of that idea, whether the work implied possible danger to the porpoise or not. They would quit before they would train porpoises for war. I also felt strongly that there was a deadly drawback in classified work. Once we were admitted to the sanctum, once we *knew* what others were not allowed to know, we would never be free to speculate again, to talk to the public and let our imaginations run loose, to try any old thing we could dream up. We'd lose our intellectual freedom, and that was not worth swapping for "black money" (the slang term for funds from espionage sources), no matter in what tens or hundreds of thousands.

Furthermore, I was sure that much of what was classified was not of military significance. If you are working in a bizarre field, doing weird and sometimes silly-looking things, criticism from a misunderstanding press or Congress can sometimes be really debilitating: witness the uproar over "kamikaze" porpoises which was provoked by a simple sonar demonstration. We might find ourselves, if cleared for classified work, unable to discuss man-porpoise teams (or some other routine matter) because Navy work in that area was classified for purposes of avoiding ridicule as well as for purposes of national security.

We were doing nothing that had not crossed the mind of every competent porpoise trainer, American or otherwise; I had no anxiety that we were really revealing "secrets." And if there were any real secrets, I didn't want myself or my team to be privy to them. So we went on training porpoises to "recover space capsules" and "drop markers on downed airplanes" and "locate missing hydrogen bombs," five times a day in our shows. I continued disqualifying myself as a good security risk at cocktail parties, and we stayed out of classified research and development.

One genuine problem for everybody who works in the ocean, both military and civilian, is locating and retrieving stuff you have accidentally dropped into the water. Even in shallow, clear water it is surprisingly hard to find something that's been sitting on the bottom for a couple of days. If the water is "beyond diver depth," that is, deeper than 200 feet, or if it is murky, locating lost objects can be nearly impossible. A porpoise, however, can work easily in dark waters, operates well at depths that are difficult for divers, can cover a lot of terrain much faster than men or little submarines and more thoroughly than boats with scanning devices; and it can search with sonar as well as eyes. When the big search was going on for the hydrogen bomb that fell into the ocean off the coast of Spain, I'm sure we were not the only porpoise trainers who swore our animals could have found it in no time.

Jon Lindbergh, son of the aviator Charles Lindbergh, had an oceanographic company on the West Coast that did a lot of salvage work. One day in 1968 I chatted with him when he came to Sea Life Park to visit Tap. Couldn't he use a salvage-seeking porpoise? Indeed so. In fact, he said, he had a problem at the time that an animal might be able to solve. An airplane had crashed into a West Coast bay; the investigation team wanted to get all the pieces back, and it was extremely difficult to locate all the pieces, scattered as they were over the floor of a murky, muddy harbor and often buried in the mud. A porpoise, presumably, could locate the pieces, even the buried ones, by sonar, retrieve the small scraps, and drop a radio beacon or some other kind of marker beside the larger pieces so that divers could find and recover them.

Jon was not willing to put any money into this enterprise, but he allowed himself to be inveigled into saying he *might* hire such an animal, if one were developed. That gave me the leverage I needed to pursue the matter, if I could do so without expending any actual cash.

By this time, the Oceanic Institute's successes with small ocean engineering projects such as the chamber had led to the formation of a new commercial company, Makai Range, Inc., an ambitious organization aimed at working on the sea floor in new and efficient ways. Makai Range had built and successfully tested a large yet portable undersea habitat, *Aegir,* a device capable of housing six men at a time at depths down to 500 feet.

The Makai Range people were not interested in porpoises and had not encouraged our participation with animal messengers or experiments in any of their work. Partly, I think, their unwillingness was caused by a realistic concern that peripheral people and experimentation might be a nuisance during the complex and truly hazardous business of conducting deep-diving tests with *Aegir.* Partly, I suspect, they didn't want the porpoises around to distract the press and TV from their own work. And partly, I suspect, divers are almost all rather concerned with masculine privileges and found distasteful the thought of female porpoise trainers in bikinis running about giving serious diving programs an air of frivolity.

However, Makai Range had built a large pier into the ocean, just offshore of Sea Life Park, a pier which made daily open ocean work easy for them and which would make it easy for us to work with a porpoise, if I could just find a way to build a porpoise pen alongside the pier.

The Oceanic Institute had a new trainer of its own, Scott Rutherford, a husky young man who could work at the pier without ruffling anyone's machismo. Furthermore, one of the Institute animals had been trained for open ocean work. On a lecture tour the previous winter I dropped in on the *Wild Kingdom* offices in Chicago, and the upshot was that they did a TV program with us about training porpoises to be domestic workers in the open sea. They used Scott and a young male Institute bottlenose named Lele (which means "jump"). Scott, under Ingrid Kang's supervision, trained Lele to fetch and carry, to obey a recall signal, and to go in and out of a cage. We had released Lele offshore, where he performed these tasks for the *Wild Kingdom* cameras, with the TV program stars Marlin Perkins and Stan Brock assisting. Makai Range cooperated to the extent of sinking *Aegir* a few feet underwater at the pier, so we could film Lele carrying stuff to Perkins and Brock alongside *Aegir*. They also let the program film its two men going in and out of *Aegir* about 50 feet underwater, offshore, so that deeper shots could be intercut with shots of Lele working.

After the filming was completed, Scott had a lot of time on his hands, and so did Lele, so setting them to work on Jon Lindbergh's problem interfered with nothing. Using Bateson's Bay as a training location—large, deep, and roomy—Scott began training Lele to drop markers next to objects in the water.

A problem in training a porpoise for salvage work is how to teach the porpoise to select what you want. You don't, after all, want him salvaging old tires and empty Coke bottles. Navy trainers told me they had gone to great lengths to teach porpoises to recognize particular shapes or to identify by sonar all things made of aluminum. I decided that how the porpoise recognized the target was going to be *his* problem. Our requirement would be "mark anything that's a piece of an airplane"; I didn't care what Lele thought about it. So a sculptor friend, Mick Brownlee, went to a junkyard and bought me pieces of airplane. Scotty threw them into the tank along with pieces of packing crates, washing machines, rocks, and so on, and rewarded Lele only for marking airplane parts. Somehow, he learned to differentiate accurately.

When Lele seemed to have the picture, Scotty and some of the other trainers, in their spare time, built a pen under the pier by enclosing four pilings with a wall of secondhand construction netting. It was not very satisfactory—Lele wriggled out of it all the time—but it was a pen. Scott also used Kai and Hou's little floating cage. When the pen was in disrepair Lele could live in the cage for a day or two. Ingrid Kang and Scott took the airplane pieces down to the pier, threw them in the water, and started training Lele to carry a marker, attached to a line on a big fishing reel, down to the airplane parts.

On the third day of work, Lele took off in the wrong direction and dropped the marker in empty water, it seemed. Two or three times the marker was reeled in, and Lele went fishless, and yet he repeated going off the wrong way. Finally Scott put a face mask on and jumped in to see what the problem was. No problem: Lele had found an old engine block buried in the coral! To him, it filled the criteria—he thought it was a piece of an airplane.

Scott and Ingrid worked Lele off and on all summer. He learned to follow a boat and to work in 50 feet of water or so. Makai Range had lost a movie camera in an underwater housing somewhere offshore, so we changed the criteria to read "Mark anything man-made and bigger than a breadbox." Lele found anchors and engines and fishing gear. One day, indeed, he found a whole airplane, the wreckage of a World War II fighter that had been lying buried in sand and coral for nearly thirty years. No one wanted it back, but we were proud of Lele.

On no budget, it was difficult to push Lele into deeper water. We had to beg for the use of a free boat, seldom got one, and thus could seldom work away from the pier. The Office of Naval Research was not likely to fund *me* any longer to buy divers' time and boat time to train Lele farther offshore. Yet without divers there was no way to check if Lele had made the right choices or not during preliminary stages of training. The Navy had lost a landing craft in the area, which sank and then shifted, owing to tides and currents, and Makai Range was looking for that with cameras and submarines. We were dying to find it with Lele, but our mobility was not sufficient.

Lele at home in the pen the Navy lent us, which he jumped out of at will in order to pester fishermen and welcome boats at the Makai Range pier.

Scotty put a push-pad under his surf board and trained Lele to push him around; it was a lunch-hour treat to go down to Kumu Cove, where the waves broke near the pier, and watch Scott and Lele surf in together, and then Lele push Scott and his board back out.

The small cage was damaged in a storm, and Lele's pen began to disintegrate in the salt water. The work had not progressed far enough to be tempting to Jon Lindbergh. We finally had to bring Lele back to the Institute tanks.

I couldn't give up the idea of having a porpoise available to Makai Range, just to see what would come out of daily association, and finally the Navy took pity on me and lent us a solidly made floating pen with a sturdy gangplank all around it. The following summer we put Lele there, and then, when solitude seemed to make him a little surly, added an almost-untrained female bottlenose, Awakea. That summer Scott had a load of researchers to work for at the Institute and had little free time to play with offshore animals. Lele and Awakea took care of themselves. They learned to jump in and out of their pen at will. They spent most of the day hanging around the pier, amusing themselves by bothering divers and fishermen. Some of the Makai Range divers did not enjoy having a porpoise zooming around while they were engaged in repair work on *Aegir* or other underwater tasks. Some of them did enjoy it, though porpoises, being curious, have an annoying way of sticking their noses between your face and your work all the time. The porpoises soon learned who liked their company and who didn't, and they were on the whole very polite. They jumped back into their pen obediently in the morning and the evening when Scott or some other trainer came down to feed them. They usually spent the night in the pen. They clearly regarded it as a refuge, and would jump into the pen if anything frightened them, such as the arrival of a strange boat.

It did not occur to us that there were any real hazards to the porpoises in the shallow water around the pier. Scott realized the value of the pen as a refuge for the porpoises when he was about to jump off the pier into the water, looked down, and saw that had he jumped he would have landed on the back of a large hammerhead shark that was passing by.

The Makai Range work boat, the 60-foot *Holokai,* had a sharp prow and a good turn of speed and made a fine bow wave. Lele and Awakea loved to ride on its bow, and they took to escorting the *Holokai* away from the pier for a couple of hundred yards, and then going out to meet her when she came home and escorting her back in. A long project was going on at *Aegir*'s 200-foot test dive site, more than a mile offshore. Every day the *Holokai* went back and forth, and finally Lele and Awakea were making the whole trip with her and spending the day at the dive site.

There was no trainer to keep an eye on them, no fish bucket or recall to bait them home again, and they had each other for company and presumably had no reason to fear being loose in the ocean. Yet they came back to the pier and jumped in their pen every night. A domestic animal.

Lele was thus at liberty at the Makai Range pier for months, Awakea for weeks. One day when they were hanging around the dive site a Navy cutter with an even better bow wave than the *Holokai* came over. When she left, Lele and Awakea went with her. They stayed with the boat for about 10 miles and then disappeared. Whether they tried to find their way back and couldn't, or whether they chose to go home to the sea for good, is uncertain. They wore no tags; they were not officially in my jurisdiction, at that time, and I had no authority to tag them. But as far as I was concerned it was an informal but highly successful experiment. For an amazingly long time Lele and Awakea deliberately chose to join the family of man.

What the most valuable domestic use of the porpoise is, I don't know. Perhaps he will come into his own when farming the fish in the sea becomes a reality. Our open-ocean work convinced us only that, if and when we need him, the porpoise is ready, willing, and able to be of help.

12. NEW BEGINNINGS

When I had spent about five years giving most of my attention to porpoise work, I began to realize that the work had become repetitious. I had no new, serious research ideas I wished to pursue myself. The trainers knew how to do the shows better than I did. Ingrid was taking marvelous care of the animals and the staff. I no longer enjoyed teaching one more porpoise how to eat, one more swimmer to dive with her feet together neatly, one more narrator how to speak the English language over a microphone. It was time for me to move on to other things.

I spent a couple of years studying exhibit design, developing new ideas for Sea Life Park, and writing, directing, and editing films for all of Tap's many enterprises (filmmaking turned out to be another skill, like porpoise training, in which practice is useful but naïveté is an advantage, too).

Sea Life Park was sustaining itself. The Oceanic Institute was growing. Makai Range seemed to be doing well. Tap and his original management team at Sea Life Park had expanded the company's business interests tremendously. Bob Haws, the Park's operations manager, now also ran a commuter airline between the Islands. Tom Morrish, the sales manager, developed a delightful little tourist railroad, the Lahaina, Kaanapali, & Pacific, on the island of Maui. The three men brought together a group of investors which purchased Hana Ranch, on Maui, a sizable operation with 9,000 head of cattle. They also ran the Hotel Hana Maui, a luxurious little resort, like a country club in heaven, I always thought, which was located on the ranch. The Institute had projects all over the Islands and sent its research vessel *Westward* on expeditions into the South Pacific.

All of this was tremendous fun for wives and families. The children and I spent summers on Maui. The boys learned to work on the ranch as they got older, and I spent some of the happiest moments of my life galloping up and down Hana Ranch's green hills trying to help the cowboys herd cattle. We cruised on the *Westward* and flew on company business to Samoa, Fiji, Australia, the Cook Islands, and often to the mainland.

During the early period of the Park's operation Tap spent two interesting but overwhelmingly demanding years as a senator in the state legislature, appointed to fill Patsy Mink's seat when she went to Washington, D.C., to Congress. Then he was named to a presidential commission on the oceans. I took a lecture tour every winter, speaking to women's clubs and colleges, showing porpoise films and talking about the oceans. We built a large house, with a swimming pool designed to make it possible to have a porpoise in the living room. Since the pool was filled with fresh water, we couldn't keep saltwater porpoises there very long; two days was the limit or their skins would get sore and flaky. We brought an animal down a couple of times for parties. One we tried didn't care for the experience and sulked, but another one loved it, fraternized with everyone, and practically cadged drinks.

In 1971 I officially resigned from the Park, the Institute, and the rest of the operation, and from the various and multiple duties with which I had been earning my salary: writing reports, drawing up research proposals, costing out construction, and so on. "Good," said my daughter Gale, when I told her I'd quit: "You mean you're going to be a real mother?"

In 1971, also, things began to go to pieces. The various companies were in financial difficulties. The stockholders rebelled.

Finally they had a series of palace revolutions. Sea Life Park was sold to a new set of investors. Makai Range folded, unable to survive without government contracts for ocean research, funds which had dried up completely under the Nixon administration. The Oceanic Institute underwent some peculiar form of bankruptcy. The railroad failed. Hana Ranch and the railroad and Royal Hawaiian Air Service split up into separate entities again. Tap not only lost control but lost his salaried positions and his place on the board of almost every enterprise.

This was not all necessarily bad. Almost every project, it turned out, had a life of its own, and revived and flourished. Sea Life Park is doing beautifully. The new owners have improved and upgraded it with a sorely needed influx of fresh capital. The Oceanic Institute rose from its own ashes and is now a thriving and solvent research organization, concentrating on farming the sea. It is run by a dedicated group of bankers and scientists who were personally unwilling to see it die. Even the Makai Range project shows a stir of life, with a handful of the most creative people from its old staff now running a number of innovative undersea projects, such as the profitable collection of gem corals using a small submarine.

Tap and I had grown a great deal through these years, but in different directions. We were no longer the shy biologists who dreamed of an oceanarium of our own; we had new interests and goals, but they were no longer interests and goals we could share. We were divorced in 1972. Tap set to work on a new dream, a profitable venture in farming the sea. I settled down with the children in a suburb of Honolulu and began catching up on a big backlog of writing, including this book. Also at last I had time to pursue a long-dormant interest in music and theater. I sang in the chorus of Hawaii's A-rated opera company. I became the drama critic on the morning newspaper in Honolulu. I grew a garden and enjoyed new friends.

"But don't you miss the porpoises?" No. I give Malia a pat if I take visitors to Sea Life Park, but I don't miss her or any of them. My work with the porpoises seems to be complete; perhaps my imagination has stretched as far as it will go in their direction.

There are dogs (Gus, Prince, Holly) and horses (Echo, Flustre) that I miss more.

I still have questions about porpoises. I would like to know if they see color. They like music; I would like to know what kind they like best, and if it is melody, harmony, or rhythm that attracts them most. I wonder about the intelligence of the great whales. Bill Schevill once played me a wonderful tape of a humpback whale in the Bahamas toying with an echo in an underwater canyon. The whale went "Mroomp!" and the echo went "Mroomp!" The whale tried it again, one note higher, until it had gone up the octave as far as it could reach. The echo answered. Having tried out higher and higher "mroomps," the whale essayed a few other roars and gargles, waiting for the echo each time. Then other whales could be heard on the tape, calling in the distance. The whale answered them and departed. Now any animal that thinks that is fun *has* to be an intelligent animal.

I wonder, too, about the meaning of the beautiful whale songs that Roger Payne, of the New York Zoological Society, has recorded, songs that are varied, rich, and patterned, and that may last as long as nine minutes and then be repeated accurately from the beginning. You can overlay a sonogram of the first nine minutes and the second nine minutes and they will match almost exactly. The only other phenomena that match it, as far as I know, are human music and human oral literature: the eddas, the sagas, the genealogical poetry of Polynesia. I would like to know what that's all about, and why the whales do it. But these are problems for other researchers, not me.

Not that I don't *like* porpoises anymore. You never get over that. Once I was at a conference at Point Mugu with F. G. Woods, William Evans, Scott Johnson, Carleton Ray, and a number of other distinguished scientists and aquarists, all of whom worked with cetaceans practically every day of their lives, and someone cried out that there were porpoises in the surf just outside the building. We all rushed out like children, dropping our weighty discussion, all thrilled to see the bottlenoses body surfing, for fun, along the shoreline. One doesn't become blasé, after all.

The Sea Life Park experience taught all of us a great deal.

Most of the people who worked at the Park have made exciting careers out of what they learned there. Bob Haws is now president of Royal Hawaiian Airlines. Tom Morrish runs a huge resort development organization. Ken Norris is a professor at the University of Santa Cruz, spearheading research and development programs, consulting to other organizations, inspiring a new generation of students. We work together occasionally. I helped him plan an oceanarium for Hong Kong. It was fun thinking up shows with a Chinese flavor and emphasis, shows for a multilanguage audience in which you would not be required to understand the narrator in order to enjoy the performance. Sea lions playing mah-jongg underwater—wouldn't you like to see that? And a duck race. And pelicans trained to perform on the wing.

Al Takayama, our vet, still takes care of my cats and dogs. Chris and Gary I have lost track of. Dottie Samson married Howard Baldwin, the scientist who helped her look for Pono. They were later divorced, and Dottie, after teaching school in Alaska and having various other adventures, is currently the secretary for Tap's sea-farming company. Jim Kelly, who brought us our booby birds, ran an oceanarium in Galveston and is now an airline pilot, I hear. Randy Lewis married Pat Quealy, and they are running a ranch in Utah. David Alices is the porpoise trainer for a hotel in Honolulu, the luxurious Kahala Hilton, where David puts on a show with his animals twice a day. Danny Kaleikini is still a headlining nightclub entertainer, with a solid gold five-year contract, a radio show of his own, the famous "Hawaii Calls," and dozens of other projects. Ingrid Kang, Kerry Jenkins, Diane Pugh, Marlee Breese, and Wela Wallwork still work at Sea Life Park. Lehua Kelekolio married a Makai Range scientist. I run into her and some of the other swimmers now and then.

Georges Gilbert died, tragically, leaving a wife and three little girls, but he died as he would have chosen, I feel sure. He was felled by a stroke on the deck of the *Imua* in the midst of catching a spinner. The spinner, named Kamae ("sorrow"), still performs in Whaler's Cove.

Once a swimmer, now a trainer, Cindy Rhys feeds Mamo, the *Tursiops x Steno* hybrid, and her *Steno* mother. Mamo, well grown, now performs at the Ocean Science Theater. *Roger Coryell*

Fred Skinner is retired but still extremely active; Konrad Lorenz likewise. Gregory Bateson is, like Ken Norris, teaching at Santa Cruz. Debby Skinner is an artist, married and living in London. Scott Rutherford, the young trainer who supervised Lele and Awakea in their life of domestic freedom, is running an oceanarium in Singapore.

Malcolm Sargeant was very ill on his last visit to Hawaii, and died soon after. I promised him that I would put him in a book someday, and now I have.

Makapuu, the false killer whale, is still the star of Whaler's Cove. She has learned wonderful new behaviors from Ingrid and Diane: Roman riding, with Diane circling Whaler's Cove with a foot on the back of each of two whales; a "whale chase" from a boat, in which Makapuu pretends to be harpooned, takes the boat on a "Nantucket sleigh ride," capsizes the boat, and then rescues the whaling men in it.

Malia, the genius *Steno,* is still the star of the Ocean Science Theater, revered and respected by a new generation of young trainers, who call her "the Dart" because she works so fast. Keiki was carried off by pneumonia in his ninth year. Makua, who was an old animal when captured, died of old age, still stubborn and crotchety.

Hoku and Kiko are gone. I still think of them sometimes. When we moved Pono and Keiki to the Ocean Science Theater to show off their research training, we took Hoku and Kiko back to the training facility for a much-needed rest. One Friday evening as I ran them through their six-bar work just to keep them in practice, I noticed that Kiko was not eating her fish, although she was performing with her usual verve and sparkle.

On Monday, when I came back to work, Kiko was dead. The autopsy showed a massive lung abscess that must have been developing for weeks; she had been mortally ill on Friday but gave no sign of weakness until the very end. A heroine.

Hoku's grief was heartbreaking. He refused all food and swam in slow circles with his eyes squeezed tightly shut, as if he did not want to look on a world that did not contain Kiko. After two days we gave him a new companion, a pretty little female kiko named Kolohi ("rascal"). She did everything she could to charm him, caressing him respectfully and swimming hour after hour at his side. Finally he opened his eyes. Then he began to eat again. At last he accepted Kolohi, though he was never as attached to her as he had been to Kiko. The two of them went to Whaler's Cove, where they performed for years. Hoku also took on a paramour, Olelo the whale. Though Olelo was ten times Hoku's size, he bullied her abominably. When Olelo earned a mouthful of fish, Hoku was right beside her, glaring, until she gave one or two to him.

Gus, my Weimaraner, died long ago on the highway. Echo, the pony stallion that made a trainer of me, is a proud herd sire on a pony ranch in California. The rest of the ponies are scattered around Hawaii, each one cherished by some new owner. One of Wayne Batteau's smart animals, Maui, is dead, but the other one, Puka, now works at the University of Hawaii porpoise research facilities.

Ingrid Kang, at Sea Life Park, keeps me up to date on her

work. She has now had a chance to work with two animals I always wanted to try, California sea lions, those bad-tempered but highly trainable circus favorites, and the Atlantic bottlenose porpoise, *Tursiops truncatus,* which oddly enough I never handled personally, though it is by far the commonest oceanarium porpoise. Ingrid finds the Atlantic species to be very different from the Pacific species in temperament, far more skittish and irritable and, in fact, in her opinion, rather difficult to train. Perhaps it is all in what you're used to.

There are ideas still to be discussed, about behavior and learning, creativity and intelligence, and the grace of individuals, whether animal or man. They need not be pinned to porpoises. What continues to interest me is the borderline between the art and the science of training. I am intrigued whenever I see events occurring on that borderline, whether between a falconer and his hawks, a psychologist and an autistic child, a lion tamer and a lion, a shepherd and his dog, a symphony conductor and his orchestra. It's time to forage out and see what other people are doing; and I suspect there's another book in that.

WHAT HAPPENED THEN...

13. DIVING IN THE NETS: THE TUNA/PORPOISE PROBLEM

The original *Lads Before the Wind* was published in 1975. When I wrote it I was divorced, with three teenage children. Sea Life Park was under new management. The old team, including me and my ex-husband, Tap Pryor, had left or been ousted. I myself had, in essence, been fired for insubordination, which was curiously satisfying.

There were no other jobs for porpoise trainers in Hawaii. Even on the mainland it was low-paid work, and I had three children to support. My most marketable skill, it seemed, was writing. I began with *Lads Before the Wind*, for Harper & Row, who had published my successful book *Nursing Your Baby* some years earlier.* When the new book was completed I got a day job as an advertising copywriter and a night job as the Honolulu newspaper's theater critic. In 1976 my oldest children, Mike and Ted, went off to college. Fifteen-year-old Gale and I moved from Honolulu to New York City, where I planned to keep working as a writer.

Sea Life Park continued to do well under new ownership. It remains one of Hawaii's most successful and popular tourist

---

* Karen Pryor, *Nursing Your Baby* (New York: Harper & Row, 1963).

attractions. Tap Pryor, who started the whole place, now lives in the Cook Islands, working for the government on new avenues for economic development. Although many of the friends and mentors from my Sea Life Park days have died—Konrad Lorenz, Ken Norris, and Gregory Bateson among them—some of the trainers that started with me still work at the Park. Ingrid Kang became curator and head trainer after me, married Park manager Eddie Shallenberger, and eventually moved to the Pacific Northwest; we continue to be colleagues and friends.

Visitors to Sea Life Park today see shows and exhibits that are much the same as those that we opened with. The buildings and grounds are certainly very spruced up, and the training is imaginative; the shows, however, still include large chunks of the scripts I scribbled on scratch paper in 1963. (They seem to have become a sort of trainers' oral tradition. I have heard pieces of our original Ocean Science Theater shows, lame jokes and all, in dolphin shows from Canada to Japan.)

Malia, the brilliant *Steno*, Makapuu, our star false killer whale, and many of the other dolphins lived long and, I think, happy lives. Some reached far greater ages than are usual for their respective species in the wild. Sea Life Park became known for its successful breeding programs with dolphins, whales, and penguins, and for its work in rehabilitating and caring for the endangered Hawaiian monk seals. The Park's sibling organization, the Oceanic Institute, is still a large and successful private research center.

When I moved back to New York I assumed I had seen the last of the dolphins. I didn't miss them. I certainly had no interest in continuing to work in the oceanarium field. (Shortly after the move I turned down a job as director of the National Aquarium in Baltimore, then in the planning stages.) I planned to find work as copywriter, a job that paid a lot better in New York than it did in Hawaii, and perhaps do some more freelance writing as well. But it seemed as if the animals were following me around. No matter what I did or where I went, for the next two decades I was to remain in the dolphin business, whether I planned to or not.

The day after I arrived in Manhattan I was offered a job as a consultant to the tuna fishing industry. In the Pacific, the American tuna fishing fleet was using porpoises—more visible from the surface of the water—as locators for the valuable tuna that swim with them. With swift vessels and huge purse seine nets half a mile long, they surrounded whole schools of porpoises and tuna, sometimes amounting to thousands of animals and tons of fish. Then the porpoises were let out over the tops of the nets and the tuna were harvested.*

Sometimes things went wrong, however, and porpoises were tangled and drowned. The mortality rate was alarming. Environmental groups were up in arms. The government, especially the National Marine Fisheries Service or NMFS (pronounced "nymphs") was struggling to come up with ways to reduce the kill. The species involved were not clever bottlenoses, who could and in fact did just jump over the tuna nets if they happened to be caught inside the circle, but timid, flighty spotted and spinner porpoises who didn't understand barricades at all. These species had been trained and maintained in captivity only at Sea Life Park. That made me a natural choice for scientific advisor.

I thought that the problem seemed solvable. Some boats and some skippers had excellent safety records and could catch and release school after school of porpoises without a mishap. If some could do it, others could learn. Though I took some criticism from the environmental community for touching the industry's tainted gold, it seemed to me that working with the fishermen might be more fruitful than picketing on the docks.

The work involved mostly meetings, speeches, report writing, and testifying at congressional hearings. Meanwhile I also did some freelance magazine writing, some dolphin-related work for the National Geographic, and a stint at the National Zoo in Washington, D.C., teaching keepers how to use dolphin training techniques to handle and manage other captive animals, including

---

* A seine is a long net with floats on one edge and sinkers on the other, so that it hangs vertically in the water and can be used to encircle a school of fish. A purse seine is constructed so that its bottom can be pulled shut before it is hauled in.

birds, rhinos, and polar bears.* Dolphin-related research kept coming up, too. I coauthored a research paper on training and the trainability of various species for a book edited by Louis Herman.† I presented and published a paper on training as communication, and dolphins as "normal" rather than magical animals, for the New York Academy of Sciences.‡ That particular talk hit about a hundred newspapers across the country, under headlines such as "Scientist Says Flipper Not So Smart After All," and "Dolphins Dangerous, Researcher Warns." A reporter in Miami set out to prove me wrong by going swimming with the dolphins in a nearby oceanarium and phoned me later to report ruefully that he had gotten thoroughly knocked around for his trouble.

One summer the National Marine Fisheries Service offered me a research contract to go out to sea on a tuna fishing vessel and personally study the behavior of the dolphins in the nets. The government wanted to find out if the animals were dying of fright, or in such a state of shock that they might die later. Were the researchers missing something if they only counted the casualties actually found in the nets?

The fishing took place in the Eastern Tropical Pacific, a vast piece of ocean off the coast of Central America, two thousand miles from land in every direction. Just getting researchers there and back was a major undertaking. But I had already had experience of that.

The year before, Ken Norris and several other senior marine mammal scientists had gone out into the Pacific on a government research vessel, the *David Starr Jordan*, to rendezvous with one of the biggest and best tuna seiners, the two-hundred-foot *Elizabeth C.J.*, and watch twenty sets of the net.

Two voyages were planned. If the senior scientists did not see twenty sets during their scheduled trip, a second trip would take

* Karen Pryor, "The Rhino Likes Violets," *Psychology Today*, April 1981.

† R. H. Defran and K. Pryor, "Social behavior and training of eleven species of cetaceans in captivity," in *Cetacean Behavior: Mechanisms and Functions*, ed. L. Herman (New York: Wiley-Interscience, 1980).

‡ Karen Pryor, "Why porpoise trainers are not dolphin lovers: real and false communication in the operant setting," *Annals of the New York Academy of Sciences*, 1981.

place, for NMFS employees, graduate students, a photographer, and other riffraff; Ken Norris had offered me a spot on that second cruise. For all of us it was an unprecedented chance to see wild dolphins close up and to watch the fishing in action.

When the *Jordan* put the senior scientists ashore, in Mazatlan, Mexico, one set was still left of the twenty allotted for the project. Ken Norris called to tell me not to bother coming for just one set; but I knew that diving among the dolphins in the net, and seeing them under water in that situation even just once, would tell me more than all the research statistics and government reports in the world. Gale was in Hawaii with her father, so I was free to go—and the industry was paying. I was on the plane to Mazatlan the next day and aboard the *David Starr Jordan* soon after that.

We spent a week just getting out to the fishing grounds. When we finally met up with the *Elizabeth C.J.*, we went aboard for the day. The fishermen found some spotted dolphins right away and made a set of the net. I went down the ladder into a skiff, with one of the NMFS people as crew, and drove out into the net's vast circle, the equivalent of three football fields in size, toward the animals. I put my mask on and slipped into the water.

Magic. Right in front of me was a young female spotted dolphin, nursing her calf. She gave me a friendly look and rolled sideways in a dolphin greeting gesture. Other females and babies were lolling around us, touching noses, caressing each other, playing in the sunshine. They were completely at ease. Not only that, I could see all the rest of the school going about its business behind them. What an incredible opportunity to see how these deep ocean animals really live! I went back to the government ship extremely elated; we had another week's travel homeward, on the slow, uncomfortable, and unfriendly *Jordan*, but it had all been worth it.

Now, the following summer, there were to be half a dozen research cruises, not on a government boat but on a tuna seiner, refitted to accommodate a scientific party of six as well as the usual nineteen crew members. I was thrilled at the chance to be on one of these trips.

I already had an answer to the government's question: Are the dolphins in a net in a state of shock and panic? Well, certainly not on the single set I had seen. I myself was curious about something else altogether. In the Eastern Tropical Pacific, spotted and spinner dolphins travel in vast congregations, sometimes containing thousands of animals. Our spinners at Sea Life Park had been pretty gregarious, but our spotted dolphins were aristocratically snobbish, swimming only with selected favorite companions; in fact they often snubbed and ignored new spotted dolphins for weeks before letting them into their ranks. How could the haughty spotters travel in these big pelagic schools of hundreds and thousands, where they couldn't possibly all be acquainted? Now I would have a chance to go to sea again, and dive in the nets over and over. We might find out.

I had asked Ingrid to join me. She had a degree in animal behavior, which I did not, and a keen and clear eye; she was also a fearless swimmer and knew more about spinner and spotter behavior than anyone. We met in San Diego, where the tuna fleet docked, including our particular ship, the *Queen Mary*. We bought our supplies, listened to instructions from the NMFS people, and went on board.

The San Diego tuna fishing fleet is owned and manned largely by descendents of Portuguese families, including our skipper, Captain Ralph Silva. Tradition was strong; it would be easy to offend by accident. I knew that some scientists and government observers had indeed gotten into trouble and been hazed on fishing vessels. A NMFS official drove me privately to the docks in order to tell me all about the things other scientific teams had done wrong. As I stepped from the car onto the pier I had a truly awful feeling inside; it took me a while to identify it. It was the feeling you have on being wheeled into the operating room: dread.

I am sure the fishermen were worried, too. Having women on board was a huge break in tradition, and the very idea had caused uproars during the planning of this voyage, about which I, blessedly, had not been informed. The end result, however, was that the rules were broken again, and not only were we two woman scientists allowed aboard but the captain's wife, Evelyn Silva, also came along, an unprecedented event. (She was not there to chaperone us, but to protect the crew from our wiles.)

We got on board, put our gear away, shook hands with the ship's officers, met Evelyn and her family on the aft deck where a farewell party was going on, and immediately went to the galley to locate our names on the dishwashing roster. Everyone saw us do that. It was the beginning of a very happy trip.

Tuna clippers are well built, incredibly fast, and have phenomenally powerful engines. We reached the fishing areas by the third day, and began finding dolphins. Ingrid and I had prepared an ethogram, a list of all the behaviors we knew spinners and spotters to do. Whenever the vessel set the net, Ingrid and I went over the side, traveled out into its circle in a little motorboat, put on masks, fins, and snorkles, and swam with the dolphins. There was no need for scuba gear; the dolphins were mostly at the surface, and scuba diving would just have added to the risk. The net itself was the biggest danger. A little countercurrent could cause buckling and folds that could trap a human diver as easily as a dolphin. Watching from just below the surface made sense.

We had roughly an hour of observation time while most of the net was being gathered aboard preparatory to spilling the dolphins out the back end. We each picked one dolphin at a time and watched it for five minutes, a technique called focal animal sampling. We had invented a sort of behavioral code that allowed us to jot down underwater—using an ordinary pencil on a plastic slate—whatever that dolphin was doing during that five minutes. The data could then be entered into a computer later.

Getting on and off the tuna boat was a nervous business every time. The *Queen Mary* rolled horribly, and the steel-rung ladder down her two-story side was slippery. You had to cling tight, dangling from the ladder as the ship rolled toward you, and then climb up or down fast while she rolled away. Philippe Vergne, a young industry biologist who acted as our boat driver and shark guard, went over the side on our inflatable boat each time, swinging wildly from the davits as the boat was lowered, a trip he did not enjoy. It would have been much easier for all three of us to just jump from the deck into the warm sea and then climb into the lowered boat, but the captain wouldn't let us. Once the net was deployed and the ship was stationary, there might be sharks loitering under the hull.

When we got out into the circle of net we moved tactfully alongside the dolphins, who were usually clustered on the far side. Philippe swam with us, looking for sharks. Chapo the cook was assigned to watch us from the ship's port rail and notify someone if we appeared to be in trouble. Captain Ralph also assigned the first mate, his son, Ralph Jr., to join us in another boat and dive with us, acting as a second shark guard, as soon as his onboard duties were done. This was a real kindness to us but a great distress to Evelyn, who was unable to watch a set if her son was in the water.

After observing our first dives, the skipper decided we were roaming too far from our shallow inflatable boat. He gave us each twenty feet of net cord and ordered us to tie ourselves to the boat, so we could go no further away from it than that. That net cord was quite a nuisance; I got tangled in it many times. But we appreciated his concern, so we coped.

Spinner dolphins were present on just a few sets. They swam in big noisy gangs, males and females, adults and young all mixed up; they were hard to study. We therefore concentrated on the spotted dolphins. I was far more curious about them than about the spinners anyway, and they tended to stay in one place throughout the set. They often hung at the surface, heads up, tails down, in large groups, a behavior dubbed rafting. In that state they seemed quite unafraid, and let us swim up to them and even touch them. They were alert but calm, breathing slowly and eyeing us attentively; they certainly weren't in shock.

Usually the schools we saw seemed to be doing whatever they would normally do at that time of day: flirting, playing and socializing; moving about restlessly in organized clumps probably preparatory to feeding; or resting and moving slowly, not doing much of anything. The animals seemed to know when it was time to be let out of the net. They traveled to the right area, marked by floats and special netting, and waited for the top edge of the net to sink and turn them free. They had, very obviously,

Using a pencil and a plastic slate, Ingrid records a single dolphin's activities over a five-minute period as other spotted dolphins circulate around and behind her.

been in the nets before. (The implications of this, and particularly of the possible long-term effects on the animals of being repeatedly pursued in high-speed chases, were unsettling to me and still remain an open question twenty years later.) We did see one school that was apparently new to the experience; they were, indeed, dreadfully upset, whistling, dashing about, head-slapping, and going out of the net sideways and in disorganized clumps. Even in that set, however, all the porpoises were safely released.

And how were those spotters managing to deal with large numbers of strangers? By the third or fourth set we had worked it out. There might be five hundred spotted dolphins in the net but in that incredibly transparent tropical water under the surface we could see that they were all divided into separate clumps or tribes. Each tribe, containing perhaps thirty to two hundred animals, remained in its own cluster, with open water between them and the next tribe. As in a sold-out football stadium, the crowd looked like an amorphous mass of individuals from above, but close up, one could see that the Joneses swam with the Joneses and the Smiths stuck with the Smiths. That made spotter sense to us.

On the net deck, I'm taking notes as the net is lifted back aboard for restacking. Steel cables can snap and whiplash, and big tuna can fall from the webbing onto the deck; a hard hat is mandatory when the net is coming in.

On the ship, meanwhile, the crew was folding the net in a big stack as it came aboard, amidst squealing winches and dangerously taut steel cables: the net deck was a hazardous place to be when the net was coming in. When most of the net had been brought back on board, the ship started its engines in order to drag the now manageable remaining portion of net backwards, thus spilling the dolphins out the back, a procedure called backing down. At this point we had to get out of the water and into our raft. The hubbub as dolphins were shunted out of the net could and did attract sharks. In that confused environment you didn't want to get backed out of the net yourself.

There was no time to get aboard the mother ship at this point, so we were instructed to tie up to the net's corkline until backing-down was completed. If it was rough, this could be difficult. The corkline sometimes sank, pulling our little boat under and swamping it while we scrambled frantically to keep our data slates and diving gear and camera from floating away. A couple of speedboats were usually assigned to the release area to watch for any trouble, and to manually extract any dolphins that managed to get their noses stuck under the corkline as they slithered out of the net.

After the backdown procedure was over, one of the speedboats would usually tow us back around to the other side of the *Queen Mary* so we could climb aboard again and our raft could be hoisted back on deck.

During one set our inflatable boat started to deflate, and we had to get onto a speedboat and drag the raft up on it as well. Then that speedboat sprang a leak and we had to clamber onto to another speedboat. It was certainly a bit perilous, moving from boat to boat in tossing seas. Even a sprained ankle would put you out of business, and sprains or fractures were a real possibility. We divided the worrying: Ingrid worried about sharks, I worried about drowning, and both of us worried about injury. Luckily we were never hurt except at the bandaid level. One day in the shower I counted forty-seven visible bruises, scratches, and scrapes on myself, and that was just on the front side that I could see.

If there were fish in the net, they were gathered into the last of the webbing, lifted aboard in a sort of bucket on a crane, and shunted into the icy brine in the hold, to be frozen until delivery to the canneries in San Diego. Meanwhile, Ingrid and I showered and changed, washed and stowed our snorkeling gear, and then, using the big tables in the galley, copied the data and comments for each focal animal from our slates onto paper forms while the set was still fresh in our minds. Often we were still working when the men were through, something they remarked on with additional comments about certain other scientists who had spent whole voyages reading novels in their bunks.

We dove on twelve out of seventeen sets in the course of the three-week voyage, and recorded data on 134 focal animals. Now and then we knew it might be too rough to work, but we always went out in the net anyway, unless the skipper forbade us. Once we made three sets in a day, but mostly the pace was manageable. The focal animal sampling system, which I had learned about during my job at the National Zoo, proved to be a great way to untangle the structure of the spotted dolphin schools. If you just look at a bunch of animals, your eye is attracted to big, obvious activity—fights, for example—and you tend to miss small but equally important events, such as who is quietly swimming with whom. By following one animal at a time we learned that each animal belonged not only to a tribe but also to a special subgroup within that tribe. Mothers with calves, for example, hung out in groups of three or four females and young, while teenagers went around in little gangs of their own.

The nucleus of a tribe was not a single dominant male, as we are used to seeing in terrestrial animals—the stallion or the bull or the alpha wolf—but three or four big burly males in a group. They moved through the school shoulder to shoulder, like gang members walking down a street, and the other animals parted and made way for them. Everything they did, they did in unison. If they surfaced to breathe, they did it as one; if they dove, they dove in tight formation.

Some tribes had one gang and some had several. If two gangs met face to face, as once happened about six feet in front of me, they stayed in lines like two football teams, made extremely disagreeable screeching noises, and sometimes fenced with open jaws—one could hear the teeth clashing. Then one group passed under the other and they went on their way. The confrontation was impressive but so formal and stylized that it was hilarious, too; one could not feel afraid.

I thought the other dolphins must feel the same way— impressed but not afraid. Once I saw an adult female swimming in the middle of a male gang. She was "holding hands," by overlapping pectoral fins, with the males on either side of her, while with her tail she reached down and patted a third male, swimming below her, on the back. Was she everyone's girlfriend? Or maybe their mom? Spotters change color with age, but these were all in the final, most senior color pattern, so I had no clue.

These gangs of males, while not exactly leading the schools, were definitely important to survival. Ingrid and I both happened to be watching the same tribe underwater when a speedboat started up nearby and frightened them. All the animals instantly plastered themselves around the senior male squads. That was the place to be if trouble came.

We had observed that different schools had different ways of escaping the initial chase. Some just tried to outrun the speedboats.

Some dove. Some tried hard to get across the bows of the *Queen Mary,* to the starboard side. (The net was set to the port side, and if the dolphins got across the speedboats couldn't easily drive them back.) One school turned in its flight and ran right into a little rain shower, where they became invisible. Another superb defense was simply to scatter all over the face of the ocean and refuse to school up and be chased. This would be hard for the animals to do, given their natures, but it happened often enough that the fishermen had a name for those schools: the Untouchables.

It seemed to us that the male squads were probably the source of such maneuvers. The oldest and most experienced animals in a school would have had the most opportunities to find out how to deal with boats and nets. A group of males that by accident had hit on a good maneuver would certainly try it again, and whatever they did, the rest of the school would do too. A cultural tradition would be born, differing, of course, from school to school, depending on what its particular males had learned.

We made good friends on that trip. The crew treated us like respected family members—cousins or aunts, perhaps. In a way, we hated to leave the ship and its smooth-running community. Ingrid and I both visited Ralph and Evelyn Silva and the fishing community in San Diego in following years. Evelyn had had such a good time that she and Ralph went to sea together from then on; she sent me a postcard once from Samoa, where the fishing was good—and did not involve dolphins.

Out of the photographs I took in the sets that summer, I put together a paper on dolphin communication systems that do not involve sound.° Like us, dolphins can indicate their wishes and intentions to each other by glance, touch, positioning, and gesture. Very much unlike us, however, they also communicate by blowing different sorts of bubbles. (I've always wondered if this is one reason why among humans smoking is such an easy sell: you can express yourself with a smoke display!) Dolphin bubble displays we had seen in captivity included the basketball-shaped sphere

---

° Karen Pryor, "Non-acoustic communication in small cetaceans: glance, touch, position, gesture, and bubbling," in *Sensory Abilities of Cetaceans*, ed. J. A. Thomas and R. A. Kastelein (New York: Plenum Press, 1991).

that indicates surprise, and a long bubble trail accompanying whistles, which no doubt helps identify the whistler. On the *Queen Mary* voyage we saw at least two more: the smoke screen, in which a male defeated in a squabble with another male blows a sort of curtain and vanishes behind it, and a frequently seen torus, a perfect doughnut shape, the meaning of which we couldn't discern.

I presented slides of these dolphin signals at a scientific congress in Rome shortly after the trip. It was a wonderful conference, partly because we Americans met a number of Russian dolphin researchers long known to us only through their work. (One of them brought me a copy of the Russian translated edition of *Lads Before the Wind* to autograph, as well as a great training present: a carved wooden whistle in the shape of a bird.)

After the trip, I also showed slides and explained our findings to the government scientists, to fishing industry representatives, and to some environmental groups. I presented the slides and data on spotter school structure and social behavior at several colleges and universities in the New York area, including Rutgers, Adelphi, and Rockefeller University. The work was useful in the tuna/porpoise congressional hearings. It somewhat demystified the animals, and it helped put an end to some totally impractical speculative solutions. Using this research as my thesis topic, I also began working toward a Ph.D. in zoology, first at New York University and then at Rutgers.

One thing we certainly did not learn on the trip was how to solve the whole "tuna/porpoise problem." Many protective measures were taken, from economic sanctions to on-board government observers to fishing lessons for new skippers. The purse seine fishing is now largely in the hands of foreign fleets. There is much government oversight and regulation. The mortality rate for porpoises is certainly reduced, but the stocks are not recovering as well as expected.

And then there's the tuna. They too are long-lived, intelligent and observant. If any adult yellowfin tuna were caught in a set, they were always the first creatures Ingrid and I saw when we dove. As soon as we got in the water, a dozen or so hundred-pound fish, sleek and silvery as if made of metal, would hurtle past us, their huge round eyes looking us up and down as they zipped by. They always checked us out just once and then went on looking for a way out of the net. Even eight or ten such fish constituted a welcome catch—half a ton—making the set well worth while. The fishermen were careful to keep the net well mended; if there was the smallest rip or hole anywhere in the net, these fish found it and were gone.

There's evidence that these schools of breeding-size tuna, perhaps ten years old or more, come from the same spawning. They may be relatives, even siblings. Those that have survived to breeding size may have stayed together all their lives, constituting a social and genetic tribe as unique as any group of dolphins. Is there an unlimited supply of them? I don't think so. While you are fretting over the dolphins, say a prayer for the tuna as well.

14. THE DREADFUL DOWAGER: CONVERSATIONS WITH A DOLPHIN

The tuna/porpoise issue wound down at least temporarily in the early 1980s, and my consulting obligations came to an end. My sons were living their own lives, one back in Hawaii and one in the banking business in New York. Gale went off to college, and then to a job in publishing. Once again my life swerved in a new direction. I married an old friend, Jon Lindbergh, an aquaculture consultant and expert on salmon farming. I left my graduate program, gave up my New York apartment, and settled down with Jon in his terrain, the little mountain town of North Bend, Washington. We had a new puppy, a fireplace, a garden, and lots of wildlife to enjoy. I thought that surely I had seen the last of my dolphin duties now.

Wrong. No sooner had I moved to Washington State than the White House appointed me to the Marine Mammal Commission. This government agency, created in part by Ken Norris, was devoted to the protection and management of marine mammals. Being a Commissioner was a low-paying, at-home job of overseeing research permit applications and reading dozens of reports; but it was interesting. Things had really changed. No longer could you just go out in the ocean and catch some kind of dolphin you couldn't even identify. First of all, they had all been identified by now. And secondly, you now needed justification, a plan, and a collecting permit, which wasn't easy to get (Hey, you needed the approval of Commissioner Pryor . . . plus that of about forty other people).

The open ocean work we had so blithely engaged in twenty years earlier was now illegal, at least in U.S. waters; not only did you need a permit to catch a dolphin, you needed a permit to turn one loose. Virtually anything you did to a captive animal, from research training to simply moving an animal to a new tank, required permission in writing from the government. The new regulations certainly protected the animals from sideshow exploitation or incompetent care, but privately I was glad I hadn't worked under those restrictions.

Except as a photocopied government report, I still hadn't published what would have been my doctoral thesis, the bulk of the tuna/porpoise research, and it was proving difficult to do so without a university affiliation. Perhaps I could make it part of a book, an edited collection including other studies of wild dolphins. The University of California Press loved the idea, especially since Ken Norris—by then at UC Santa Cruz—decided that he'd like to be coeditor with me. Ken visited us in North Bend and he and I thrashed out the details. What we thought would be a two-year job took more like seven, but the result was *Dolphin Societies: Discoveries and Puzzles*, a collection of papers about dolphins and dolphin field research, with some additional essays by me and Ken, that is still in print ten years later.*

Ken Norris and I were working on the last bits of *Dolphin Societies*, mailing manuscripts back and forth between North Bend and Santa Cruz, when he phoned me one day to say he had a dolphin training problem. He didn't know what the problem was, just that the sonar experiment he'd planned wasn't getting done. Would I come down to Santa Cruz "for a day or two" and fix it? I very much doubted that I could fix the problem in a day or two, but perhaps I could at least identify it. I pointed out that I was waiting for his final essay for *Dolphin Societies*. If he'd write the essay, I'd look at his problem. So a deal was struck.

---

* *Dolphin Societies: Discoveries and Puzzles*, ed. K. S. Norris and K. Pryor (Berkeley: University of California Press, 1991).

Ken had been a pioneer in dolphin sonar studies. I didn't know exactly what kind of continuing work he planned, but it would almost certainly involve training dolphins to echolocate on specific targets, on request. In tanks at the University's marine laboratory Ken was housing his proposed research partners, two large, old female dolphins named Josephine and Arrow, who had been transferred to him from the U.S. Navy's dolphin research program.

Teenage bottlenose dolphins love a puzzle and eagerly participate in this kind of study, with its many repetitive trials. Arrow and Josephine, however, were of grandmother age. They had been captured many years earlier off the coast of Florida. In the wild, by this time each of these dolphins would probably have been the matriarch of her own female-calf band of sisters, daughters, nieces, granddaughters, and babies. They would be making decisions, keeping the peace, and driving off nosy boyfriends. They would not be taking tests and obeying commands day after day for some research program. It would not be the first time, I thought, that the Navy had foisted crabby old lady dolphins off on some innocent researcher.

I flew to Santa Cruz. Ken drove me to the lab and dropped me off near the dolphin tanks. I found Ken's post-doc, Randy Wells, and some helpers draining a small holding tank in order to strand the two dolphins on the bottom to medicate and force-feed them. The dolphins seemed to be sick; apparently they were not eating, a little detail Ken had not bothered to mention. (Of course, one would be having difficulties using food to train animals that are not eating.) I peered down into the tank. The dominant animal, Josephine, was thrashing the last bit of water with her tail and flinging her head and jaws about at the handlers. She was furious at being stranded. She didn't look all that sick to me.

The trainer, Michelle Jeffries, and I sat down and got acquainted. She had some straightforward logistical problems that I could help her with. Visitors, guests, and faculty at the lab, including Ken, were interrupting training sessions to pat and play with the dolphins; that could be stopped if Michelle was given the authority to do so. The dolphins' fish supplies, which Michelle thawed and prepared carefully each morning, were sometimes purloined by sea lion researchers in another section of the lab; that too could be stopped, once Ken was made aware of it.

By late afternoon, when everyone else at the lab had left, Michelle planned to try again to see whether the animals would eat. The dolphins' tank had been refilled and they had been released into their somewhat larger main pool. I asked Michelle if she'd like to do a little training together; she said she'd love to.

We stationed ourselves in separate places on the tank edge. Even if dolphins are not eating, they are often willing to perform simple tasks they know well just for the contact and stimulation. And performing those tasks sometimes gives a non-eating animal an appetite again, as Michelle and I both knew.

I suggested we start by calling the animals back and forth and having them carry toys between us, behavior which was certainly well within their repertoire. Each animal had a small sound-maker that was supposed to be their "name-cue": a little bell for Jo and a toy cricket clicker for Arrow. These noisemakers work great when you hold them underwater; one can't hear the sound in the air, but it is very clear below.

It was quickly obvious that we weren't going to get anything in the way of such organized behavior, if indeed we got any behavior at all. Both animals swam by a couple of times, eyed us, and then retreated to the center of the tank. We changed our plan; I would work with Jo and Michelle with Arrow. But then Arrow began coming to me while Jo sulked with her back to us. Michelle suggested I work Arrow alone. Fine.

I called Arrow over and tried to get her to touch a little hoop, neck-ring size, which I was holding in my hand underwater. I blew the whistle, the universal conditioned reinforcer for dolphins, each time she even came near, and then tossed her a fish. She let her fish fall to the bottom of the tank.

Jo now came over and began exhibiting aggression toward Arrow—horrible raspy sounds, streams of bubbles, and threatening movements in Arrow's direction. I have never heard worse dolphin language, even among the wild spotted dolphin male gangs. I was shocked. Michelle shrugged. "She does that all the time." Tsk tsk.

As I had hoped, Jo now wanted to have all the attention for herself. She barged in and did the behavior I was asking Arrow to do: she touched the hoop. I blew the whistle and gave her a fish, which she ignored. Nevertheless, she touched the hoop again when asked, and again was reinforced.

Jo now drove Arrow away from me to the far side of the tank. That was fine with me. I was beginning to suspect that Arrow was not going to be able to work anyway unless Jo was occupied, but now I had Jo mad enough to want to work herself. Jealousy and dominance may not be virtuous states, but they can be useful to the trainer. Josephine was now actively interested in getting reinforced, if only to prevent Arrow from having that pleasure. If Josephine could be made to work, Arrow would get her chance in time.

Since I had Arrow's cricket in my hand, I called Jo with that sound, making it clear that I meant her by making a string of clicks when she happened to come toward me and stopping the sound when she turned away. I was using the cue to say, in effect, "Come here to me," and also, "Yes I mean you, not Arrow." She finally came over to me. I held out the hoop. She touched the hoop and got the whistle and the fish (which she ignored again). Of course I didn't intend to stick with the simple behavior of hoop touching forever; I wanted to get Josephine doing lots of different things. But we'd had a small success with this hoop, so with this hoop we would continue.

Whoever designed the dolphin tanks at this facility had not consulted a trainer. Dolphin tanks should be raised above ground level, making the water's surface waist-high so that people can easily interact with the animals. These tanks were flush with the cement deck, like a swimming pool. To hold the hoop in the water I finally lay down on the concrete with my arms over the edge, a damnable position to work in but less wearing on the whole than crouching or kneeling. Josephine immediately swished by briskly enough to send a wash of water over the concrete, effectively soaking the front side of my body; if there's one thing dolphins are good at, it's making waves.

"She got you wet!" Michelle exclaimed. So what? I thought. It wasn't a cold day. Part of the job. If I recoiled, or objected, or went away to change my clothes, Josephine would win, and we couldn't have that. Josephine also apparently recognized this as a draw; she didn't do that again, though I continued to work lying prone on the concrete.

Again I held the hoop in the water for her to touch. This time she touched my hand, instead of the hoop, very gently with her rostrum. This is dolphin con artistry: "Poor little me, I don't understand quite what you want, but won't you give me a fish anyway?" I was big about it; I reinforced Jo for touching my hand and asked her to touch the hoop again. This time she touched the cricket. I did not reinforce that (two can play at being unpredictable, can they not?) Jo immediately went and sulked in the middle of the tank: "If you won't play my way I won't play."

"If you won't play with me, fine—I'll play with the *other* dolphin." I got up and tossed a plastic floating baseball bat toward Arrow, and from another location started reinforcing Arrow for going anywhere near the toy. Jo immediately started yelling at Arrow and threatening her. Arrow retreated to the middle of the pool, afraid to move. Poor, bullied Arrow. I'm sure she hadn't asked to live in the same tank with Josephine.

I went back to the spot I'd chosen as Jo's training station, lay down, and went back to work with the hoop. With each repetition Jo's behavior improved. She came to me more briskly and touched the hoop promptly. And she began taking and mouthing her reward fish before letting them sink: a very good sign!

Then she tried another familiar dolphin game. She swam briskly up to the hoop and stopped dead about a quarter of an inch from actual contact. This is a fine stunt. An elephant at the National Zoo tried this game on me, too. Maybe the animal just made a mistake, you think. You are tempted to move the object toward the animal and complete the contact, and then reward the animal.

The contact reinforces the trainer's behavior as well. It *seems* as if you got the behavior you wanted, after all. The next time, the dolphin stops a half-inch away, then an inch away (they have fabulous control of where they are in the water). The naïve trainer then moves the target toward the animal again. At Sea Life Park I once saw a dolphin play this trick on one of Ken's graduate students. Over a period of days she got him leaning so far over the tank that eventually he actually fell in.

In this case I had no illusions that Josephine didn't know what she was doing. I thought of a countermove. The next time Josephine swam up and didn't *quite* touch the hoop, instead of being lured into reaching toward her I moved the hoop briskly six inches further away from her, toward me. She let out a bucket-sized bubble (that indication of dolphin surprise) and sank backwards two feet or more (sinking tail-first is a dolphin sign of annoyance).

I called her again with the cricket and offered the hoop once more. Instead of quitting on me, as I thought she might, this time she came briskly, touched the hoop firmly, and got a whistle and a fish (which she held politely but didn't eat). I took that to signify that she'd enjoyed the little duel between us. This level of communication, even with an animal you have never seen before, is one of the great pleasures of using operant conditioning. Ingrid describes it as having the ability to say to the animal, "I know what you're up to. And now you know that I know." And Josephine could say back, "Oh. Damn. Oh well, okay, let's continue."

Now and then during this session Josephine quit on me and went to hang motionless in the middle of the tank. When that happened I got the pool broom and started netting out the fish she hadn't eaten. I was not giving her a time out, exactly, but I was not hanging around coaxing and waiting for her either. I made eye contact with her from time to time, so she knew I was not through with her.

I thought of another trick to stir her up. At the end of one of these pool-tidying periods I came back to the training station, lay down, put the hoop in the water, and once more called Jo over with the *clickety-clickety-clickety* sound of the cricket. This time I held a large herring in the middle of the hoop and asked her (by positioning the cricket and thus the sound source right next the fish) to touch that instead of the hoop. Asking a dolphin who won't eat to touch a fish on command? What a dirty trick!

Josephine looked at the herring and then echo-located on it, swinging her nose back and forth and up and down as she scanned the fish acoustically. When she had to believe her senses—that I was training her to touch a fish—she barged by me and rapped the hoop sharply with her rostrum as she passed. She hit it just hard enough to make my hand sting a little—as clear a statement of opinion as you could possibly wish.

I decided to end the training session at that point. Jo had eaten nothing from me (although once, when I surprised her by giving her *two* fish, she had looked them over very carefully).

Michelle then stepped in. Jo's usual evening treat was a mackerel. Essential daily medications were tucked into the body cavity of the fish, so it was important that Jo actually eat it, and that was more likely to happen if she'd done something to earn it than if Michelle just handed her the fish. Michelle gave Jo a hand signal to jump, which she obeyed very nicely, with a high, arcing leap. Jo then wolfed down two mackerel, the first vigorous eating she had done in days.

The next morning Michelle and I met at the lab again. This time we agreed that I would take Jo from the start. When I came into the training area, Jo stood half out of the water on her tail. She followed me around with evident excitement. I put down my fish bucket and hoop and noisemaker at the place on the side of the tank that I had chosen as my training station. Jo stood up on her tail again, right in front of me, making the most penetrating eye contact. She was not looking at me sideways with one eye, as dolphins usually do, but belly-forward with both eyes meeting mine, looking around her jaws, a startling sight (dolphins have binocular vision straight down, but I had never seen one use it to make social eye contact before).

How should I respond? The hand signals and acoustic cues we give dolphins are very clear in their meaning, and both sides agree to what that meaning is. Conversation, on the other hand, and in my opinion, is a jumble; you may think you are encouraging the animal or pleasing it, when what you are doing is in fact quite meaningless. So normally I don't talk to dolphins. But here, with this unusual eye contact, I felt Josephine deserved some sort of social greeting. I would have greeted her by stroking or petting, but she wasn't permitting me to touch her, so a big cheerful "Good morning! How are *you!*" was all I had to offer.

I started where I had left off, with the behaviors of coming to the cricket sound and touching the hoop. At one point, Jo touched the hoop and I whistled and gave her the jump cue instead of a fish. She jumped and got another whistle and her fish.

So of course I then asked her to jump two times for one fish. And of course she turned away and sulked. "Let's work Arrow," I said to Michelle. We tried reinforcing Arrow for almost any behavior in any part of the tank. By this means Arrow was able to do a few little flops and get rewarded for them, although she did not eat her fish.

As I had hoped, Jo got so mad at Arrow for earning fish that she began stealing the fish that Arrow had earned and defiantly swallowing them. (I was later asked how much of this improvement was from the training encounters, and how much was due to medication taking effect on whatever was ailing her, so her that appetite was increasing. Who could tell? Anything from 100 percent to zero for both causes.)

After stealing Arrow's fish, Jo came back to work with me and at last began eating the fish I gave her. In fact she was really gulping them down. Maybe she wanted to get them out of the way, I thought, so she could hurry back and see what I had up my sleeve next.

I uncovered a couple of other behaviors she already knew— a "pec wave," or flip of the pectoral fin, and stationing, or holding still with her chin on my cupped hand. She also volunteered some vocalizations, but I didn't reinforce the sounds; we didn't need any more of that, thank you.

Usually each behavior earned a whistle and a fish. Once I reinforced her with three little sardine-sized fish. She positively counted them, aiming her rostrum at one, the next, the other, back and forth, as if truly astonished. No one ever gave her three fish at once, apparently. Another time, on purpose to surprise her, I gave her just one especially small fish. She chewed on it, mangled it, and then zoomed around the tank and spat it out at me as she went by. "Here's what I think of your gift! Take it back!"

Why was I working so hard to surprise Josephine? Was it fair to make her mad? Well, I thought it was a sign of progress. I'd far rather have her telling me off than beating up Arrow or sulking in the middle of the tank. Furthermore, I was short of reinforcers since she wasn't eating. Novel events are reinforcing in themselves, at least in small quantities, so I was using surprises to reinforce Jo for interacting with me at all.

In fact, I thought that boredom, exacerbated by seniority, was a large part of Josephine's problem. She had no doubt been trained, in her long Navy career, by many, many trainers. Training had become predictable, and inept training had become especially predictable; she was a whiz at introducing novelties of her own, indicating a past career of skilled trainer harassment. Rebuke, anger, or dominant behavior on my part would just make things worse; surprises, however, could help.

Josephine only quit on me twice on the second morning, in comparison to half a dozen times the previous day. She was much more active, attentive, and responsive, though her responses were not always beneficent. Once, after I had won in some training exchange, she breezed by me a yard away, lifted her large tail from the water, and sailed it past my nose. I assumed she was going to slap her tail on the water right in front of me and get me wet again; a big tail slap will soak you even if you are not lying on the deck as I was. But she just glided by with her tail up as if to say, "See what I could do if I wanted to?" Perhaps Jo had been given time outs in the past for wetting people that way. So she didn't quite dare actually slap, since right now she didn't want to stop the fun.

Once I gave Josephine the jump cue and she took off but then didn't actually jump. Of course I had seen that ploy before, especially from Sea Life Park's old male bottlenose, Makua. I did not reinforce the behavior with the whistle. I also did not move, change my facial expression, or react physically in any way. After she had looked at me and registered my non-reaction, I talked to her with laughter and eye contact, reasoning that socializing might convey "No hard feelings" without reinforcing the faked jump.

I asked for and reinforced a pec wave, and then asked her to jump again. This time she did jump; but she took off with a speed-building rush right in front of me, and accidentally on purpose made such a big splash in doing so that she got Michelle and me both soaking wet. Josephine then rocketed into the air, completed a fine big jump, and stuck her head out of water and cocked an eye at us: "Oh, what a shame—you're all wet! But I was doing what you told me to, lady, wasn't I?" You bet. I wouldn't dream of punishing such a nice jump by withholding reinforcement. She'd gotten her whistle in midair, and now I tossed her a fish while I wiped the water out of my eyes, laughing.

Meanwhile I put Arrow's name-cue, the cricket, aside, and started calling Josephine with her own name-cue, the bell. Of course Jo had initially responded more vigorously to Arrow's cue than her own, just being obnoxious to Arrow and trainer both—but I couldn't let her go on doing so forever, now could I? Josephine, I am happy to say, accepted the switch without discussion.

Now that we seemed to be getting on working terms, to add variety and keep things moving I decided to ask Jo to retrieve the hoop instead of just touching it. I called her over and let the hoop float away a foot or so. Jo went over and touched it. Then she stuck her nose into it. I ran the cue-sound: "Good, now come here with it!" She knew what I meant, all right, but pulled away from the hoop and turned her back on me. The hoop floated quite far away, beyond my reach even with the pool net.

There was another toy in the pool, a floating bat, and she now tried to bring me that instead. I refused to reinforce that behavior. She let the bat float away and then went and got it again and brought it to me. Again I refused. She retreated to the center of the tank and sulked. I got the pool net and cleaned some leaves from the bottom of the pool, giving her a break and me a moment to think.

The hoop was still out there, unretrieved. I got another hoop from the toy box and let it float, not a foot or a yard away, but just a few inches from my fingertips (that way at least I could get it back if she turned me down). When I invited Josephine to retrieve that one to me she pushed the new hoop gently into my hand. I reinforced that response, put the hoop back in the water, and asked her to do it again, just to make sure. She brought it to me again, and ate the fish she earned.

Josephine had saved face, and so had I. She was docile, almost purring. She came a little closer, and let me pat her on the forehead. I thought that this was a great time to end the session, so I got to my feet. Jo presumably felt it was a nice time to stop too, since she went over and floated peaceably next to Arrow, having a lot to think about, and a slightly full stomach.

Michelle and I and Carol, a volunteer who had watched the session, sat down together and talked over what had happened. Most of it had gone by so fast that it was hard for even Michelle to see. Also, of course they hadn't heard the underwater cues, so they missed the crucial starts and stops that told Josephine "Yes, I mean you," "Yes, I like that behavior, keep it up," and "Nope, that's not what I want." But they had certainly witnessed Jo's change of attitude. We finished our discussion and put the toys away. To say goodbye I called Jo with her name-bell and gave her a jump signal. She jumped, I whistled and then tossed in the last four fish in the bucket with a dramatic sweep, a nice jackpot.

Carol was stunned; she'd never seen anyone give that many fish. I told her it's a question of individual style, which is true. But an occasional or final jackpot is also good technique; it keeps the animals excited and slightly off balance, and it ends the work on a high note so that the next session begins with happy expectations. We left the tank area. Jo stood up on her tail and watched us go.

Michelle threw her arms around me, saying, "Thank you!" just as Ken Norris showed up.

"What happened?" Ken asked. Michelle told him that the animals had started working again. Ken wanted details. I picked my favorite episode, Jo's well-expressed indignation, the day before, when I had told her to touch a fish for a fish reward. Ken was bewildered; much as he loved his dolphins, he did not interact with them personally as trainers do, so he perceived only that the animal had been upset. He said—and meant it—"God, you're tough. God, you're *mean*."

But I knew Jo felt differently. Jo thought I was a friend, and more than a friend: a worthy opponent. I felt much the same about her. What Michelle saw and Ken missed, and I didn't manage to put into words at the time, was that Josephine and I were playing. She was playing dolphin jokes on me, and I was playing trainer jokes on her. She wasn't really mad when she rapped the hoop. Had she felt truly aggressive, she could have struck my arm and could easily have broken it. She was just telling me, "I know what you're up to; and now you know I know."

Ken went into his office and finished his essay. I advised him that in my opinion Arrow and Josephine were not really appropriate for the kind of work he wanted to do. He should locate some younger dolphins. These two should be either retired or released.

I'm happy to say that that's what happened. Ken got some other dolphins. Arrow and Josephine were shipped to Florida. Arrow was freeze-branded with an identifying sign on her dorsal fin and then released in her natal waters, where she has successfully taken up life with other female dolphins. Jo proved to have a chronic kidney ailment requiring lifelong medication, which precluded release under the provisions of the Marine Mammal Protection Act. She was established in a breeding female band at the Dolphin Research Center, in Grassy Key, Florida, where she still resides, and is said to be doing well.

I went back to North Bend marveling at Jo. People are always asking dolphin trainers, "Do you think we'll ever be able to communicate with dolphins?" I always answer, "I can communicate just fine with a whistle and a bucket of fish." But this brief encounter was the best example I'd ever had of just how rich that communication can be, at least in experienced hands . . . or fins.

15. THE BRAZILIAN FISHING DOLPHINS

Wild dolphins kept crossing my path as well, not in North Bend, of course, but in South America, where Jon and I traveled regularly for his aquaculture projects. Waiting for the ferry beside the Magellan Straits I saw the dramatic black-and-white Commerson's dolphin, a life-first for me: I screamed so loudly with excitement that I frightened everyone else in the car. Visiting the salmon farms sprinkled amongst the islands off Chile, we often saw the cute little Chilean dolphins, *Cephalorhynchus chilensis*. They were colored exactly like a Siamese cat, light brown with dark brown tails, fins, and noses. I once impressed some fish farmers by banging on a pipe in the water and luring the dolphins over for a closer look.

We stayed several times with marine mammal expert Natalie Goodall in Tierra del Fuego. I pored over her enormous and beautifully prepared research collection of whale and dolphin skeletons, collected from the beaches of that Antarctic-facing island, and wondered at the biological puzzles many of them presented. Why do these twenty pilot whales have holes in the same place in their skulls? Why is this solitary beaked whale built like a battering ram? How does this strap-toothed *Mesoplodon*, whose teeth, in adult males, hold the jaws almost closed, get anything to eat?

One day Jon invited me to go to Brazil with him, on a fisheries-related consulting trip. *Dolphin Societies* had gone to press, and my three years on the Marine Mammal Commission had just ended. I was due for a vacation. I said I'd go absolutely anywhere, provided it did *not* have any dolphins.

With Jon's brother, Scott, and his Brazilian wife, Raquel, who are both field biologists living in Brazil, we drove from city to city along the Atlantic coast down toward Uruguay, looking at port facilities, fish processing plants, and the like. One evening we pulled into Laguna, a summer beach resort town named for the huge, muddy coastal lagoon it sits next to. Here in the Southern Hemisphere it was winter, so most of the beach hotels were closed. We found a run-down commercial hotel in the center of town, with a café next door that served rice, beer, and shrimp from the lagoon. Period. Over platters of shrimp cooked five different ways I heard the waiter saying something enthusiastic about *delfines*. Uh-oh.

Scott translated. It seemed the local attractions included wild "fishing dolphins" who helped the local fishermen; wouldn't I like to see that? I said that if such a thing occurred (as it does, sporadically, in West Africa) it would be unpredictable and looking for it would be a waste of valuable time. Besides, I added conceitedly, if it had ever happened in such a modern, populous, industrialized area, I'd already know about it, and I didn't. So let's forget about it and just look at the harbor facilities as usual.

The next morning, a chilly, drizzly day, we drove down to the harbor, where a long breakwater created a narrow passage between the sea and the lagoon. There on the lagoon's shore we saw a curious sight. About forty men, most of them wearing yellow waterproof jackets, were standing hip-deep in a line in the muddy water. Each man held a throw net over his shoulder. And beyond them, patrolling up and down the line, was the unmistakable gray dorsal fin of a bottlenose dolphin. There was   crowd of spectators on the beach. There was even a man selling sandwiches. It was right in the middle of town.

We drove up, parked, and got out to watch. By and by the dolphin disappeared. The men braced themselves. Then with a

A curious sight: a long lie of throw-net fisherman, standing hip deep in the water, wait for a dolphin to drive fish into net range.

rush, the dolphin came back, made a curious sort of twisting splash toward the line of men, and turned away. The five or six men directly in front of the dolphin cast their nets. When the nets had been gathered up again, we could see that each man had caught about a dozen big fat mullet.

Another dolphin showed up and began working another part of the line. Then a third arrived, this one greeted by a shout from the fishermen: "*Bate Cabeza!*" A name. They knew these dolphins by name! Raquel hit the beach and started talking to people while I studied the animals.

Here's how it worked. Mullet were coming into the brackish lagoon from the sea. They were hard for the fishermen to spot because the lagoon water was so muddy. A dolphin, detecting a school of mullet coming into the lagoon, would go out, round them up, and herd them back into the line of fishermen. The dolphin swerved away at the last minute, just out of net range, which effectively told the men when and where to cast their nets. The catch could be substantial, we learned later—perhaps a hundred pounds per man on a good day. The fish were trucked on ice to the nearest urban markets, and this provided cash income for the fishermen and their families.

And what was in it for the dolphins? Even a dolphin finds it hard to catch schooling fish in open water. But the fishermen's presence halted the fleeing fish momentarily, and the falling nets disorganized them. Those fish that were not actually netted became easy for a dolphin to grab. It was an almost effortless way for a dolphin to earn a living.

We extended our stay in Laguna. We found the fishermen's bars, interviewed fishermen, and hired a boat so we could watch and photograph the action from the water. The fishing families, who, like the tuna fishermen of San Diego, were mostly Portuguese, lived in neighborhoods around the lagoon. We visited homes and talked with wives and children. On a second trip a year later I got into the town records and discovered that the fishing with dolphins had begun in 1847.

We learned that the same fishermen, and their fathers and grandfathers before them, had been fishing with the same dolphin tribe all their lives. They knew the animals by sight. They often knew their individual histories. One fisherman said he could be sure that the dolphin named Chinela was fifty years old because she had been born on the same day as his own father. Young teenage boys turned out to be a great source of information; they were not old enough to fish yet, but some of them knew the different dolphins the way an American teenager might recognize different makes of cars. Bate Cabeza, for example, had a curious habit of banging his head on the water to chase fish; and now his younger brother, Bate Cabeza II, was taking it up.

Marks and scars also provided identification. Sometimes, we were told, an excited calf would dash ahead of its fishing mother and get caught under a net. In that case the fishermen untangled it carefully and notched the dorsal fin with a penknife before setting the baby free, so that they could recognize it later and be sure it survived. Thus many animals could be easily identified all their lives.

There were also tribes of dolphins in the lagoon that did not participate in the human/dolphin fishery. From a skiff out in the middle of the lagoon we saw one group of dolphins circle a school of *anchovitas*, or sardine-sized fish, to bunch them up. Then they took turns feeding on the closely packed fish. Other resident tribes of dolphins, we were told, spent most of their time hunting out in the open sea and seldom came in the lagoon. Maybe these also used traditional skills passed down from mother to calf. It was the same, I thought, with Laguna's human fishing families. Some were shrimpers, fishing from small boats in the lagoon at night with lanterns. Others pooled the family resources for bigger boats and diesel engines, and went offshore. Not everyone wanted to stand around in cold water all day waiting for dolphins.

The dolphin fishermen had little interest in other dolphin lifestyles. In their view, some dolphins were good, and all the rest were *ruim*, or rascals. Some *ruim* harassed the fishing dolphins and beat them up; others tore and destroyed the men's nets. Once, as we were going past some beach houses along the shore of the lagoon, a mother and juvenile dolphin leaped together right beside the stern of the boat where I was sitting; I could almost have touched them. They each made eye contact with me, a glittering, mischievous glance. I laughed, and the fisherman driving the boat muttered, "@%°$# *ruim*." These two were, Scott interpreted, a particularly wicked pair.

I was amazed that no one seemed to have published anything about this in the scientific literature. Across the next year or so I found several American scientists who had been to Laguna before me, but they had apparently had other interests. One senior professor asked me if I'd been able to collect any dolphin skulls. Another said, "Oh yes, those Laguna dolphins, aren't they interesting. Now did you see any right whales?"

I was also amazed that no American journalist had happened upon what was to me a great nature story. As soon as I got back I contacted my friend Bill Curtsinger, a wildlife writer and photographer who does a lot of work for the *National Geographic*. He was very excited, as was his editor. On their instructions I shipped all my dolphin film to the *Geographic* to be processed by them so they could see it right away and perhaps send Bill to Laguna to shoot some more.

Then I got a call from the photo editor. "Why is the water that funny color?"

"Well, it's full of silt from the land runoff. That's the point. That's why the cooperative dolphins are so important to the fishermen."

"But have you seen all our beautiful stories on the Caribbean, with that beautiful blue water?"

"Yes, of course. But that's a different ocean. This is the South Atlantic. It's cold and gray and this part of it is muddy." Nope. No sale. Too much geography!

I never did succeed in selling a story on the Laguna dolphins to a magazine, though a couple of TV shows were made on the topic. I believe Jon's brother Scott worked on one of them as a consultant. Eventually I satisfied myself by publishing a scientific paper on the cooperative fishery and presenting several talks and posters at scientific conferences.[*] I'm happy to say that these efforts gave ammunition to a number of young Brazilian scientists who found support for long-term studies of dolphin populations and behavior, both in Laguna and up and down the coast.

---

[*] K. Pryor, S. Lindbergh, and R. Milano, "A dolphin-human fishing cooperative in Brazil," *Marine Mammal Science* 6:1 (1990).

16. DOLPHIN TRAINING FOR EVERYONE: THE CLICKER REVOLUTION

For years I kept assuming that I had not only seen the last of the dolphins but was also through with the topic of training. No one else seemed interested. Contrary to my expectations, *Lads Before the Wind* had not been received as a book about training, but as a book about dolphins—and a rather upsetting book to some people, since it demonstrated that dolphins were not all lovable floating hobbits.

Nor were the trainers themselves spreading the word. When I started in 1963 there were perhaps thirty dolphin trainers in the universe; now the International Marine Animal Trainers Association had two thousand members. But the training principles they used remained the province of these trainers; few were interested in working with other species or with the general public, and in any event no one was asking them to do so.

Most marine mammal scientists and animal intelligence researchers were equally obtuse, from my point of view. At an elite Office of Naval Research conference on dolphin cognition I drew on my experiences at the National Zoo to demonstrate that lots of species could be very "cognitive" when trained the way dolphins are trained. I told of hyenas and polar bears inviting their keepers to play, and of a chimpanzee using celery and carrots to reward its keeper's behavior.* My presentation made a chapter in the conference proceedings, but it was not well received at the meeting itself. One participant, a famous brain scientist, huffed, "That's all Skinner stuff, totally out of date. You'll never get a grant with those ideas." Since I didn't want or need a grant, I wasn't much moved by this statement, but it was indicative.

I decided I needed to write another book, one that would spell out how the principles of operant conditioning apply not just to animals but also to human situations and daily life. After several false starts I produced a salable proposal and got a contract from Simon & Schuster. I wrote most of the book after I moved to North Bend. Both my editor and I struggled to find a title; I finally settled on *Positive Reinforcement*. I was told, however, that Dick Snyder, the boss at Simon & Schuster, had picked up the galleys and said, "What is this? This will never sell!" So Simon & Schuster named the book *Don't Shoot the Dog!*

The title was a clumsy reference to a minor joke in the book. I had written in jest that one of the eight ways of getting rid of behavior you don't want is to shoot the animal—then you definitely won't see that behavior from that individual again. I was furious that my serious book about training without coercion was saddled with this hostile title. Don't? Shoot? Exclamation point? Arghh! Not only that, the title was totally misleading: the book was about people and about basic principles of learning, not at all about dogs.

I had to agree the title was catchy, though; probably more so than anything I had thought up. Tony Burbank, an editor at another big publishing house, Bantam Books, picked up the paperback rights. In paperback the book began to sell steadily, in spite or perhaps because of the name.†

Some psychology professors began using *Don't Shoot the Dog!* in their courses on learning theory; it was popular with students

---

* K. Pryor, "Reinforcement training as a method of interspecies communication," in *Dolphin Behavior and Cognition: A Comparative Approach*, ed. J. A. Thomas and F. G. Wood (Hillside, N. J.: Erlbaum Associates, 1987).

† Karen Pryor, *Don't Shoot the Dog!: The New Art of Teaching and Training* (New York: Bantam Books, 1985); Revised Edition 1999.

because unlike most textbooks it was fun. The book also became a "bible" for marine mammal trainers and an increasing number of zookeepers. When some falconers realized that operant conditioning could improve their procedures in this highly traditional sport, I was asked to address their national convention. I had a chance to go hunting with the experts and their birds in the wheatfields and waterways of eastern Colorado. Watching young birds just learning how to use men and dogs to help them hunt, I was able to make some operant suggestions that the falconers found useful, particularly in signaling to birds in the air. (Instead of a whistle, they sometimes use a photographer's strobe-light flashgun. *Blink!* A hawk can see that a mile away.)*

I visited, and Jon videotaped, top shepherds in New Zealand and their brilliant "huntaways," dogs that work at great distances with thousands of sheep, in teams of several dogs, each of which responds to its own set of whistled commands. Horse owners also began using the techniques I described, so very different from traditional horse training, and inviting me to watch or to help; Jon videotaped some of that as well.

But by far the biggest application of my book and its principles was to dogs—initially, I suppose, because of the misleading title, but then more generally because it was truly useful. In 1984, shortly after *Don't Shoot the Dog!* was published, I gave the first of what would be many all-day seminars for dog trainers, to the annual meeting of the National Association of Dog Obedience Instructors. I was nervous, but they seemed to like the information, and I made a lot of new friends, including a delightful Norwich terrier named Busy, who jumped into my arms for the final group photo (I have owned terriers ever since).

Soon I found myself speaking to groups of dog trainers at humane societies and dog clubs across the country. Two dog trainers in the Seattle area, police officer Steve White and

* K. Pryor, "Click!: Falconry and modern operant conditioning," *Hawk Chalk*, April 1997; K. Pryor, "Come back but don't come down: An advanced exercise in cueing," *Hawk Chalk*, August 1997.

animal control officer Gary Wilkes, showed up on my doorstep and became students, then practitioners, then operant teachers themselves. Hungry for information about shaping and reinforcement, the dog trainers began asking me for copies of *Lads Before the Wind*, then ten years out of print. At last someone wanted it for the information on training, not just the stories about dolphins.

I tried without success to interest some publisher in reissuing the book. Finally, Jon and I decided to reprint it ourselves and sell it by mail order. Our first printing sold out, to our amazement, and we ran another. In 1989 we arranged with the owner of a little North Bend business, Sunshine Secretarial Services, to take phone orders, do the paperwork, and handle the packing and shipping of books. (We used her mailing address, so we named ourselves Sunshine Books to make things easier for the local post office.)

In 1992 I was invited to give a speech to the annual meeting of the Association for Behavior Analysis, which was held that year in San Francisco. These behaviorists are the scientific descendents of B. F. Skinner, and I had always hoped they would be interested in our kind of training. I worked hard on my speech.[*] I also presented a panel of operant conditioners at the conference, to show the academics what we trainers were doing with their science.

During the panel discussion, Ingrid Kang Shallenberger and I talked about shaping behavior in dolphins, whales, and free-flying birds. Gary Wilkes, now a full-time dog behaviorist, repeated the "creative porpoise" experiment with his cattle dog, Megan. Gary Priest, a former killer whale trainer who had become the behavioral curator at the San Diego Zoo, showed elegant videos of training zoo animals for husbandry procedures (blood sampling, foot trimming, and so on).

The zoo trainers used whistles when training elephants, just as we did with dolphins. With a diabetic ape, Priest used a toy cricket or clicker (not as a cue, as we did with Arrow, but as a marker or conditioned reinforcer, in place of the whistle.) The

---

[*] Karen Pryor, "If I Could Talk to the Animals," President's Invited Scholar's Address, Association for Behavior Analysis, 1992.

crucial element was the same in every case: some distinctive stimulus was used to identify the very instant that the animal was doing exactly the right thing. What you use for the signal doesn't matter much as long as it is sharp, brief, and clear. (The human voice, therefore—fuzzy, slow, and loaded with emotion—is a very second-rate marker signal.)

After the ABA meetings I agreed to give an all-day *Don't Shoot the Dog!* seminar for an audience of two hundred and fifty dog trainers in the San Francisco area. I invited Gary Wilkes and Ingrid to participate. Years earlier, Skinner had suggested that a clicker would be an ideal training tool for dogs. Gary had found a good source for nearly indestructible steel-and-plastic clickers. We ordered a few hundred and gave them away to our audiences, both at ABA and at the dog event. (Giving out clickers, we discovered, temporarily brings any program to a complete halt. Even with a roomful of professors, you have to wait out a cacophony of clicking as everyone tries their new toy.)

While the ABA psychologists were intrigued, I thought, by both my speech and the panel, they were still mystified, confusing what we were doing with their preconceptions about conventional animal training. We modern trainers would present panels and symposia at the annual ABA meetings every year from then on, but it would take nearly a decade before the behavioral community really began to make use of our new technology.

The dog seminar, meanwhile, was an instant success. Two hundred and fifty people went home with clickers in their pockets and a brand-new way to train dogs in their heads. Gary and I were soon getting and accepting invitations to do more *Don't Shoot the Dog!* seminars across the United States and in Canada.

The ABA office had asked me to make videos of my presentations at their meeting, so members could buy them for classroom "enrichment." I arranged to videotape both the speech and the panel discussion, found a production studio near North Bend, edited the two videos, and had duplicates made up. The psychologists were not very interested, as it turned out; but I took copies of the tapes to the next dog training seminar. The dog trainers bought them gladly and found them useful.

I began giving *Don't Shoot the Dog!* seminars three times a year, initially with Gary Wilkes and his wife Michele (who sold the clickers, books, and videos), and later on my own. Jon always came with me, acting as manager, video cameraman, and producer. We put together a mail order catalog. We made more videos based on the seminars themselves, and they sold well too.

I was fascinated by the problem of teaching this kind of training. The training game that we used at Sea Life Park, in which people use a whistle or clicker to shape behavior in each other, was very illuminating. My own favorite variation consisted of building a chain of several behaviors in a human being—turn, clap, sit, stand, etc.—and then wrecking it by omitting or altering a cue. For example, using the clicker as the marker signal and wrapped candies as treats, I would reinforce someone from the audience for turning left or right until they were turning circles. Then I would train them to wait for a starter signal to start turning. As the starter signal, I held up a large red sign with the letters TURN on it in blue. When the behavior was well established—that is, when the person was turning on cue, stopping at the click, and waiting for the next presentation of the cue before starting to turn again—I substituted a large blue sign with the letters TURN on it in red.

Even a human being, who can read, will freeze in confusion if the familiar red sign with blue letters suddenly becomes a blue sign with red letters. It looks like the same cue. It gives the same information. But something important has changed, and the cue is now, at least briefly, meaningless. This kind of training error often affects the behavior of dogs in obedience competitions, and of course the dog gets the blame: "I *know* he knows it, he's just being stubborn."

Some people went away from these seminars with a very clear grasp of the operant method. They understood this totally new system for communicating with their dogs. They could use it spontaneously and creatively. These quick-minded folks (who tended to use the word "epiphany") started teaching classes, giving their own seminars, making their own videos, and variously spreading the word. A trainer of police dogs, Kathleen Weaver, started an Internet clicker "list," or e-mail discussion group, for dog owners;

soon two thousand people were participating. Via the Internet people around the planet were reading, learning, trying out, and reporting back on this new way to interact with dogs, and by extension, any living being.

The box-shaped clicker became the talisman of the new technology, now universally dubbed clicker training. In 1999, I'm told, the Minnesota novelty company that manufactures the clickers sold 1.5 million of them—almost all to clicker trainers.

A new friend from the Association for Behavior Analysis, Mt. Holyoke professor Ellen P. Reese, persuaded me to put together a collection of my training-related articles and research. The result, *Karen Pryor on Behavior*, for which Ellie Reese wrote a wonderful foreword, contains most of the articles mentioned in this chapter, and some others besides.* To bring the price per copy to a reasonable level, we had to print 3000 copies. That's a serious investment, and that's also 180 cases of books, or six pallet loads, to find room for in the basement.

Sunshine Secretarial had gone out of business. Jon and I found someone else to handle the shipping, but that was now only a small part of the work. We'd opened a website, which needed constant tending. I was writing, editing, lecturing, and teaching trainers. Jon was doing the bookkeeping, tracking the inventory, assembling and labeling packs of clickers, and carrying cases of books and videos from car to basement and basement to car. He was determined to do it all himself, but not enjoying the pressure.

We had been married nearly fifteen years, and happily so; but I now was entering a very busy and public time in my life. Commercial, professional, and scientific opportunities were coming my way that I really couldn't turn down. Jon, meanwhile, was looking toward retirement and the quiet country life he preferred. The solution was an amicable divorce. As a result, I alone would be responsible for Sunshine Books.

I moved back east, to a suburb of Boston where my daughter Gale had settled with her architect husband, Kolya Leabo, and their three little boys. I found a comfortable old house within what the

* Karen Pryor, *On Behavior: Essays and Research* (Waltham, Mass.: Sunshine Books, 1995).

Japanese call hot-soup-distance from my family. Sunshine Books was now too big to run from home. I either had to shut it down or let it grow. I hired a wonderful manager, Sandra Hoagland. We moved Sunshine Books into offices in nearby Waltham and began building a staff and turning into a real company. Perhaps the Sea Life Park years of watching other people developing other businesses would pay off; I was now an entrepreneur myself.

Back in 1991, *Nursing Your Baby* had undergone a thorough overhaul, resulting in a new edition written jointly by me and my daughter Gale.* Now Bantam asked for an update of *Don't Shoot the Dog!*. Luckily, in Boston I finally had access to all kinds of behavioral experts, so I was able to improve the terminology and the science in the book. I also added a new chapter on clicker training.

Meanwhile, on the scientific front, it was becoming clear to me that something new was happening with the training. There now existed a big "sample population" of thousands of people interacting with thousands of animals, using strictly dolphin training methods. They were reporting, sharing, and discussing their observations and results on the Internet. There was a lot of agreement. All over the world, clicker trainers, no matter what kind of animal they clicked, were getting exactly the same results we had gotten with the dolphins at Sea Life Park.

Take the "creative porpoise" experiment, for example, described in Chapter 10 of this book. That experiment had become quite well known in academic circles, but previously only other dolphin trainers had actually used the procedure. Now, however, it became a standard training exercise with dogs, so much so that in a little instruction book on clicker-training dogs I gave it a name: "101 Things to Do with a Box." (You put a cardboard box on the floor and click the dog for touching the box, pawing the box, dragging the box, getting into the box, and anything else the dog can think up.)†

---

* Karen Pryor and Gale Pryor, *Nursing Your Baby, Updated for the '90s* (New York: Pocket Books, 1991).

† Karen Pryor, *A Dog and a Dolphin* (North Bend, Wash.: Sunshine Books, Inc., 1995), reissued as *Getting Started: Clicker Training for Dogs* (Waltham, Mass.: Sunshine Books, 2000).

In the spring of 1997 I gave a big seminar in Great Britain. An Englishwoman who had learned her clicker training from the Internet, and was now running advanced clicker classes, offered to show us the box game with her border collie. I didn't have a box, so I put a chair on stage. We let the audience suggest the behavior, and they decided the dog should crawl under the chair and out the other side.

The dog sniffed the chair. *Click*. The dog checked back with the owner to get its treat, and then sniffed the chair again. This time, no click. Hmm. The dog circled the chair and nosed the other side. Nothing. It pawed the chair. It put its front paws on the chair. It jumped up on the seat of the chair. It stood on the seat and put its paws on the back. Nothing.

The dog jumped down and tried again from the floor, standing with front paws on the back of the chair. Nothing. By now the audience was beginning to mutter. "The poor dog! It's working so hard!" The owner was silent. "She knows her dog," I admonished the audience. Personally, I thought the dog was behaving much like my terrier in a woodpile: "I know there's a mouse in here somewhere!" The dog was having fun. You'd have to drag it away from that chair.

Then the dog happened to stick its nose under the chair seat. *Click!* Ahah! The dog ran back, took its treat perfunctorily, and stuck its nose under the chair again. Nothing. Laid its nose on top of the chair. Nothing. Stuck its whole face under the chair. *Click*. Without returning for the treat this time, the dog crouched— *click*—and then crawled under the chair and out the other side. *Click!* Cheers from the audience, cheers from the owner, and dancing and tail wagging from the dog: "I got it! I got it!" Just as with the dolphins, food rewards weren't even in the running compared to solving the puzzle successfully.

The border collie is a breed highly regarded for intelligence, but many dogs can excel at the box game, including Scotties, chihuahuas, and Alaskan malamutes, none of them known to be especially trainable. Not to mention cats. And parrots. In fact, on the bird-click list on the Internet, new parrot owners are advised to make the box game the very first thing they teach their birds.

A horse trainer and riding instructor, Alexandra Kurland, who had come to a *Don't Shoot the Dog!* seminar and caught on to the system, developed some wonderful clicker training applications for horses. My company published the ensuing books.* Now thousands of horses are being trained dolphin-style. We are discovering that although people regard horses as stupid, they are not; and they too have the ability to initiate, to be creative.

One of my favorite personal observations was of a beautiful Arabian show mare newly introduced to clicker training. She was being taught to prick her ears and look alert while posing at halter. Someone else had tried to accomplish that more traditionally, by swishing a whip around her face. That made her lay her ears back and look very ugly indeed. She had been sent to a clicker trainer for repair.

The mare had learned that the click means treats. She had learned that she could make the trainer click. And she had learned that it had something to do with ears. But what? As her trainer stood calmly in front of her, waiting for a clickable behavior, the mare pointed one ear forward and one back. Then she reversed that. Then she rotated her ears like searchlights. Then she flopped both ears to the sides like a rabbit, something I didn't know a horse could do on purpose. Then she pointed them both forward. *Click!* "Oh. Is that all you want?" And from then on she had it.

I found this charming but a little poignant. We don't often ask horses to think; in fact we usually ignore or even punish them for any self-initiated activity. But horses turn out to be great innovators, given the chance, and extremely fast learners. Like dolphins, cats, parrots, and primates (and a surprising number of clicker-wise dogs), they can also learn by watching each other. If you shape a behavior in one horse, any horses looking on will learn it too. "Oh. He got clicked for picking up a foot and holding it in the air? Hey, I can do that, watch me! Click me, too!"

I used to think it might be only dolphins (and people of course) that got so interested in a task that they would practice it without

<hr>

* Alexandra Kurland, *Clicker Training for Your Horse* (1998); *Getting Started: Clicker Training for Horses* (1999); and *Clicker Training for Riders* (forthcoming)— all from Sunshine Books, Waltham, Mass.

reinforcers, as Malia the *Steno* had often done. But clicker trainers are seeing this behavior in lots of species. Alexandra recently taught her young horse, Robin, to kick a soccer ball with his front legs. Robin, without being clicked for it, has since been working on aim and distance, lining himself up deliberately to get a good shot back to Alex, nosing the ball out of corners until he can get behind it, and tossing his head and prancing when he's pleased with the results. No clicks, but an equine gold star in soccer ball management.

My nine-year-old border terrier, Twitchett, confidently follows a target stick over a totally unfamiliar obstacle, for a click and a treat. (Photo: Bonnie Johnson)

This system of training seems to me to tap into what animals naturally do in the wild, when they learn how to hunt, forage, and utilize the environment. No one "trained" the Laguna dolphins in any traditional way. The fishermen didn't even try to feed them. But the lives of the Laguna dolphins, and of the spotted dolphins in the tuna nets for that matter, depended on learning, initiative, exploration, discovery, and recognition of cues. When we use operant training we give animals, and indeed any learner, a rich environment full of potential reinforcers and intelligible ways to get at them. We don't ask the animals to kowtow to us and obey us, but to use their natural skills in a natural way. In return, we get the benefit of the best thinking the animal can do.

Thinking! An awfully anthropomorphic word, is it not? But thinking is a behavior. One can observe the outcome, if not the internal process. Over and over again I've been impressed—staggered would be more like it—to see clicker-wise animals in the act of figuring things out. The marvelous thing about these events is that they are not just anecdotes from a doting pet owner; they are outcomes common to many clicker trainers. They are, like any good scientific finding, predictable and replicable.

I did not know, when I left Sea Life Park, that the simple fundamentals of the training—the use of a marker signal, shaping, and stimulus control—could be easily transferred to anyone with an interest and an open mind. I didn't know that the Internet would give us all a way to share and develop our skills communally. I didn't imagine that we would have a grassroots explosion of normal people, not specialists, demonstrating with glee that just about any animal can be as remarkable as a dolphin. What began with marine mammal trainers and their dolphins has opened up a new way of communicating with animals for everyone.

The past few years have been the most fascinating, productive time in my life since my first years as a trainer almost a generation ago. Sunshine Books continues to grow. We have several clicker training authors, a great staff, and two websites, clickerpet.com for shopping, and clickertraining.com, for in-depth information, stories, and links to other sites. My daughter Gale, an editor at a much bigger publishing house in Cambridge, is our advisor. All my children are happily married to people I love. My sons and their wives, one couple in Connecticut and the other in Los Angeles, have provided me with delightful granddaughters. Ted keeps an eye on our growth from his Wall Street viewpoint, while Michael and I work by e-mail on his uses of operant techniques and technology as a flight instructor. Running a company is a demanding job, so I seldom do seminars now, but I still do a lot of writing, and training with friends, both human and animal, here in Boston and around the world.

Last month I took my twelve-year-old grandson Max to the Florida Keys. We visited some long-time trainer friends at the Dolphin Research Center, where Ken Norris's dolphin Josephine still lives. First the trainers allowed Max to swim with two of the baby dolphins, Pandora, two years old, and Pax, three. These friendly babies had dozens of trained behaviors. They got talked to a lot, too, and understood a surprising amount. When the trainer told Max to get in the water, Pax startled and came over; he thought she meant him.

Then Max and I paid a social call on Josephine. Jo, looking quite serene, was lolling with a couple of friends in a big wire-walled pen built in the sea itself, with minnows swimming in and out. Max and I got down from the dock onto the trainers' floating platform. I spoke to Josephine and fed her a few little fish. I couldn't see any sign that she remembered me, though she let me stroke her and even hold her tail out of water and rub it, something all dolphins enjoy but only a very relaxed dolphin will allow. But she took a definite interest in Max, and solicited his attention by hanging around beside him making eye contact. When he sat down she actually played with him, spitting water and fetching toys, in a very gracious and grandmotherly way.

At the Dolphin Research Center in the Florida Keys my grandson Max gets acquainted with a young dolphin named Pandora. (Photo: Linda Erb, Dolphin Research Center)

The head trainer told me that Josephine is an important part of the Center's female-calf band, and may choose her companions and her dwelling place. Interestingly, she prefers one of the medium-sized pools and is very uneasy in the largest spaces; she might well have hated being released. Also, in addition to enjoying her retirement she has two jobs: helping newly arrived dolphins get used to their new surroundings, which she does well, and humbling new trainers. She does that well, too.

I'm shortly going to take the next grandchild in line, Ted's eleven-year-old Gwen, to Norway, Sweden, and Finland; and Ingrid Shallenberger is coming, too. We're going to give clicker seminars with the Scandinavian clicker experts, of whom there are now many, and we will go north of the Arctic Circle to clicker-train reindeer. After that, Wylie, Ellie, Michaela, and Nathanial will reach traveling age, one by one—and then maybe Michaela's little brother or sister, whichever it turns out to be.

My own next writing task is a little book about clicker training for cats. I haven't owned a cat in years, due to allergies in Jon's family; perhaps I need to get a cat while I'm writing. That will certainly be a surprise for my company spokesdogs, Twitchett, a now-elderly terrier, and my young spotted poodle, Misha. Since they are clicker-wise, however, I can teach them on their first encounter that a great new way to get clicked is to turn your face away from this eminently chase-worthy animal. You think it won't work? Oh, it will, and quickly, too. To quote my grandchildren, "Clicker *rules!*" Ask any dolphin.

Karen Pryor
Watertown, Massachusetts
June 8, 2000

INDEX

ABOUT THE AUTHOR

Karen Pryor is a scientist with an international reputation in two fields, marine mammal biology and behavioral psychology. Through her work with dolphins in the 1960's she pioneered modern, force-free animal training methods. She is the author of many scientific papers and monographs and seven books, including *Nursing Your Baby*, with two million copies in print, and *Don't Shoot the Dog! The New Art of Teaching and Training*. She is a founder and leading proponent of 'clicker training,' a world-wide movement involving new ways to communicate positively with pets and other animals. She is the founder and CEO of a behavioral publishing company, Sunshine Books, Inc., and its on-line divisions, www.clickertraining.com and www.clickerpet.com. Karen has three children and seven grandchildren. She lives in Boston with two dogs and a cat.